LGBTQ PEOPLE & ISSUES
AN INTEGRATIVE APPROACH

REVISED FIRST EDITION

Edited by E. Cabell Hankinson Gathman
University of Wisconsin–Madison

cognella®
academic publishing

Bassim Hamadeh, CEO and Publisher
Michael Simpson, Vice President of Acquisitions
Jamie Giganti, Managing Editor
Jess Busch, Senior Graphic Design
Mark Combes, Acquisitions Editor
Mirasol Enriquez, Project Editor
Luiz Ferreira, Senior Licensing Specialist
Mandy Licata, Interior Designer

First published in the United States of America in 2015 by Cognella, Inc.

Cover: Copyright © See-ming Lee (CC BY-SA 2.0) at http://commons.wikimedia.org/wiki/File:Rainbow_Flag_Gay_Pride_New_York_2008.jpg; Copyright © Anastasiarasputin (CC BY 2.0) at http://commons.wikimedia.org/wiki/File:Balloons!_%289181632461%29.jpg; Copyright © Victor Grigas (CC BY-SA 3.0) at http://commons.wikimedia.org/wiki/File:San_Francisco_Pride_Parade_2012-12.jpg; Copyright © 2013 by Depositphotos/SUNG KUK KIM; Copyright © 2013 by Depositphotos/SUNG KUK KIM; Copyright © 2012 by Depositphotos/Yelo34; Copyright © 2013 by Depositphotos/Mariusz Prusaczyk; Copyright © 2012 by Depositphotos/SUNG KUK KIM; Copyright © 2012 by Depositphotos/Narcis Parfenti.

Printed in the United States of America

ISBN: 978-1-63487-119-8 (pbk)/ 978-1-63487-120-4 (br)

www.cognella.com   800-200-3908

CONTENTS

INTRODUCTION

By Cabell Gathman

This book would not exist without the encouragement and support of Joseph Elder, Professor of Sociology, Languages & Cultures of Asia, and Integrated Liberal Studies at the University of Wisconsin-Madison. I was assigned in 2008 to serve as a teaching assistant for the Introduction to LGBTQ Studies course that Joe had originally developed. I was already hard at work on my dissertation, but it was only my second semester teaching at the university level. Not only did Joe request that the department reassign me to the course in subsequent years, but he allowed me to substantially revise the course syllabus on a yearly basis, introducing a great deal of new material which he then incorporated into his own lectures as the professor. He always welcomed my contributions to the course, encouraging me to lecture on selected dates and happily experimenting with new materials and mechanisms for student assessment from year to year.

As the course has evolved, so has my own understanding of LGBTQ issues, as well as my personal identity as a bisexual woman, an activist, and a teacher. I will always be grateful to Joe for both the opportunities and the model of a teacher as a partner in learning and growth that he has provided.

Two less personal but equally crucial influences on my selection of readings for this book are Kimberlé Crenshaw and Patricia Hill Collins, Black feminist thinkers who developed the concepts of **intersectionality** and the **matrix of domination,** respectively. Crenshaw described intersectionality in a 2004 interview with *Perspectives: A Magazine for and about Women Lawyers*:

> It grew out of trying to conceptualize the way the law responded to issues where both race and gender discrimination were involved. What happened was like an accident, a collision. Intersectionality simply came from the idea that if you're standing in the path of multiple forms of exclusion, you are likely to get hit by both. These women are injured, but when the race ambulance and the gender ambulance arrive at the scene, they see these women of color lying in the

1

intersection and they say, 'Well, we can't figure out if this was just race or just sex discrimination. And unless they can show us which one it was, we can't help them.'[1]

I don't call this reader "intersectional" because unlike Crenshaw's work, its focus is not primarily on race and gender; similarly, Collins applied her ideas of the matrix of domination, which included aspects of race, gender, class, sexual orientation, etc., primarily to the experience of Black women. However, without Crenshaw and Collins's work, I would not have learned to seek out research and accounts that complicate the mainstream image of LGBTQ people as White, middle-class, abled, thin, and otherwise privileged aside from their sexual orientation and gender.

As Crenshaw highlights, it is not possible in practice to separate marginalized aspects of an individual person's identity. Black women are not only affected by racism and sexism, but by a particular cultural strain of anti-Black racialized misogyny that is more than the sum of its parts. Similarly, LGBTQ people of color (some of them Black women), LGBTQ people with disabilities, working class and poor LGBTQ people, fat LGBTQ people—all LGBTQ people who also experience marginalization and oppression based on aspects of their identities other than gender and sexuality—need to have their voices heard. We cannot develop a meaningful understanding of the "LGBTQ community" unless we seek out these voices, especially the ones who belong to groups that we ourselves do not.

Many students enter LGBTQ Studies courses with a fairly narrow view of the problems that LGBTQ people face; if that's true for you, it's not your fault, and I commend you for taking steps to learn more. I do want to caution students, however, to resist the natural human impulse to reject or ignore information that conflicts too sharply with one's established worldview, including one's existing view of what the field of "LGBTQ Studies" should include. The voices of multiply marginalized LGBTQ people are not "supplementary" to an introduction to LGBTQ Studies, but **necessary.** As the cultural critic and political analyst Flavia Dzodan, a woman of color living in Amsterdam, proclaimed in 2011: "My feminism will be intersectional or it will be bullshit!"[2]

As a sociologist, I have taught various courses on inequality, and I always remind my students that structural inequality works specifically to render marginalized people, or at least their experiences, invisible to the dominant group. If you live your whole life in a house without entering the basement, you may never know that it's flooded—but there's still a foot of standing water down there, getting deeper every year. And if you don't want that house to eventually collapse, you need to first see, and then try to understand and repair, the damage that is causing the flooding.

If you actually live in the basement, you probably know how bad things are, but you may end up wondering if anyone else does when media portrayals of your "house" almost never show the part you're in. This metaphor can only extend so far, so I'll just point out that even now, it's noteworthy not only that a trans woman of color is featured on a popular *Netflix* series, *Orange Is the New Black*, but that she is actually portrayed by a trans actress, Laverne Cox, instead of a cisgender person as the majority of trans roles still are. Despite making up slightly more than half of the LGB community, bisexual and pansexual people are rarely featured in television and movies. The majority of those characters remain White cisgender gay men. In news media

---

1   Crenshaw, Kimberlé. "Intersectionality: The Double Bind of Race and Gender." *Perspectives* 12.4: 4. I first encountered this particular quotation through so-treu's Tumblr blog: http://so-treu.tumblr.com/
2   http://tigerbeatdown.com/2011/10/10/my-feminism-will-be-intersectional-or-it-will-be-bullshit/

coverage, attention is still heavily focused on a narrow range of LGBTQ issues like marriage equality and adoption, and even then, you would never know that people of color in same-gender relationships are twice as likely to be raising children as White same-gender couples.[3] When celebrities like Tom Daley date same-gender partners, gossip blogs and even popular gay publications rush to label them "gay" without even acknowledging the existence of bisexuality and pansexuality.

As a bisexual woman with physical and mental health problems, I am marginalized within both mainstream US society and the broad LGBTQ community. As a White, cisgender, middle-class, well-educated, thin person approaching middle age, legally married to a man, I am also a member of several dominant groups. I have a great deal of **privilege**, unearned advantages that improve my life and outcomes in innumerable and sometimes difficult to quantify ways, whether I want to admit it or not. My access to certain necessary pain and anxiety medications, for instance, while sometimes unnecessarily complicated, would likely be insurmountably blocked if I were Black and poor.[4] At the same time, as a bisexual woman, my physical and mental health is already statistically likely to be poorer than that of an otherwise demographically comparable cisgender man, or that of a straight **or** lesbian cisgender woman. I have attempted to provide in this reader LGBTQ perspectives from a number of different intersections of marginalization.

One of the great limiting factors in creating a reader like this one, unfortunately, is striking a balance between cost and utility. In order to produce a book that was not prohibitively expensive to students, who already bear the burden of increasingly high costs in the US, I had to make hard choices about which pieces to include and how to condense many of the pieces that I did include. I encourage interested students to seek out the unabridged versions of pieces that interest them, further work by the authors and others included here, and even more broadly, further work by others on the topics that are raised here. As bell hooks points out in her seminal critique of the documentary *Paris Is Burning*, there are serious problems with a member of a dominant group controlling representation of the very marginalized people over whom they have privilege. I prefer readers to single-author textbooks specifically because they allow for a multiplicity of voices, but the selections included here are still limited by my own perspective as well as cost considerations.

As an academic, an activist, and specifically a sociologist of digital media, I am often frustrated by the levels of professional gatekeeping in academia: access to college and university education is severely limited by socioeconomic class, race, and ability, research is frequently confined behind paywalls that essentially require elite institutional membership, and while technical language and jargon serve important purposes in the communication of ideas, too often academic writing is pointlessly, mystifyingly dense. I have benefitted immensely as an activist and a person from my use of social media platforms like Twitter and Tumblr.

Despite sometimes intense harassment from people who don't want marginalized voices to be heard, these platforms allow marginalized people to speak out and connect with each other. Despite much-publicized fears that technology is eroding community and critical thinking (a reaction that, as any social scientist of technology could tell you, dates back to Plato's response

---

3   Gates, Gary J. "LGBT Parenting in the United States." *The Williams Institute*. February 2013.
4   Studies have repeatedly found that Black and Hispanic patients are less likely to be prescribed opioid pain medication for the same conditions and symptoms as White patients. This is true even after controlling for socioeconomic status (SES), although lower SES is also associated with reduced opioid prescription. Joynt, M. et al. "The Impact of Neighborhood Socioeconomic Status and Race on the Prescribing of Opioids in Emergency Departments Throughout the United States." December 2013. *Journal of General Internal Medicine* 28.12:1604-1610.

to the invention of writing and repeats predictably in response to virtually every new communication medium), social media provide those who are open to new perspectives on culture and social issues with an inexhaustible supply of them.

As a teacher, I find that Tumblr especially is a great place to collect and share news articles, blog posts, and other media relevant to the topics that I teach. I encourage instructors using this book to consider creating a class Tumblr with a submission box, so that they can provide additional relevant content to students and also give students an opportunity to contribute content for their peers.

A class Tumblr or other blog could also be a useful resource for providing basic 101 overviews of topics like White privilege or common-but-inappropriate questions to avoid asking trans people. When I teach Intro to LGBTQ Studies, I typically provide a list of terms; I decided not to do so in this reader because community standards in regard to language change often enough that it would be impossible to keep such a list up to date. A class blog or Tumblr, however, would be a good place to provide such a reference, and would also allow for discussion, including criticism or counter-examples from people to whom the language applies.

This reader is a jumping off point, and I believe that it provides an overview of many aspects of LGBTQ experience that are too often overlooked. It is, however, only one person's collection of relevant pieces at one particular point in time. I hope that you will learn from it and go on to seek out more ideas and perspectives than any single textbook can provide.

GENDER, IDENTITY, THEORY, AND ACTION

By Talia Bettcher

As a philosopher, I am acutely aware of the stereotype of philosophy as utterly disconnected from the everyday world. Therefore, when I introduce philosophy to students for the first time, I am concerned to show its relevance to daily life. Central to my approach in teaching philosophy of gender is the concept of "identity" (or "sense of self").[1] I see individuals as possessing a sense of who and what they are (how they "fit into the world"). Such a sense of self involves a "map" of the world that is largely value laden and action guiding. Our identities are built upon beliefs about the world: about gender, sexuality, race, and religion, which may not always be true or well grounded. Philosophy can help us examine such identity-central beliefs with a critical eye. Just as Socrates asked questions about the nature of piety, justice, and the like, we can also ask questions such as "What is a woman?" and "What is a man?"

Identity in Theory

Using this approach, I encourage students to think reflectively about their identity-founding beliefs and the ways in which these beliefs guide their behavior. Here it is important to stress that our sense of who and what we are and how we fit into the world generally involves norms, which can govern our behavior. For example, often women may find themselves evaluated according to prevailing cultural aesthetic norms, which are supposed to connect in deep ways to the overall sense of self as valuable. Again, men may find themselves evaluated according to prevailing norms about excellence in various sorts of achievements. The point is that such norms can have a taken-for-granted status; they can guide our actions in ways that go largely unquestioned. To the extent that philosophy as a discipline takes seriously reasoning about moral, aesthetic, and other norms, it is the ideal discipline for examining the grounding (or lack thereof) of such gender-regulated behavior.

Identity in Practice

As a transsexual woman, I am aware of how unreflective views about the nature of gender and sexuality can have an impact on the day-to-day lives of real people; I have also seen how theories about gender have failed to capture my own experience of gender, or else reduced transsexuality to an abstract object of investigation.[2] Indeed, there is a long history of research and scholarship that regards transsexuals and other transgender people as exotic and problematic objects of investigation.[3] Contemporary trans studies have involved, among other things, a departure from the historical objectification of trans people in theory and research, such that trans people themselves have emerged as subjects/authors instead of just as objects. In this way, some of the extreme transphobic aspects of theory and research have been removed (or at least thinned out), and trans studies have taken on a kind of political liberatory dimension.[4]

The now-dominant model of trans theory and politics is itself fairly specific and open to dispute. It evolved simultaneously with (and in relation to) the queer theory and politics of the early nineties. While the relationship between queer theory and transgender theory and politics has certainly witnessed tensions, current transgender theory and politics borrows many of the key themes of queer theory/politics, not the least of which is an attack on gender/sex binaries, and the view that all gender/sex is socially constructed.[5] As an interdisciplinary field, trans studies draws on history, psychology, sociology, anthropology, philosophy, and biology (to name a few).

Central to my approach in introducing students to trans studies is the notion that theory is political, and that the very course itself is inevitably bound with political considerations. For example, I make it clear at the outset that a starting point of the course is that the lives of trans people are valid and legitimate. In this day and age, however, such an assumption is inherently problematic and controversial. Likewise, the decision to teach a course problematizing the validity of trans lives is a political decision. In general, one important theme of the course is the relationship of theory to politics. How does it actually relate to the lives of the people it is designed to examine? Who is developing the theory and for what purposes? Can the theory help guide or promote resistance? For whom?

Intersectionality

A concept that is essential to both courses involves the recognition that various forms of oppressions are deeply bound together, and that as a consequence, any discussion of gender or sexuality must be embedded within a broader sociocultural discussion of race, class, religion, and the like. The gender norms, which govern identity, are surely deeply bound with racial and class-based stereotypes as well as very specifically located cultural norms. For example, it is pretty hard to talk about a beauty ideal that (young) women are supposed to attain in our culture without noticing that this ideal tends to be *White*. Similarly, racist stereotypes of Black men and women tend to involve masculinization and hypersexualization.[6] In this way, gender and racial oppression are deeply blended. What this means is that attempts to investigate issues of gender and sexuality, abstracted from considerations such as race, are in danger of coming from a place that takes race, for example, as ultimately unimportant and detachable from issues of gender. In effect, it is to come from a privileged *White* place in which race appears to be no problem.

These issues and concerns are central in the course Philosophy, Gender, and Culture, weaving throughout it as a major theme. They are also quite relevant in the course Introduction to Transgender Studies. One of my concerns with current trans studies is the fact that it emerges from a fairly specific cultural location (White, academic, American, Anglo). While there has been some critique of the biases inherent in the prevailing framework, there remains a dearth of writing from people who do not come from that location, and the discussions of transgender issues for the most part appear to be abstracted from related issues such as race.[7]

"World"-Traveling

The notion of "world"-traveling is also important in both of these courses— indeed it informs my approach to service learning and civic/social engagement more broadly. This concept, introduced by philosopher María Lugones (1987), involves the view that people may move within very different social realities or "worlds."[8] Integral to this "world"-traveling is the fact that one has a different self (or is a different person) in different worlds. Indeed, a change in "world" is basically defined through a change in self. The insight derives from the experience of being bi- or multicultural: moving between different cultures and sometimes occupying several at once. One of the important features of this view is the recognition that sometimes who and what we are can be to some degree determined by others. Sometimes conceptions of who we are may be imposed upon us from without, and sometimes we may be blind to how we appear to others. Thus, our own sense of self (self-conception) may blind us to some of our actions, to their meanings, to their effects upon others. This is especially important because insofar as our own identities involve a larger picture of the world and how we fit into it, they also include a conception of other people and our relations to them. Because of this, there is a danger that we view others only in terms of ourselves—a danger that is only augmented if our map places other people in categories that are racist, sexist, or in other ways harmful to them. One of Lugones's points is that in order to be open to see others as they see themselves—and to be able to identify with them—it is important that one be open to seeing oneself differently, open to the fact that one may be viewed by others in a way that does not necessarily accord with one's own self-conception. In a word, one must "world"-travel.

Service Learning

In both courses I offer students the option of service learning. This is one strategy among many that I use to help promote course objectives. In the course Philosophy, Gender, and Culture we focus specifically on topics such as domestic violence, sexual assault, homophobia, and regulations of intersexual and transgender bodies. One of my goals is to argue that much of these forms of violence flow in part from harmful gendered conceptions of self. Some of the agencies that we work with include ones addressing domestic violence and sexual assault (such as the East Los Angeles Women's Center, Prototypes), and ones that have specific programs for lesbian/gay/bi/transgender/queer (LGBTQ) people (such as the Los Angeles Gay and Lesbian Center, Asian Pacific AIDS Intervention Team, Bienestar Human Services). For the most part, students perform various activities that are needed by the agencies at the time they are placed. They have worked in the planning of domestic violence vigils, been involved in outreach activities, provided assistance during support groups, helped organize events, and provided child care and assistance in compiling and distributing resource materials. Through service learning, students are not only given the opportunity to experience the connections between the issues discussed in class and the real world, they are also hopefully led to challenge beliefs that ground their own sense of the world and their place within it not only through reflecting upon what they have learned, but by effectively "world"-traveling.

When I teach Introduction to Transgender Studies, most of the students who take it are not themselves transgender, and many have not had any real interaction with transgender people and do not know very much about them. As a consequence, the course is inevitably a kind of introduction to trans realities and what it is to be trans. Naturally, this raises the difficulty that transgender people are often exoticized and marginalized. Obviously classroom assignments and a transgender instructor are themselves insufficient to undermine this tendency. So, it is for this reason that I think service learning is an important way of encouraging "world"-travel on the part of the students.

Additionally, beyond introducing students to trans theory and the history of trans studies, it is important to illuminate the connection between such theory and the real-world politics in trans communities. Because of that, I think that it is important for students to have an experience being involved in trans community organizing at the grassroots level. By doing this, students are not only enabled to go beyond the theory to real flesh-and-blood people, they are able to see the limits, advantages, and disadvantages of transgender theorizing and the political nature of theorizing about trans people. For example, it is a sad fact that much of transgender theory fails to adequately centralize issues of race and class. As a consequence, it ends up using problematic assumptions that go largely unquestioned. By having students work with agencies and organizations that provide services for transgender people in Los Angeles, they are thereby enabled to see the limitations of a culturally situated theory.

In this course, the agencies we worked with included members of the Los Angeles Transgender Youth Consortium (TYC). The TYC addresses the impact of HIV on young transgender people (ages 13–29) and comprises several organizations including Asian Pacific AIDS Intervention Team, Bienestar Human Services, Children's Hospital Los Angeles, Minority AIDS Project, and Van Ness Recovery House (Prevention Division). Additionally, we worked with FTM-LA Alliance, a Los Angeles–based community-building organization for FTM-identified individuals.[9]

In this course, students who chose the service-learning option helped conduct outreach, provided backup supportive services for support groups, conducted various forms of information gathering/resource building (concerning trans-friendly resources, trans-friendly surgeons, relevant funding opportunities), and also developed brochures with some of the information they had researched. Prior to their service, all students were required to participate in an HIV 101 training session led by representatives from the TYC. Additionally, students had received basic transgender 101 training by the time they started working in their placements. What students seemed to get out of the service experience was not only what they learned through the specific services they provided for their agencies, but also the fact they had basically entered an unfamiliar world. In entering this world they had the chance to interact with trans people as real people in real communities, working to improve their lives.

Because I offer the service learning as an optional component in both classes, it is especially imperative that additional work be done to integrate student community work with what is happening in the classroom. In both classes, I offer panel presentations and guest speaker presentations on most of the topics that we cover. For example, in Gender, Philosophy, and Culture, we have a guest speaker from the East Los Angeles Women's Center present on issues of domestic violence and sexual assault. I have found this essential in breaking down the model of professor as chief information source. By drawing on expertise from the community (particularly agencies that we are working with in service learning) a kind of knowledge is brought into the classroom that cannot come from books. Clearly, the point is not merely for students to learn about the realties of sexual violence. How do they address them in their daily lives? What sorts of forces and situations do they contend with in reality? By having experts who address these issues by leading conversation in the classroom, an important gap between theory and actual student life can be breached. Indeed, we have had occasions when students in the classroom came to confront personal issues of domestic violence or abuse. Because there were experts present, these situations could be handled effectively and professionally.

This has proven even more important in Introduction to Transgender Studies. By inviting transgender leaders involved in grassroots community activism in Los Angeles, an important counterpoint can be offered to the nature of the theory that grounds most of trans studies. Some of the topics that were covered included an introduction to trans issues (Trans 101); the medical/psychiatric model of transsexuality; Camp Trans and the Michigan Womyn's Music Festival; and transphobic violence. Additionally, in Introduction to Trans Studies, I required that students who did not choose the service-learning option attend at least one community-based event and write about it. While I understand that for some students a full service-learning commitment is not a reasonable option, it seemed essential to me that students be required to at least physically travel at least once during the course to a world that was not necessarily their own. While I do not have a similar requirement in the Philosophy, Gender, and Culture course, I do require that students attend specific cultural events that are being held on campus during that quarter. For example, one year our class attended the campus National Coming Out Day. It turned out that I was one of the speakers, so I used this opportunity to come out to my students as transgender.

To be sure, one of the major reasons that work with community partners has been so successful, and facilitated a tighter integration of course content and community service, is that I have had independent relationships with and commitments to many of the agencies. For example, I have had a long relationship with the East Los Angeles Women's Center, serving on its board of directors for over five years. I am also an active member of the Los Angeles transgender community and have played a role in grassroots organizing and community work. Because I have a community vantage point on some of the issues as well as that of an academician, I think that I am better enabled to guide the students. I also think that it is important that the instructor demonstrate a commitment to civic/social engagement. Short of this model, it is hard to see how an instructor can authentically promote this in her or his students. Additionally, I think that it goes some considerable distance in undermining tendencies of marginalizing or objectifying the community. I found this especially important in Introduction to Transgender Studies, where objectification is always already a pressing danger. Indeed, the fact that I had already engaged in many projects with our partners, and had formed meaningful friendships, helped move the entire class from something located on the UCLA campus, to a kind of genuine trans community intervention. In this way, a possible two-sidedness on the part of the instructor can be important in helping to open doors for student "world"-travel.

Reflections

Because I have taught Philosophy, Gender, and Culture over the course of several years, it has changed and evolved, and I have had the opportunity to explore several different types of reflection activities. Perhaps the most effective is the weekly journal, which I have used in the past to guide students in reflecting on the connection between specific concepts discussed in class and their service experience. As class size increased, however, it became more realistic to assign short response papers. I also have students complete a set of reflection questions at the beginning of the course and the end of the course. I have also worked in collaboration with our mostly student-staffed volunteer placement organization on campus (Educational Participation in Communities) conducting group reflection sessions for our service-learning students. These exercises led by student facilitators involve, among other things, having students select objects (from their backpacks, etc.) to represent who they are in relationship to their service (which they then share in groups), as well as putting together collages from magazines about their service experiences. One reflection activity that I have found successful in service learning is when students answer the question "Who am I?" By focusing on a few aspects of their identity (such as "What does it mean for me to be a man?" etc.) and then relating this to what they have learned in their service experience, students are enabled to connect concepts and experience directly to the notion of identity. Students can then work together in groups to stage presentations, which end up being dialogues between the different identities.

In Introduction to Transgender Studies, I have students complete a term paper that integrates many of the different features described above. Some of the general questions they are expected to answer included the following:

- In which agency have you been placed? In which program?
- Whom does the agency serve?
- What is the mission of the agency?
- What do you think some of the major issues are that confront the clientele? The agency itself?
- What are some of the strategies that the agency uses to address these issues?
- Describe some of the activities that you did for the agency. What was the point of the activities? How did they fit into the agency's mission?
- Describe some of the interactions that you had with clients and with coordinators.
- What sorts of things have you learned about "trans issues" that you did not know before?
- How has this experience challenged you personally (if at all)?
- Are there any particular experiences that were especially meaningful to you? Discuss.

Students are then asked to reflect upon some of the issues presented and discussed in class in lectures and in readings. In particular they are asked to reflect upon the following questions in their paper: Does the theory illuminate the actual experience? Does the actual experience challenge a rethinking of the theory? What does this have to say about "trans issues" and the relationship between those issues and academia? And what does this reveal about you and your own relationship to gender?

The paper assignment involves three stages. First, the student met with me in person to discuss his or her service-learning experience and to talk about the overall direction of the paper. Then, the students wrote rough drafts. This enabled me to give fairly detailed comments on their work, encouraging them to explore issues that they may not have paid enough attention to. Finally, they submitted their final drafts. Because the assignment also had specific questions requiring students to gain certain information about the agency they were working with, this also seemed to encourage some focused, meaningful dialogue with their supervisor.

Engagement

In the case of civic/social engagement, my objectives are limited to the following: First, I intend for students to come away with an increased sense of social/cultural responsibility. Second, I intend for students to be more capable of moving beyond their own perspective, being sensitive to the perspective of others, and being capable of critiquing their own subject position.

Third, I intend for students to develop a deepened, more nuanced knowledge of the play of gender (sexual, racial, class) politics in everyday reality—including in the classroom and in the very deployments of theory.

The last of these is the easiest to determine, and I have certainly found that in general the students who have engaged in service learning have been able to make certain observations and critiques that they would not have been able to do in the classroom alone. For example, a student in my Philosophy, Gender, and Culture course who was doing outreach for the transgender program at Asian Pacific AIDS Intervention Team saw firsthand racial division and fragmentation among trans women, and the ways this gets played out even in the occupation of space (e.g., at dance clubs). He had been under the impression that the category "trans" was more homogenous and unified. While I can try to explain in class how the issues of race and class intersect transgender issues, I can also only go so far as a White, Anglo trans woman. A reality, which goes well beyond the classroom, is required.

The second of these, in my experience, is the hardest for students to actually achieve. Students—well, all of us, I suppose—are generally reluctant to engage in a kind of self-assessment or to see themselves from the perspective of another. Yet I continue to believe that this is an indispensable exercise (for all of us). Indeed, it is the key to successful world traveling. I have found that very good service-learning students can move in this direction. For example, a student in Introduction to Transgender Studies wrote in her paper:

> Before this class, I never questioned the fact that I was female or what being a female entails, yet that has changed. After some self-contemplation, I realized that I held both masculine and feminine traits yet in the same vein, questioned whether or not labeling the traits as such even mattered. Whether the attribute was masculine or feminine it did not change the fact that I had it.... This re-evaluation of my own relationship to gender allowed me to become even more accepting of different types of people and value the incredible diversity of human beings.

Students are often enabled to move beyond an easy objectification (especially in the case of transgender people) to the recognition that they are in the presence of genuine, flesh-and-blood human beings. Thus, one of the students working with Bienestar in Introduction to Transgender Studies writes: "What I did at Bienestar was converse with the transgender women and come to realize that transgender women are like everybody else. I did not have a note-pad ... it was actual conversation that took place."

Finally, we genuinely want our students to become more motivated to engage in social/political issues. Yet, to be sure, short of serious long-term follow-up, this is not easy to measure. One measure is that many students continue volunteering well after their service-learning experience. Indeed, some of my students have been recognized at volunteer recognition events and even found employment at some of their placement agencies. However, I think one of the most powerful example of this sort of impact came from a student who worked with Bienestar Human Service during the Introduction to Transgender Studies course. At the end of the quarter, we discovered that the transgender program was not going to receive funding, and as a consequence the program would have to close. The transwomen who worked at Bienestar organized a staged response to this. This student showed up at this event to speak from his own firsthand experience and to point out the valuable work that he saw performed in this program. His presentation was informed by the realities he had experienced and the empathy and the friendships he had developed with the women he had worked with. This young man—whose ambition was to become a lawyer and advocate for those sometimes forgotten—seemed to have already learned something important and to have already taken a stand. It was a sharp example of informed reflective social/civic engagement in a truly deplorable situation. It was an example of somebody who had clarified who he was and why that was important.

Evaluation

Community partners evaluate student participation and their success in community service through attendance sheets, evaluation forms (often coordinated through Educational Participation in Communities) and discussions with me. My general principle is that students are awarded an A for this component of the course and their grade is lowered only in case they fail to perform their tasks responsibly and in good faith. Through the reflection activities, I evaluate student success in achieving learning outcomes (including the civic outcomes mentioned above). I have found that students tend to be reluctant to engage in deep reflection and so it is important that the reflection activities be rather explicit and directive in order to encourage this type of inquiry. For example, a very simple way of measuring journal entries is to assign three points: one point for a discussion of in-class concepts, one point for discussing community-based experience and learning, and one point for reflecting upon the connections and disconnections between them (half and quarter points are used). Student paper topics include (as part of the assignment) specific sections, which require reflection on connections between theory and practice and on the overall sociocultural context. I take this sort of reflection as a necessary requirement of completing an assignment satisfactorily, I am not as demanding in my expectation that students demonstrate the capacity of challenging their own subject position. Rather, this I take this as a hallmark of a strong paper (B plus and above).

Conclusion

This coming year I will have the opportunity to teach Philosophy, Gender, and Culture again for the first time in a couple of years. I am looking forward to it, and I also eagerly await the next opportunity to teach Introduction to Transgender Studies. In the future, my intention is to clarify more distinctly the relationship between identity, "world"-travel, reflection, and social/civic engagement outcomes. I suspect that by fine-tuning these connections, I will be better enabled to guide students in examining themselves in ways that may not always be comfortable. I also hope to work even more closely with community partners in creating a truly integrated course. Greater attention to these features will help both courses become true vehicles of identity reassessments, "world"-travel, and social engagement. What I have learned, at any rate, is that by being both an instructor and a community activist, I am in a better position to help students increase their capacity for social engagement through thinking about identity, by partaking in "world"-travel, and by recognizing that even theorizing itself can be deeply political.

Notes

1. For a brief discussion of the notion of *identity* I have in mind and its relation to gender, sexuality, and homophobia, see Hopkins (1996). In my understanding of it, *identity* involves the following features: (a) reflexivity (i.e., it is a conception of oneself); (b) implication of others (i.e., a picture of the world that includes more

than oneself; (c) temporality (i.e., an interpretation of the past and expectations and plans directed toward the future); and (d) agency (i.e., the view of oneself as a moral subject).

2. *Transgender* is often used as an umbrella term, which brings together different kinds of individuals who have gender identities and/or expressions and performances that are taken to differ from "the norm." For example, transsexuals, cross-dressers, drag kings and queens, and some butch lesbians may be viewed as "transgender." Sometimes the prefix *trans* (as in *trans people*) is used as a way of avoiding the sometimes contested assimilation of transsexuals under the term *transgender*. MTF is often used to refer to male-to-female trans people and FTM is often used to refer to female-to-male trans people. All of this terminology is subject to political contestations and I do not intend to use it to attribute self-identities.

3. For an introduction to the notion of "trans studies" see Prosser (1997).

4. The move in this direction is best captured by Hale (1997).

5. For one of the most influential popular formulations of these ideas see Bornstein (1994).

6. For a discussion of such issues see hooks (1992, pp. 145–156).

7. For critiques see Namaste (2005, 2000) and Roen (2001).

8. See Lugones (2003). For a discussion of the relevance of "world"-traveling in the context of trans studies, see Hale (1998).

9. For an explanation of FTM see note 2.

I would like to thank my former students Alice Bui and Derek Murray for their kind permission to cite passages from their work. I would also like to thank Marie Auyong, Miguel Martinez, Alva Moreno, Alexis Rivera, Sonia Rivera, Bamby Salcedo, Kimberly Scott, Lauren Steely, Terri Tinsley, and Alexander Yoo for the various ways in which they helped bring many of the service-learning projects or in-class discussions to life. I give special thanks to Susan Forrest for her continued support and her invaluable comments and criticism.

References

Bornstein, K. (1994). *Gender outlaw: On men and women and the rest of us*. New York: Routledge.

Hale, C. (1997). Suggested rules for non-transsexuals writing about transsexuals, transsexuality, transsexualism, or trans. Retrieved from http://sandystone.com/hale.rules.html

Hale, C. (1998). Tracing a ghostly memory in my throat: Reflections on FTM feminist voice and agency. In T. Digby (Ed.), *Men doing feminism* (pp. 99–128). New York: Routledge.

Hopkins, P. (1996). Gender treachery: Homophobia, masculinity, and threatened identities. In L. May, R. Strikwerda, & P. Hopkins (Eds.), *Rethinking masculinity: Philosophical explorations in light of feminism* (2nd ed.) (pp. 95–115). New York: Rowman & Littlefield.

hooks, b.(1992). *Black looks: Race and representation*. Boston: South End Press.

Lugones, M. (2003). Playfulness,"world"-traveling, and loving perception. *Hypatia, 2*(2), 3–19. Reprinted and updated in M. Lugones (2003), *Pilgrimages/peregrinajes: Theorizing coalition against multiple oppressions* (pp. 77–100). New York: Rowman & Littlefield.

Namaste, V. (2000). *Invisible lives: The erasure of transsexual and transgender people*. Chicago: University of Chicago Press.

Namaste, V. (2005). *Sex change, social change: Reflections on identity, institutions, and imperialism*. Toronto, Ontario, Canada: Women's Press.

Prosser, J. (1997). Transgender. In A. Medhurst & S. R. Munt (Eds.), *Lesbian and gay studies: A critical introduction* (pp. 309–326). London: Cassell.

Roen, K. (2001). Transgender theory and embodiment: The risk of racial marginalization. *Journal of Gender Studies, 10*(3), 253–263.

ARE YOU A BOY OR A GIRL?

By Roe-Anne Alexander

Roe Anne Alexander, "Are You a Boy or a Girl?" *Gender Outlaws: The Next Generation*, ed. Kate Bornstein and S. Bear Bergman, pp. 72. Copyright © 2010 by Perseus Books Group. Reprinted with permission.

THE SELF I WILL NEVER KNOW

There are times when I wish I didn't know so much. And I realize that what I know, I learned too late. Reclaiming a childhood of medicalization can be challenging at best, but key to my survival. The challenge is not that I was born with atypical reproductive anatomy—but the power of others to question and correct my natural anatomy.

My treatment became white-coat violence the moment I lost my choice. The reason for 'corrective treatment' is to prevent emotional trauma associated with diverse anatomy. Yet quality of life and emotional support were never part of my care. Living in a body that raised all these questions left answers beyond my reach. Medical treatment is focused on correcting intersex variations, not advice for living with them.

I was not told of the frequency of intersex—it's actually more common than cystic fibrosis. At the age of 13, I was scheduled for surgery. I was not allowed to accept myself; I was told what is normal and how I should be. I was never told that I was viable; or that who I was is all I had to be.

Once deemed a 'medical success' I was left to feel that I had drastically failed, because corrective surgery did not make me feel normal. My feelings became irrelevant and I have feared success from that moment on. I survived by denying I had any feelings at all. My body was altered to meet social values, but my values were never discussed. My puberty was focused on vaginal function before I had a chance to care.

Children Who Don't Conform

Every day throughout the world children are born who challenge social values. And every day the response has been to make those children conform. This is not about children in medical crisis, but about children who are intimately invaded because their genitals aren't 'up to standard'. These kids are called intersex. Their genital or reproductive anatomy is treated as an emergency that must be *corrected* immediately. Genital variation is not medically threatening, but cosmetic surgery is the medical standard in most 'civilized' societies. In the United States alone, genital surgeries are performed on at least five children every day, probably more. Many will have to have surgery repeated several times throughout their lives.

In the year 2000 the American Academy of Pediatrics issued a statement that 'ambiguous genitals', the global term for intersex, constitutes an emergency. In fact, intersex includes anyone born with atypical genital or reproductive anatomy. Treating an emergency does not require parental consent even when cosmetically derived. This brings to light some curious questions about what is atypical, and who has the right to decide what acceptable genitals are. Are medical professionals standing by with rulers and stamps of approval? To some extent they are, and we are all subject to their judgement. The majority who pass are sent on their way; but, for the sacred few who don't measure up, the silent nightmare begins.

Intersex occurs as often as once in every 1,000 to 1,500 live births. Incidence is unusual, but not rare. Treatment refers to medical intervention to make atypical genital or reproductive anatomy normal. Normal is defined by medical standards determined by anatomical dimensions. The medical criteria for genital and reproductive anatomy are: a clitoris cannot be larger than 3/8 of an inch at birth … Or … visible? The recommendation is that an 'enlarged' clitoris be surgically reduced to match the medical standard. A penis is 'too small' if it cannot be stretched longer than one inch at birth. The recommendation for a child with a penis considered too small is to reassign the child female, and then create typical female anatomy. An 'adequate' vagina is one that will accept an average size penis. When a vagina is 'inadequate' various treatments are recommended to promote heterosexual intercourse. Medical treatment is deemed successful once these intimate dimensions are met.

Elusive Data

The data surrounding intersex is difficult to determine for many reasons. Doctors disagree amongst themselves regarding what conditions are considered intersex. Treatment for their 'intersex' patients could easily match treatment for patients with a different diagnosis. Many former patients avoid medical care because their medical histories are painful to explain to new doctors, or they have lost their trust in providers. These people are 'lost to follow-up' and data is unavailable.

Even as an insider, performing follow-up research has been difficult because many people cannot discuss their medical histories, do not know their medical histories, or have been used as research subjects during their intersex treatment. I suspect the incidence of intersex treatment is much higher than we imagine. Statistics on various diagnoses include:

- People whose bodies will not categorize them as male or female: 1 in every 1,000
- People with chromosome types that are NOT 'normal' XX (female) or XY (male): 1 in every 1,666
- Male-defined bodies with XXY chromosomes: 1 in every 1,600
- Female-defined bodies with XXY chromosomes: 1 in every 10,000
- Vaginal agenesis (or absence): 1 in every 4,000
- Number of people who have some form of genital surgery: 1 or 2 in every 1,000

There are dozens of intersex conditions that are medically corrected. Though techniques vary, the treatment goals remain the same:

- Enlarged clitorises are surgically removed or 'reduced'
- Treatment for vaginal agenesis includes a variety of vaginal reconstruction techniques to increase vaginal size and depth for penile vaginal intercourse
- Treatment for hormone differentiation involves lifelong hormone therapy and/or genital surgery
- Treatment for urethras that are not at the tip of a penis involves multiple surgeries to lengthen the urethra to allow urination while standing up
- Treatment for 'gender ambiguity' usually entails infant genital surgery and surgical sex assignment at birth.

Losing Sensation

The caveat of current protocols is that adults who have received successful treatments claim a loss to their quality of life. Others lose sexual sensation as a result of removed, reduced, enlarged or scarred genitals, in addition to loss of self. People are generally too young or traumatized to make the immediate decisions required upon discovery, so parents and providers are left in charge.

Treatment histories are not always disclosed, so children grow up in confusion. Since treatment is irreversible and permanent, discerning what is important to the child is essential for the parents or physicians who wish to do no harm. How can we ascertain what is best for the child when they are still too young to speak?

The medical community believes people will be traumatized by their atypical anatomy and need corrective treatment to lead happy and healthy, or normal, lives. Many adults argue that correction creates its own stigma that leaves them struggling with identities and loss of self. The growing number of support groups and patient advocacy groups (currently 3,012 appear in an internet search) endorse the position that corrective treatment does not resolve the issue of psychosocial adjustment.

Many people believe that corrective treatment created problems they didn't have before. Others believe that the foundation of their discontent is the treatment itself; and the values that overlook medical needs in the rush to correct intimate anatomy. Although doctors have produced a number of studies that support the current protocols, the reports contain limited definitions of physical normalcy. There is currently no data collected that includes quality of life for intersex outcomes. The intimate nature of intersex is complicated by the stigma around genital anatomy. We are not so quick to judge other parts of anatomy. We teach our children to respect diversity, yet adults create a 'state of emergency' over the size and shape of genitals. The real phenomenon is that the prevalence of genital and reproductive variation is kept such a secret. Intersex variations are so quickly 'disappeared' that we don't get a chance to know about them, or how they might mature.

Break the Cycle

The panic of discovery is real, and based in a perpetual cycle of ignorance. Discovery invites panic because intersex is unheard of. Panic invites correction to make it go away. Correction invites a conclusion that out of sight is out of mind. Doctors will admit to the wide range of variation, but the standard for what is acceptable has been determined by social and medical values rather than human nature. Removing intersex variation tips the scale to override diversity.

By normalizing genital and reproductive anatomy, we lose awareness. With each altered child, another will be born into the panic of ignorance.

The truth is that we need to move intersex away from the medical context and into our social consciousness. I think of intersex as a civil rights movement still in the stage of breaking the silence. I compare intersex awareness to other movements that have earned their place in the world. You cannot remove our existence by removing our anatomy. The panic that people feel at discovery comes from silence and isolation. Inclusion of diversity could prevent emotional trauma without physical or emotional scars. Educating families would provide time for children to decide what they want for themselves.

When I talk to people about intersex they are stunned by what they did not know. Their ignorance is genuine and their concerns hopeful. They see the benefit that intersex awareness can liberate everyone from rigid standards. History reminds us that social values can change with awareness. Just like homosexuality, which has finally been removed from the Diagnostic and Statistical Manual for mental disorders, intersex cannot be cured. Corrective treatment will never change who we really are: it only prevents others from knowing us.

The invasion I feel now is the need to feel my past and the fallen hope that I would find my 'self' in a medical diagnosis. Nary a day goes by that something doesn't remind me that I am a misfit in a normal world. When I am strong, I revel at being a misfit, and know that normal is no-one's reality. When I am strong I challenge ignorance and educate those who care to know. But I feel invaded when my strength dwindles, and I return to a solitary world. I feel invaded by pain and health concerns that never were addressed during treatment. I feel invaded by the ignorance of experts. I feel invaded by depression that takes too long to wane. I feel invaded by the theft of my former self whom I will never get to know.

Equality Watch: Sexual & Gender Minorities

Pictures of lesbian weddings and exuberant gay Mardi Gras parades suggest that equality for sexual minorities has come a long way in the past 20 years. Campaigners have fought for and won rights in Europe, Australasia and the Americas.

But the overall picture is mixed—and extreme. The UN, more than 50 years after the Universal Declaration of Human Rights was drafted, still denies these rights to the world's estimated 40 million homosexuals. Repeated attempts at inclusion have been derailed by powerful rightwing and religious interests.

In no country in the world today do lesbians, gays and transgender people enjoy full and equal civil rights with heterosexuals—rights, for example, relating to employment, housing, parenting, partnership, inheritance and protection from abuse and discrimination.

However, many states have made significant steps towards equality in recent years. South Africa and Ecuador have written anti-discrimination clauses relating to sexual orientation in their constitutions. In 43 states of the Council of Europe, discrimination against sexual minorities can be challenged under the European Convention of Human Rights. And in 2003 the US Supreme Court finally overturned an anti-sodomy law which had applied in 12 states.

But steps have been made in the opposite direction too. In the past three years the number of countries where homosexuality is punishable by death has risen from 7 to 10. All are Muslim-majority states, with Saudi Arabia, Afghanistan and Iran especially inclined to execute. The number of countries where homosexuality is recorded as illegal has gone up from 70 to 80.

Some impose prison sentences of 20 years or more. Gays and lesbians in Uganda and Russia have been tortured and forced into exile.

Street violence towards lesbian, gay and transgender people is alarmingly high. In Brazil some 90 are murdered each year. Police often fail to investigate such killings—or are involved themselves. Some religious fundamentalists in the US preach that it is a Christian duty to kill gays.

We know about these things because the issue of homosexuality is being openly discussed.

For people born with intersex conditions, their struggles remain little known. While there is public outcry over the African practice of Female Genital Mutilation (FMG), Intersex Genital Mutilation is practiced in hospitals of the rich world under the name of 'corrective surgery'. This is usually medically unnecessary, often carried out on babies of under 18 months, and may continue throughout the patients life.

Intersex campaigners are calling for an end to this. The child should be assigned a sex, says the Intersex Society of Northern America, given a name that corresponds to the sex, and raised with counselling and age-appropriate explanations of their condition.

Awareness is increasing. In 1999 the Constitutional Court of Colombia restricted the ability of parents and doctors to resort to the scalpel when children are born with atypical genitalia. It was the first time a High Court anywhere in the world considered whether Intersex Genital Mutilation was a violation of human rights.

Colombia's court also recognizes that intersex people are a minority which enjoys the constitutional protection of the State and that every individual has a right to define his or her own sexual identity.

INTERSEX 101

By Cary Gabriel Costello

What is Intersex?

OK, it's important that I get the basics out for blogreaders unfamiliar with intersex conditions. In our society, it's common to think that all people are born either male or female. But the biological truth is that sex is a spectrum. It's typical for people to lie near the male or female ends of the spectrum, but many people are born with bodies closer to the middle. Sometimes this fact is immediately clear at birth, because a baby has intermediate genitals. Sometimes a person may look male or female on the outside, but have different internal organs than would usually be expected. And sometimes a person may have a body with typical female or male organs, but have chromosomes that do not match expectations.

How Common is Intersexuality?

About 1 in 1000 babies are classified at birth by doctors as intersex because their genitalia appear atypical. This is more babies than are born with Down's Syndrome. Many more babies are diagnosed as having a "disorder of sex development" based on variant genitalia, yet not given an "official" intersex diagnosis. Other individuals are not diagnosed at birth, as their genitals appear fairly standard, but later are found to have an intersex condition. It is commonly estimated that 1 in 150 people has an intersex condition. Some find out because they encounter fertility problems, or have a medical scan done for some unrelated reason. Some people never know—do you know if your chromosomes are XX, XY, XXY, or some other variation?

What is the Gender of an Intersex Person?

The way to tell the gender of an intersexed person is to ask them. Often intersexed people identify as either male or female, because that is how contemporary Western society understands gender. Some of us do not identify as male or female, however. You can't tell by looking at an intersex person's body what their gender identity will be—different people with similar looking intermediate genitals will have different identities. Simply respect each individual's sense of self.

What are Central Concerns for Intersex People?

Intersex status has been treated as a source of shame in the U.S., which means that most intersexed people are in the closet about their status. We have been called "freaks" and "monsters," have been treated as sexually titillating, have been excluded from international sporting competitions, and have been subjected to medical treatment without consent. Intersex people deserve to have their bodies, their gender identities, and their choices respected.

A major complaint of many intersex people is that they were subjected to childhood surgery that they are unhappy about. Every day in the U.S., 5 babies are given sex assignment surgery to "correct" intermediate genitals to look more typically female or male. Doctors choose the sex they see as appropriate for the infant based on appearance or surgical ease—and quite often, their choice is wrong. In addition, many cosmetic surgeries are given to try to "normalize" children's genitals. Although doctors say they have gotten better at these surgeries over time, they usually produce loss of genital sensation. I don't know about you, but I and many others would rather have sensitive genitals than somewhat-more-average-looking ones. Advocates for the intersexed urge that no sex assignment or cosmetic surgery be performed on children. Instead, intersex children should be allowed to grow up to make their own decisions about what surgery, if any, they would like.

Intersex people may suffer from gender dysphoria if they were assigned by doctors to a sex but do not identify with it. If so, they should be assisted in securing hormonal and/or surgical treatment so that they can transition to the sex that is the same as their gender identity. Intersex people who develop at puberty in ways that conflict with their sense of identity should be given access to hormonal treatment to suppress unwanted periods, beard growth, etc. In dealing with managing our bodies with surgery and/or hormone therapies, intersex people share experience with trans people, and that commonality should be respected.

Intersex people and their families may also need supportive therapy. When a mother gives birth to an intersex baby, the family may be thrown into distress. It is especially important that the family receive support so that hasty decisions about "normalizing" surgery are not made. Adults who discover that they are intersexed may also be thrown into an identity crisis and need support. And since all intersex people have to face lack of understanding and pressure to hide our sex status, many of us need access to counseling.

There is a myth that intersex people are almost always infertile. Sadly, many of us are infertile not because of how we were born, but because of surgical intervention in infancy. In fact, intersex people can have children (I did it …), but we may need fertility treatment and supportive medical assistance during pregnancy and birth.

What are Some Common Types of Intersexuality?

There are many conditions that lead to intersex status. I have no interest in getting overly clinical and showing the sort of medical photographs of dehumanized children with their genitals exposed that are so common in discussions of intersex. We are people, not … bits for display. However, I'll do a quick run through of some of the most common flavors of intersex people, with physical description, in the name of education.

People with **Androgen Insensitivity Syndrome** usually have a clitoris, labia, and partial vagina, with testes internally. They develop breasts at puberty, but no periods. People with **Partial Androgen Insensitivity Syndrome** are born with intermediate genital appearance and internal testes.

People born with **Congenital Adrenal Hyperplasia** or **CAH** are born with a phallus, empty scrotum, a uterus, and ovaries. At puberty, people with CAH will develop breasts and get a period.

Hypospadias refers to a range of conditions in which a person has phallic tissue, but does not have the urethral opening at the tip. This can be a small displacement in an otherwise typical penis, or can occur with an intermediate genital appearance.

People who have **Klinefelter Syndrome** are born with XXY chromosomes. Individuals with Klinefelter's usually have a penis and small testes, wide hips, small breasts, and are usually tall and long-limbed.

People who have ovotestes are termed **true hermaphrodites** by doctors. Ovotestes are gonads which combine ovarian and testicular elements. Those of us with ovotestes may also have an ovary or a testis, and often have a uterus and a menstrual period.

What can Other People do to be Allies for Intersex Folks?

There are plenty of things allies can do, and I'll post more about them later. But the single most important thing allies can do is to refuse to treat intersex status as something shameful and freakish. Allies can help educate people about the fact that intersex happens and is not some sort of medical emergency requiring cosmetic surgery on infant genitals. Only an intersex person can determine what hir gender is, and what surgery if any zie wants—doctors and parents can no more decide what gender a person will have than they can pick hir sexual orientation or taste in music. Educating people about this will help lead to a day when parents welcome an intersex baby as a happy rather than tragic addition to the family.

THE "TREATMENT" OF INTERSEX AND TRANSGENDER INDIVIDUALS

By Eve Shapiro

The construction of binary genders that correspond to binary sexes is a social endeavor that, while not universal, has dominated North American and European thought since the nineteenth century. Researchers have increasingly documented, however, that this model is inadequate; it does not reflect the diversity of human bodies and lives. The hegemonic sex equals gender paradigm in North American societies asserts that male and female bodies are clearly, dimorphically distinguished by chromosomes (specifically XX for females and XY for males), internal and external biology (the presence of testes or ovaries, penis or vagina), as well as by naturally corresponding secondary sex characteristics (whether breasts or an adam's apple, and the appropriate presence or absence of body hair). In this idealized model all bodies clearly fit into one, and only one, of two possible sex categories in which each individual's genetic information matches his or her genitals and those genitals are the visible key that decodes his or her sex and attendant gender (Kessler and McKenna 1978).

This two sex/two gender paradigm so strongly structures our social scripts and meaning making that even scientists describe male biological attributes and processes as aggressive, violent, and strong and female biological functions as passive, soft, and receptive (Allen 2007). In both medical and lay publications, for example, descriptions of conception typically depict sperm that compete, race, burrow, and hunt while eggs wait patiently to be inseminated. This is held as true even though a more accurate description of biological processes would cast the egg as far more active and the sperm as more receptive (Tomlinson 1995). As Anne Fausto-Sterling, a biologist who has written extensively about the social construction of sex, summarizes, "reading nature is a socio-cultural act" (Fausto-Sterling 2000). The scripts for what "normal" bodies are and the dominant paradigm for sex and gender shape what we see when we look at the human body from a scientific perspective.

Reality is much more complex, however. Fausto-Sterling estimates that between 1 and 2 percent of infants are born intersex, possessing ambiguous genetic and/or physiological sex characteristics, but many of these cases are undiagnosed until something precipitates closer inspection. For example, in 1996, eight female bodied women, classified, raised as, and identifying as women their whole lives, failed the International Olympics Committee's chromosomal testing used to prevent men from competing as women (Fausto-Sterling 2000). This technologically advanced method of verification replaced the "primitive" method of genital inspections for women athletes, which was required until 1968. Instead of clarifying the "real" sex of athletes, however, these "advanced" technological methods only muddied the waters, so much so, in fact, that the International Olympics Committee dropped genetic testing for sex in 2000. Instead it returned to a reliance on lived experience and presentation. In this case, instead of offering clarity into competitors' "true" sex, new technologies highlighted the very instability and constructed nature of sex and gender.

Human bodies are not as clearly distinct in terms of sex or gender as most think. There are more physical and mental similarities than differences between men and women, and the considerable presence of intersex bodies challenge the veracity of a bipolar model of sexed bodies. This variation is viewed as disordered, however, and doctors—and the sciences that underlie their practice—impose a binary imperative on biological variation. Until very recently, the constructed binary was so naturalized that this diversity of sexed bodies was not allowed to exist. Instead, parents of intersex infants were pushed into surgical "correction" of their children's bodies, even when the surgical intervention served no purpose whatsoever outside of the construction of clear bodily distinction between male and female.

We as a society are so invested in this binary sex system, this notion that bodies come in only two forms, male and female, that we surgically alter bodies that do not fit this model simply because they do not fit. Indeed, decisions about whether to make intersex infants male or female have as much to do with social beliefs as any biological truth. Shaped by gendered beliefs (for example men need sexual satisfaction, women do not), infants are much more likely to be "made" female, in part because medical guidelines sway surgeons away from selecting maleness unless the child will have a "large enough" penis. Simultaneously, "feminizing" surgeries often permanently destroy sexual sensation for the girl child (Allen 2007). This profound commitment to a sex/gender paradigm is a clear example of how dominant social paradigms for sex and gender inform technological intervention into and personal experiences of bodies. Only in recent years has activism on the part of intersex individuals (often through advocacy groups like Intersex Society of North America [ISNA]) begun to change the treatment of intersex infants.

ISNA has worked for many years now to educate doctors and parents about intersex conditions and to advocate for delaying surgical or hormonal intervention. Driven by their own experiences of dishonesty on the part of parents and doctors, surgeries that scarred their bodies and removed pleasure (often surgeries on intersex children result in the loss of sexual sensation or function), and gender identities mismatched to their surgically assigned sex, intersex activists have protested, advocated, and fought for new treatment protocols. Most significantly, activists have argued that medically unnecessary treatment should be delayed until intersex children develop their own gendered sense of self and can participate in the decision-making.

And they have been reasonably successful; increasingly hospitals have intersex advocates on call so that when intersex children are born an advocate can come in alongside doctors to offer support and counseling. In the past parents were pushed by doctors to make quick decisions about treatment, often without access to any information about intersexuality in general or their child's condition more specifically. Now, the increased access to information and support has resulted in more parents choosing to delay or refuse surgical intervention. ISNA's work is just a fraction of what must be done to refashion our sex/gender paradigm in line with the diversity of human bodies, however.

Why might we as a society reinforce a two-sex system even though evidence supports a more diverse conceptualization of sex? Answers to this question reveal a lot about the power of sex and gender as a social institution. To begin with, our social order is based around two sexes: marriage laws and norms assume only men and women; buildings are required to have single-sex male and female bathrooms and locker rooms but not private or unisex ones; schools and organizations divide individuals by male/female; and official forms all offer only two distinct sex-categories. The binary sex/gender paradigm works interactively with other social institutions such as marriage, medicine, education, and sport to structure and direct our society, bodies, and identities. In this binary system, non-conforming bodies must be "disciplined," as Foucault would say, into place by available technologies of power. Although this discipline does not work perfectly, these societal forces are so powerful that diverse bodies are forced to conform, at least on the surface. As a consequence, the social invisibility of intersex contributes to the naturalized belief in a binary gender model.

As social context shifts and communities advocate for change, these same technologies can be used in new and non-normative ways. Groups like ISNA have been increasingly successful in changing how intersex infants are treated at birth, counseling parents to leave them to develop their own gender identities and then decide whether to avail themselves of any available technological interventions later in life. In many cases, intersex individuals are now choosing to leave their bodies as they are, and in the process are manifesting new sexed bodies. Meanwhile, transsexual and gender non-conforming individuals are also using the same technologies to intentionally construct differently gendered and sexed bodies.

In response to changes in societal gender paradigms and scripts, brought on by transgender and intersex activism, medical gate keepers such as psychiatrists and surgeons are slowly relaxing medical barriers to breast and genital (re)construction surgery. These changes are creating a diverse array of gendered and sexed bodies as individuals may solicit some but not all sexed/gendered bodily modifications. For example, an individual may choose to have breast augmentation or reduction ("top" surgery), genital (or "bottom") surgery, hormones, a combination of these biomedical interventions, or none of them.

Based on evidence discussed so far in this book, it will come as little surprise to discover that rates of surgery, hormone use, and cross-gender dress and bodily comportment vary dramatically across racial, economic, geographic, and sexual communities. We can begin to understand why hormone use dominates transsexual treatment in North America, for example (as opposed to primary reliance on hair removal or transplant, social role changes, or dress), by examining dominant paradigms of sex and gender and paying close attention to the central role of hormones in defining sex, the need for distinct physical sex characteristics, and the naturalization of gender (Fausto-Sterling 2000). The United States and Canada have legislated the validity of these types of differences—but not others—by requiring irreversible bodily changes in order to legally change one's gender status on official documents like driver's licenses, birth certificates, and bank records. While the requirements vary by state, those states that do allow changes in legal status tend to require significant bodily transformations as opposed to less invasive ones like a change in personal identity or social role. This is one of many reasons that transgender women and men with class privilege in North America are more able to gain recognition for their chosen identities than poor individuals; the ability to deploy legitimized gender change scripts requires the financial and social capital to afford the required transformations.

The set of surgical procedures aimed at changing an individual's body to match a gender identity have traditionally been called sex-reassignment surgery (and before that sex-change surgery). In recent years, however, as the transgender movement has grown and activists have received more attention, this term has fallen into disfavor by some. Some activists argue that they are not changing their gender or sex, but rather correcting the alignment between their body and their internal sense of self. Many of these individuals have come to use the terminology "gender confirmation surgery" to reflect these beliefs. Similarly, some transgender individuals bristle at the term "gender identity disorder," claiming that their gender—their internal sense of self—has never changed, that only their ability to manifest this self by having their body match it has (Bryant 2008; Waszkiewicz 2006).

As this debate plays out in media and press materials, in transgender activist and organizational statements, and among scholars and medical professionals, it is clear that the debate is really about sex and gender ideologies. These new technologies and attendant new scripts for what gender individuals can be are challenging the gender paradigms utilized to structure the dominant sex/gender system. If power is the ability to have one's own knowledge count as true, then this debate reflects the growing power of transgender individuals and communities to set the terms of their own lives, in the face of hegemonic gender paradigms, and the medical institutions empowered to maintain this system. In response to this diversity it is likely we will see more shifts in hegemonic paradigms and sex/gender scripts.

Debates over sex and gender identity reflect how language and attendant explanations for gender non-conformity change alongside ever-broadening gendered and sexed selves. Shifts in dominant gender and transgender paradigms have allowed for more diverse gender and sex scripts, and in turn individuals have advocated for visibility, support, and somatechnic interventions in line with these scripts. In the past, medical gate keeping was routinely used to police transgender body work by demanding that after gender/sex changes people live in line with hegemonic gender and sexuality scripts. Now, however, increasing numbers of endocrinologists and surgeons are willing to perform surgery or prescribe hormones even when individuals do not match heteronormative identity scripts, something that was highly unlikely only ten years ago. As these doctors allow the expansion of appropriate discourses-in-practice, there is less pressure on individuals to construct their own narratives within prescribed boundaries; at the same time the language of gender itself is broader and more readily available. Whereas most individuals identified as transsexual or transgender in the past, contemporary surveys find a multitude of gender non-conforming identities including genderqueer, bi-gender, and androgene (Beemyn and Rankin 2011).

Th ese differences are also generational, which suggests that younger transgender individuals are constructing identities and coming out with very different gender paradigms, social scripts, and technologies at their disposal. For example, young transgender individuals are significantly more likely to claim a diversity of gender non-conforming identities. As Rey, a young female-to-male transgender college student, commented in a 2008 New York Times Magazine article,

> Some transmen want to be seen as men—they want to be accepted as born men ... I want to be accepted as a transman—my brain is not gendered. There's this crazy binary that's built into all of life, that there are just two genders that are acceptable. I don't want to have to fit into that.

(Quart 2008: 37)

Moreover, there is a strong correlation between age and when individuals report meeting another transgender person for the first time (and presumably when they came to know about transgenderism and gain exposure to transgender identity and body scripts). In Beemyn and Rankin's National U.S. study, 76 percent of individuals under 22 years old had met another transgender individual by the age of 19, while only 32 percent of individuals had between the ages of 23 and 32, and only 5 percent of people 63 years old and older had. That is, the lower the age-cohort a person is in, the more likely they are to have met a transgender person at a young age. In the same study, Beemyn and Rankin found that 27 percent of individuals age 63 or older were totally closeted about their transgender status, while only 10 percent of individuals 22 or younger were, and only 9 percent of people age 23–32 were. Similarly, 34 percent of individuals age 23–32 described themselves as out to all their friends, while only 17 percent of people 63 and over were (other age groups ranged between 26 percent and 30 percent) (Beemyn and Rankin 2011). These statistics alone do not imply any causality; however, this data suggests that who people think they can be, and how able they are to manifest that identity in their body are changing significantly and these changes have everything to do with shifting gender paradigms and social identity and body scripts (Grossman and D'Augelli 2006).

While there has been positive change, it is important not to romanticize transgender lives or choices without grounding them within the lived reality of transgender people. Rey experienced significant levels of harassment and institutional resistance that caused him to move out of the dormitories at Barnard and even take a leave of absence from college. Rates of violence for transgender youth are significantly higher than for their cisgender peers, as are rates of poverty and homelessness (Namaste 2006; Shilling 2008). Some studies report that 60 percent of transgender youth experience physical violence (Moran and Sharpe 2004). Researchers also find that lack of social support from family, GLBT peers, teachers, and school administrators leads transgender youth to disproportionately high rates of suicidal thoughts, loneliness, and homelessness (Pardo 2008; Pardo and Schantz 2008). Moreover, class and race both affect outcomes for young people and adults, and transgender people of color experience more violence, higher rates of homelessness, and lower social status than their White peers do (Xavier et al. 2005).

Social change continues to be a slow process. Transgender social movements have brought transgender advocacy into the public sphere, and gender scholars across a variety of disciplines have documented the complexity of gender and the inadequacy of binary sex/gender systems. However, hegemonic paradigms and scripts have not yet caught up and gender non-conformity remains pathologized. That said, even though transgender individuals face tremendous discrimination and prejudice, transgender youth are more visible and more accepted now than at any other time in modern Western history (Beemyn and Rankin 2011). As individuals live in more complex bodies and with more diverse gender identities, these paradigms will likely continue to loosen, and social gender scripts will likely expand. The biomedical technologies being used to produce embodied gender differently will slowly shape public knowledge and discourse about gender and gender non-conformity.

Discussion Questions

1. What is the difference between sex and gender?
2. What do you think about genetic testing for sex in the Olympics and other sports competitions? Is it necessary? Does sex or gender matter more when deciding who can compete?

3. How does the increased flexibility afforded to intersex and transgender individuals in creating their own identities impact the binary gender system?
4. Discuss the ideas about gender and sex presented in the reading in terms of the nature and nurture arguments.

References

Allen, Caitilyn. 2007. "It's a Boy! Gender Expectations Intrude on the Study of Sex Determination." *DNA and Cell Biology* 26(10): 699–705.

Beemyn, Brett-Genny, and Susan Rankin. 2011. *Understanding Transgender Lives*. New York, NY: Columbia University Press.

Bryant, Karl. 2008. "In Defense of Gay Children? 'Progay' Homophobia and the Production of Homonormativity." *Sexualities 11*(4): 455–75.

Fausto-Sterling, Anne. 2000. *Sexing the Body: Gender Politics and the Construction of Sexuality*. New York, NY: Basic Books.

Grossman, Arnold H., and Anthony R. D'Augelli. 2006. "Transgender Youth: Invisible and Vulnerable." *Journal of Homosexuality 51*(1): 111–28.

Kessler, Suzanne J., and Wendy McKenna. 1978. *Gender: An Ethnomethodological Approach*. Chicago, IL: University of Chicago Press.

Moran, Leslie J., and Andrew Sharpe. 2004. "Violence, Identity and Policing: Th e Case of Violence against Transgender People." *Criminal Justice 4*(4): 395–417.

Namaste, Viviane K. 2006. "Genderbashing: Sexuality, Gender, and the Regulation of Public Space." pp. 584–600 in *The Transgender Studies Reader*, eds. Susan Stryker and Stephen Whittle. London: CRC Press.

Pardo, Seth T. 2008. "Growing Up Transgender: Research and Theory." *ACT for (Trans) Youth, Part 1*. New York, NY: Cornell University.

Pardo, Seth T. and Karen Schantz. 2008. "Growing Up Transgender: Safety and Resilience." *ACT for (Trans) Youth, Part 2*. New York, NY: Cornell University.

Quart, Alissa. 2008. "When Girls Will be Boys." *New York Times Magazine*, March 16, pp. 32–37.

Shilling, Chris. 2008. *Changing Bodies: Habit, Crisis and Creativity*. Thousand Oaks, CA: Sage Publications Ltd.

Tomlinson, Barbara. 1995. "Phallic Fables and Spermatic Romance: Disciplinary Crossing and Textual Ridicule." *Configurations* 3(2): 105–34.

Waszkiewicz, Elroi. 2006. "Getting by Gatekeepers: Transmen's Dialectical Negotiations within Psy-chomedical Institutions." Master's Thesis, Georgia State University, Atlanta, GA.

Xavier, Jessica M., Marilyn Bobbin, Ben Singer, and Earline Budd. 2005. "A Needs Assessment of Transgendered People of Color Living in Washington, DC." pp. 31–47 in *Transgender Health and HIV Prevention: Needs Assessment Studies from Transgender Communities across the United States*, eds. Walter Bockting and Eric Avery. New York, NY: Haworth Medical Press.

MODELS OF SEXUAL AND RELATIONAL ORIENTATION: A CRITICAL REVIEW AND SYNTHESIS

By Jeffry L. Moe, Stacee Reicherzer, and Paula J. Dupuy

Many frameworks exist to explain and describe the phenomenon of same-sex sexuality as it applies to human development. This conceptual article provides a critical overview and synthesis of previous models to serve as a theoretical bridge for the suggested multiple continua model of sexual and relational orientations. Recommendations for how counselors can adapt the multiple continua model to improve their work with same-sex sexual clients are presented, and future directions for research are discussed.

Counselors and psychologists are encouraged to avoid discriminating against clients based on their sexual orientation (American Counseling Association [ACA], 2005), and empirical scholarship continues to support the use of affirmative approaches as the standard of care when working with clients that experience same-sex sexual romantic and physical attraction (APA [American Psychological Association] Task Force, 2009). Despite these developments, counselors continue to report overt (Matthews, Selvidge, & Fisher, 2005) and subtle biases against clients who self-identify as lesbian, gay, bisexual, transgender, or questioning (LGBTQ) of their sexuality (Israel & Hackett, 2004). These biases are influenced in part by counselors' lack of both conceptual knowledge and practical experience working with same-sex sexual clients (Israel & Hackett, 2004; Matthews et al., 2005).

Inquiry into what motivates sexual behavior, desire, and identification has a long and interdisciplinary history (Gamson & Moon, 2004), and counselors may feel overwhelmed as they review past and current developments in theory related to same-sex sexual and relational attraction. The purpose of the present article is to provide an overview and critique of models that have been and are used to conceptualize same-sex sexual and relational attraction in order to familiarize counselors with the developments in theory related to this subject. These past frameworks are (a) the heterosexual–homosexual dichotomy, (b) biological evidence for sexual orientation, (c) social constructionism, (d) lesbian and gay identity development, and (e) two-dimensional models based on sexual and relational orientations. We also describe the sexual life course development model as put forth by Hammack (2005) to serve as a theoretical base for an alternative conceptual framework termed the *multiple continua model of sexual and relational orientations* (MCM). The MCM is offered as a working model to improve counselors' ability to conceptualize same-sex sexual clients' behavior relative to sexuality and is based on a critical synthesis of previous theory, research, and our own clinical experiences.

The Heterosexual–Homosexual Dichotomy

Counselors are likely familiar with the phenomenon of same-sex attraction in human beings and with the use of the words *heterosexual* and *homosexual* to differentiate an individual's exclusive sexual attraction to members of the same or to a different biological sex (Diamond, 2003). The term *homosexual* was invented in the late 19th century to describe a type of male person viewed as an antisocial deviant, pervert, and even a criminal driven by unnatural sexual motives (Silverstein. 1996). Ultimately, the terms *homosexual* and *homosexuality* came to connote a difference in kind or type from the heterosexual norm (Gamson & Moon, 2004). The heterosexual–homosexual dichotomy rests in part on the assumptions that other-sex sexual attraction (a) is normal (i.e., heteronormativity; Gamson & Moon, 2004), (b) is superior to same-sex sexual attraction (i.e., heterosexism; Herek, Gillis, & Cogan, 2009), and (c) is dictated by strict adherence to the social roles prescribed by biological sex (i.e., sexism; Konik & Stewart, 2004).

Counselors who rely on the dichotomous model may favor heteronormative and heterosexist attitudes and strict gender role stereotyping (Herek et al., 2009; Israel & Hackett, 2004). This is problematic because expecting people to conform to rigid gender and sexual roles will cause confusion as counselors encounter masculine gay males, feminine lesbians, or same-gender attracted transgender people. The dichotomous model is closely associated with the oppression of same-sex sexual people because it creates a conceptual binary where exclusive heterosexuality is favored (Garrison & Moon, 2004). Commitment to the dichotomous and totalizing heterosexual–homosexual model leads to further confusion as counselors encounter clients who express changes in identity over the life span and/or bisexual identities, attractions, and behavior (Chung, Szymanski, & Amadio, 2007; Diamond, 2003).

Single-Continuum Models
The Kinsey Scale

The notion that many more people may experience same-sex sexuality than they do exclusive homosexuality is one important idea that draws largely from the research conducted by Kinsey and his colleagues (Kinsey, Pomeroy, & Martin, 1948; Silverstein, 1996). The so-called Kinsey Scale describes a continuum in which people's preferences may range anywhere among 7 points between 0 (*exclusively heterosexual*) to 6 (*exclusively homosexual*; Kinsey et al., 1948). Kinsey et al. (1948) also articulated the experience of bisexuality, in which a person is equally attracted to members of both sexes. Use of the Kinsey Scale permits a basic reference structure in which homosexuality is not positioned in a diminished role relative to heterosexuality. This has been particularly useful for providing clients more possibilities for describing their sexual and romantic experiences.

Although the work of Kinsey et al. (1948) revolutionized a great deal of thinking about human sexuality, overreliance on the Kinsey Scale does have some limitations. The treatment of sexual orientation as a single continuum provides limited space for describing the influence of sexual and relational identification, sociopolitical positioning, and other components of sexuality. The terms *heterosexual* and *homosexual* fail to address the experiences of transgender women and men, because many transgender people describe their sexual orientations based on gender identities and not necessarily birth-assigned sexes (Namaste, 2000). Last, a single-continuum model conflates physical and romantic attraction desire (Diamond, 2003). Counselors who view physical and relation attraction as identical may be confused by intense emotional longing or by sex-seeking behavior without emotional attachment. By focusing on the object of sexual desire and fantasy, counselors may overlook the situational and social context of how identifying as a sexual minority affects a person's motivation to engage in sexual and romantic behavior.

The Biological-Essentialist Model

The biological-essentialist model is based on a positivist epistemology that purports to measure or observe naturally occurring phenomena (De Cecco & Elia, 1993). Proponents of the biological-essentialist model view same-sex sexuality as a part of a verifiable reality that has biological and therefore genetic origins or causes (Gooren, 2006). For example, it is apparent that individuals are more likely to report exclusive same-sex attraction if a biological sibling also reports the same (Diamond, 2003). Up to 60% of identical twins who report exclusive homosexuality share this with their twin (Gooren, 2006). One highly replicated finding in humans involves the increased chance that having older brothers helps in determining whether younger brothers will identify with the gay male label in later life (Gooren, 2006). Mobilization of the framework of biological essentialism facilitated the development of the concept of sexual orientation (Gamson & Moon, 2004; Hostetler & Herdt, 1998). In tandem, the social phenomenon of self-identification as gay (for males) or gay or lesbian (for females) is partly grounded in acceptance of the concept of sexual orientation rooted in the biological-essentialist worldview (Hostetler & Herdt, 1998).

Treating human same-sex sexuality as a naturally (i.e., biological) occurring phenomenon has facilitated many gains in terms of social tolerance and recognition for same-sex sexual people, yet much biophysical research is grounded in the attempt to find a cause (and subsequent cure) for same-sex sexual and relational orientations (De Cecco & Elia, 1993; Silverstein, 1996). Additional critiques of this framework are aimed at the idea that sexuality is a static component of an individual and that commitment to biological essentialism promotes use of the heterosexual–homosexual dichotomy to classify human sexualities (Gamson & Moon, 2004; Hostetler & Herdt, 1998).

Evidence that sexuality is more fluid, unfixed, and is both situation and context dependent (Diamond, 2003; Gooren, 2006) seems to align with the current consensus in the biological sciences regarding the role that physiology and genes play in determining human behavior. Current theory on the role of genes in human development is based on the view that genes do not dictate behavior, that most human traits are linked to multiple genes, and that the ecology surrounding an organism has a powerful impact on the expression of certain gene-linked traits (Douthit, 2006). Counselors who overrely on the biological-essentialist model for conceptualizing same-sex sexuality may fall back into a dichotomous mode of thinking about sexuality (De Cecco & Elia, 1993) and may fallaciously rely on biological determinism to explain human behavior (Douthit, 2006). The causal direction for biological findings related to same-sex sexuality has not been established (Hammack. 2005), and counselors who commit to simple biological determinism will have a difficult time understanding client impulsivity, relational connections and motivations for sex, changes in self-identification, and conceptualizing the role of homo-prejudice at the individual and social level.

The Social Constructionist Model

Whereas the biological-essentialist paradigm is largely grounded in the physical sciences, the social constructionist paradigm is based on poststructuralist theory and the analysis of language, social interaction, and how both language and interaction are influenced by social power (Hostetler & Herdt, 1998). Those operating primarily within a social constructionist perspective view people as developing within multiple overarching historical and cultural contexts, or *discourses,* that define and create the symbolic field that humans use to describe their life experiences (Hostettler & Herdt, 1998). Human beings navigate various discursive influences by exercising choice and the ability to act as coauthor of their own socially constructed realities (Hammack, 2005). From this perspective, biological essentialism and sexual orientation are viewed as limiting concepts that fail to capture the textured and multidimensional richness of human same-sex sexual drives, feelings, and behavior (Hammack, 2005). Proponents of social constructionism also advocate for a critical analysis of the privileges associated with identifying as heterosexual and the subsequent disadvantages of identifying as nonheterosexual (Gamson & Moon, 2004).

One critique of the social constructionist perspective focuses on how its proponents overemphasize the sociocultural embeddedness and therefore the fluidity of sexuality because of the location of subjective experience entirely within seemingly transitory discursive and symbolic fields (Hammack, 2005). This assumption is problematic because it is often used to assert that same-sex sexual phenomena (and not just the desire to self-label as same-sex sexual) are arbitrary, and this belief repositions people who identify as LGBTQ further into a space of marginalization, diminished agency, and discounted life experiences. Counselors who adhere to radical constructionism may be overly abstract when discussing sexuality, especially when it comes to explaining bodily responses. Overemphasizing the mutability of sexual self-identification is a key tactic used by those who engage in efforts to change same-sex attraction to other-sex attraction (APA Task Force, 2009).

Lesbian and Gay Identity Development

The concept of lesbian and gay identity development involves the theory on how a person comes to recognize his or her same-sex desires and associated behaviors and subsequently to incorporate this awareness into his or her overall sense of self-identity (Konik & Stewart, 2004; Mohr & Fassinger, 2000). This phenomenon is often referred to within the research community and within popular culture as *coming out* (Hammack, 2005). The term *coming out* is generally used to connote an event where a person discloses her or his same-sex sexuality to another person (Mohr & Fassinger, 2000). According to lesbian and gay identity development models, individuals are viewed as accomplishing critical tasks within distinct phases that permit internalization of high levels of same-sex affirming attitudes (Mohr & Fassinger, 2000). The final stages or phases of coming out are conceived by theorists as typifying a healthy, adaptive, and psychosocially well-adjusted same-sex sexual person (Mohr & Fassinger, 2000).

The aforementioned framework has received both support and criticism by researchers and LGBTQ rights advocates. Individual and intrapsychic models of LGBTQ identity development are often criticized for not considering the process of identity development within the context of a sociocultural milieu dominated by heterosexism, compulsory gender role conformity, and homoprejudice (Gamson & Moon, 2004; Konik & Stewart, 2004). The sociocultural influence on identity development is important to consider because of the controversial practice of encouraging clients to come out regardless of context (Hostetler & Herdt, 1998). The selective disclosure of one's same-sex sexuality may represent a mature approach to engaging with the management of stigma related to heterosexism and homoprejudice (Herek et al., 2009).

Two-Dimensional Models

Rather than a single dimension of sexual attraction and responsiveness explainable in terms of biology, culture, or identity development, researchers such as Diamond (2003) and Chung et al. (2007) have called for the incorporation of at least two dimensions when conceptualizing sexual and relational orientation. Diamond proposed that sexuality be conceived along physical-sexual and affective-emotional lines. This configuration, according to Diamond, accounts more broadly for lesbian women's experiences of their own sexuality and is based on Diamond's research with changes in lesbian identity over the life span. Chung et al. also called for a two-dimensional model of sexual orientation based on physical-sexual and affective-emotional lines. Chung et al. supported their paradigm with a correlation-based study demonstrating the ability of their model to correctly classify participants' sexual experiences and self-identification.

Two-dimensional models are valuable for expanding understanding of same-sex orientation further. However, they do not account for orientation that is based on gender expression, the degree of willingness to participate in sexual activity, or sociopolitical context (Herek et al., 2009) because these inform subjective understanding of personal sexual and relational experiences. Counselors who commit to an exclusively two-dimensional model may be confused by the choice to not disclose information related to both a client's physical and affective attraction. The ability to identify the objects of a client's sexual and romantic desire does not in itself help counselors to understand the choice to engage in certain sexual and romantic behaviors. Interest in sexual activity changes over the life course and may be influenced by access to role models, available partners, and the sociocultural environment in which individuals must navigate to meet their sexual and relational needs (Hammack, 2005).

Sexual Life Course Development

As proposed by Hammack (2005), sexual life course development acknowledges that human experiences of sexuality are conceived in relation to multiple drives and needs beyond physical gratification or emotional validation. Sexual life courses are conceived as developmental pathways that are embedded within meaning systems (i.e., language) that create and shape awareness in a given historical-cultural context (Hammack, 2005; Hostetler & Herdt, 1998). The pathways concept includes a person's experience of romantic, relational, physical-sexual attraction, and desire between human beings of the same biological sex. The model of sexual life course development facilitates validation of the idiosyncratic ways that people connect to and express their sexuality. As with other models, sexual life course development also addresses how people integrate experience of same-sex sexuality into an overall sense of personality and self within an existing "social ecology" (Hammack, 2005, p. 268).

Table 1: Multiple Continua Model of Sexual and Relational Orientations

Continuum	Orientation
1. Desire of sex characteristics	Male genitalia---------------------------------Female genitalia Male secondary sex characteristics------------ Female secondary sex characteristics
2. Desire of gender expression	Masculine-- Feminine
3. Sexual and relational interest	Low interest---High interest
4. Relational orientation	Same gender--Other gender
5. Community identification	Low identification--------------------------------High identification

We believe that Hammack's (2005) sexual life course development model provides an advancement of theory regarding sexual orientation. Hammack's work, however, is primarily an attempt to integrate and innovate beyond the biological-essentialist versus social constructionist debate and therefore is presented with a focus on these two paradigms. Specific articulation of how people negotiate available explanations for their own sexual and relational experiences along multiple pathways within the framework of sexual life course development is warranted. We therefore have developed a series of continua to more fully represent the range of possibilities for human sexuality and thus name our model the MCM (see Table 1).

The MCM

Rather than conceptualizing same-sex attraction as a singular phenomenon or enduring and totalizing experience, use of the MCM encourages the view that sexuality is best understood as a matrix of mental-emotional-behavioral experiences occurring across a wide range of contexts. It subsumes both a biological understanding of sexuality in which a person can articulate an orientation to a type of genitals or secondary sex characteristics. In addition it allows an articulation of socially constructed sexual and relational orientations within domains of an identity or a contextually defined relationship. Attraction to gender markers that are culturally adapted (e.g., long hair for women, competitiveness for men) become definable by the client based on her or his understanding (i.e., social construction of what the words *man* or *woman* signify).

The Desire of Sex Characteristics Continuum

The desire of sex characteristics continuum (see Table 1) represents relative attractions to female body characteristics and male body characteristics (Diamond, 2003). Additionally, this continuum may be used to represent an attraction to transsexual characteristics (e.g., a male-to-female transsexual with female breasts and a penis, a female-to-male transsexual with a male chest and a vagina) or intersexual characteristics. Given the potential for desire of transsexual or intersexual characteristics, this continuum may be used for multiple situational representations including attraction to genitalia or to secondary sex features (i.e., breasts or chest and body hair).

The Desire of Gender Expression Continuum

The desire of gender expression continuum differs from the desire of sex characteristics continuum (see Table 1) in that the attraction is not based on body sex features but the identified features of masculinity and femininity (Hostetler & Herdt, 1998). Experiences of masculinity and femininity represent the socially constructed roles and behaviors that have been culturally assigned to women and men specific to speech, demeanor, patterns of relationship, and personal adornment. Although patriarchal and heterosexist ascription of masculinity as male and femininity as female has been the dominant paradigm. Halberstram's (1998) *Female Masculinity* clarifies the experiences of women who are both identified with femaleness and with masculinity. Simultaneously, it invites readers to more clearly articulate an experience of male femininity for men who are identified with both maleness and femininity.

The Sexual and Relational Interest Continuum

Positioning sexual and relational interest as a continuum that is separate from the continua of desire (i.e., desire of sex characteristics and desire of gender expression) removes the essentialist argument of whether one is lesbian or gay by desire or by action. Rather, the sexual and relational interest continuum, as a low to high scale, identifies the relative interest in engaging in sexual and relational behaviors (see Table 1). Although one may self-identify as being attracted to male characteristics and to masculinity, for example, the curiosity and interest in engaging in sex with a male may be relatively low (Gamson & Moon, 2004). Used together, the continua of desire and the sexual and relational interest continuum illustrate a more inclusive depiction of a person's sexual identity and motivations for engaging in sexual and relational behavior.

The Relational Orientation Continuum

The relational orientation continuum's distinction is that the emphasis is in the individual's relationship role as a point of greater congruence with those of the same gender, those of the other gender, or both (Mohr & Fassinger, 2000). Like the desire of gender expression continuum, this continuum is positioned largely in the roles ascribed to women and men. For a woman who identifies strongly with relational intimacy with other women, which may or may not include sexual activity, her relational orientation would be same-gendered. Likewise, a female-to-male transsexual who is relationally oriented to women would experience his relational orientation as other-gendered. In examining sexual and relational orientation the emphasis is in understanding the gender orientation for intimate relations. When identified with the continua of desire and the sexual and relational interest continuum, the relational orientation continuum allows for an understanding of an individual's experience in relationship roles relative to orientation to sex roles.

The Community Identification Continuum

Self-identification with the terms *lesbian, gay,* or *bisexual* is emblematic of a cultural identity that is highly reliant on group cohesion for a variety of needs that include survival, safety, political visibility, and personal growth (Mohr & Fassinger, 2000). The ability to identify with a lesbian, gay, or bisexual community occurs within a sociopolitical structure that instills shame in same-sex sexual and relational orientation and that actively oppresses the collective LGBTQ communities (Herek et al., 2009). Within such a structure, naming of identity is infinitely challenged and becomes a potent self-symbol in which the individual is privately and/or publicly committing to an identity for which the likely outcome is some degree of social opprobrium.

Identification with the community is expressed in this article as a continuum of low to high identification (see Table 1). In the previous continua, the relative sexual and relational positions are understood as variables that influence how an individual engages sexually and relationally in romantic relationships. A same-sex sexual and relational orientation structure, however, does not immediately ensure identification with a community identity marker. To conceptualize this, consider a woman who partners with another woman at midlife following a lifetime of marriages to men and for whom the lesbian community is not a familiar identity marker. Her naming herself as a lesbian is not the distinguishing characteristic of her romantic relationship with a woman.

Implications for Counseling Practice

If clients (adults, adolescents, or children) disclose their struggling with same-sex feelings and attraction, the proposed framework of the MCM supports affirmative practice by permitting counselors to address the needs of same-sex sexual clients through the use of a broader conceptual framework grounded in current research and theory. Mapping the experiences of same-sex attraction into a profile along the identified continua increases the explanatory options for people struggling to accept or understand their sexuality. For example, a person may find sexual arousal to another member of the same biological sex (desire of sex characteristics continuum) as an extreme embarrassment because of personal beliefs about appropriate gender behavior (desire of gender expression continuum) and fear of being identified with a highly stigmatized social group (community identification continuum; see Table 1). Education on the normalcy of same-sex arousal would be appropriate at this level, and a nondirective stance related to the topic of self-identifying as gay or lesbian would be warranted. Some individuals may be comfortable experiencing and even expressing same-sex sexual desires and attractions but may be unsure of how this informs their sense of self and their behavior in a day-to-day context. Along with issues of relationship, sexual expression, and curiosity, people may struggle with fitting into local same-sex sexual communities. The following case examples of Damien and Sarah (fictitious names associated with case material synthesized from multiple clients) further demonstrate this application of MCM mapping for work with same-sex sexual clients.

MCM Mapping Example: Damien

Damien is a man self-identified as a heterosexual who presents in counseling to address dissatisfaction in his marriage, which included a lack of sexual fulfillment. Damien is primarily female attracted, although his sexual (premarital) history has included relationships with both women and men. In his current life, Damien does not identify himself as masculinity-attracted but considers himself open to relationships with preoperative transsexual women. The majority of Damien's relationships for his life were female, and he identified a preference for female companionship in his relational structure. In addition, Damien expressed little concern about whether people think of him as gay or straight. On the continua, Damien charts his experiences as (a) desire of sex characteristics—midpoint between male genitalia and female genitalia, (b) desire of secondary sex characteristics—female end of the continuum, (c) desire of gender expression—toward the feminine end of the continuum, (d) sexual and relational interest—high end of the continuum, (e) relational orientation—other gender end of the continuum, and (f) community identification—between the low end and midpoint of the continuum. This mapping of Damien on the continua allows for a broader discussion of the role his sexual identity will play in the decisions he is making in his relationship with his wife.

MCM Mapping Example: Sarah

Sarah attended counseling to explore her emerging feelings for a man whom she was dating. Part of her struggle was embedded in the fact that, for all of her adult life, she had exclusively dated women. On the continua, Sarah's experiences are as follows: (a) desire of sex characteristics—halfway between the female end of the continuum and the midpoint, (b) desire of secondary sex characteristics—halfway between the female end of the continuum and the midpoint, (c) desire of gender expression—feminine end of the continuum, (d) sexual and relational interest—between the midpoint and the high end of the continuum, (e) relational orientation—midpoint of the continuum, and (f) community identification—high end of the continuum. Through this exercise, Sarah was able to articulate that indeed she was primarily female-attracted to women and to femininity. In addition, her identity as a lesbian woman was important to her. Her attractions to her boyfriend were creating interest and curiosity that, as she identified, were moving her from the female end to the midpoint of the continuum.

Implications for Theory and Research

The MCM represents a logical next step in developing a theoretical understanding of human sexual and relational experiences. The recognition of a broad spectrum of bodily orientations, attractions by gender, and community identities creates greater conceptual possibilities for human relationships. Through adding to the conceptualization of a variety of sexual and relationship orientations, new language and descriptions may be constructed depicting the variety of means by which people experience sexual and relational attractions. Empirical work on how people relate to sexual interest and curiosity would be an important contribution to the current discussion, as well as further articulation of how life experiences related to sexual and relational awareness develop over the life span. Because we offer the MCM as a means to explain client motivation to engage in sexual and relational behaviors, it would be helpful to know how well the MCM predicts behavior in a manner similar to how Chung et al. (2007) used their conceptual model. Finally, it is important to empirically compare the MCM to models of gay or lesbian identity development to see if a relationship exists and, if so, to what extent.

Conclusion

Scholarship, research, and newly developed standards of care continue to support the use of affirming approaches for clients who self-identified as LGBTQ (ACA, 2005; APA Task Force, 2009), and these developments encompass counselors' ability to conceptualize same-sex sexual and relational orientations across a variety of social positions and life experiences. The presented MCM facilitates the implementation of affirmative approaches based on cultivating rapport and grounding interventions within client experience using an expanded conceptual framework. The MCM further helps counselors to avoid stigmatizing clients for having self-doubt, low self-esteem, and ambivalence related to self-identification as LGBTQ, engaging in sexual and relational encounters, or confusion related to how sexual and relational desire informs their sense of connection to different communities. Becoming aware of the advances in theory related to human same-sex sexual and relation orientations that form the basis of the MCM promotes sensitivity and competency for counselors striving to meet the needs and promote the development of same-sex sexual clients.

References

American Counseling Association. (2005). *ACA code of ethics*. Alexandria, VA: Author.

APA Task Force on Appropriate Therapeutic Responses to Sexual Orientation. (2009). *Report of the Task Force on Appropriate Therapeutic Responses to Sexual Orientation*. Washington, DC: American Psychological Association.

Chung. Y. B., Szymanski, D. M., & Amadio, D. M. (2007). Empirical validations of a multidimensional model for assessing sexual orientation. *Journal of LGBT Issues in Counseling. 1*(3), 3–13. doi: 10.1300/J462v01n03_02

De Cecco. J., & Elia, J. (1993). A critique and synthesis of biological essentialism and social constructionist views on sexuality and gender. *Journal of Homosexuality. 24.* 1–26.

Diamond, L. M. (2003). What does sexual orientation orient? A biobehavioral model distinguishing romantic love and sexual desire. *Psychological Review. 110.* 173–192. doi: 10.1037/0033-295X.110.1.173

Douthit, K. (2006). The convergence of counseling and psychiatric genetics: An essential role for counselors. *Journal of Counseling & Development. 84.* 16–28.

Gamson. J., & Moon, D. (2004). The sociology of sexualities: Queer and beyond. *Annual Review of Sociology. 30,* 47–64.

Gooren, L. (2006). The biology of human psychosexual differentiation. *Hormones & Behavior. 50.* 589–601.

Halberstram, J. (1998). *Female masculinity*. Durham, NC: Duke University Press.

Hammack, P. (2005). The life course development of human sexual orientation: An integrative paradigm. *Human Development. 48.* 267–290. doi: 10.1159/000086872

Herek, G. M., Gillis, J. R., & Cogan, J. C. (2009). Internalized stigma among sexual minority adults: Insights from a social psychological perspective. *Journal of Counseling Psychology. 56,* 32–43. doi:10.l037/a0014672

Hostetler, A., & Herdt, G. (1998). Culture, sexual lifeways, and developmental subjectivities: Rethinking sexual taxonomies. *Social Research. 65.* 249–290.

Israel, T., & Hackett, G. (2004). Counselor education on lesbian, gay, and bisexual issues: Comparing information and attitude exploration. *Counselor Education and Supervision. 43.* 179–191.

Kinsey, A. C., Pomeroy, W., & Martin, C. (1948). *Sexual behavior in the human male*. Philadelphia, PA: Saunders.

Konik, J., & Stewart. A. (2004). Sexual identity development in the context of compulsory heterosexuality. *Journal of Personality. 72.* 815–843.

Matthews, C. R., Selvidge, M. M. D., & Fisher, K. (2005). Addictions counselors' attitudes and behaviors toward gay, lesbian, and bisexual clients. *Journal of Counseling & Development, 83,* 57–65.

Mohr, J., & Fassinger, R. (2000). Measuring dimensions of lesbian and gay male experience. *Measurement and Evaluation in Counseling and Development, 33,* 66–90.

Namaste, V. (2000). *Invisible lives: The erasure of transsexual and transgendered people*. Chicago, IL: University of Chicago Press.

Silverstein, C. (1996). History of treatment. In R. P. Cabaj & T. S. Stein (Eds.), *Textbook of homosexuality and mental health* (pp. 3–16). Washington, DC: American Psychiatric Press.

COMING TO AN ASEXUAL IDENTITY: NEGOTIATING IDENTITY, NEGOTIATING DESIRE

By Kristin S. Scherrer

INTRODUCTION

One of the most pervasive social assumptions is that all humans possess sexual desire (Cole, 1993). A related assumption about sexuality is that sexuality is not only something one *does*, but an identity, or something one *is,* usually biologically (Foucault, 1978; Weeks, 1986). While scholars of sexuality have theorized the social constructions of sexuality and sexual identity, there remains a relative paucity of academic literature exploring the identities and experiences of people who do not experience sexual attraction or desire.[1] Individuals who identify as asexual challenge these notions of the pervasiveness of sexuality and present a unique opportunity to explore the negotiation of identity and desire. Asexuality, a relatively recent emergent sexual identity, has been developed with the aid of internet technologies which have allowed for the formation of community by otherwise geographically isolated individuals.

Social scientists conceptualize their interests in sexuality in three common ways: behavior, desire and identity (Laumann et al., 1994). In this project I have chosen to focus on asexual identities. Inquiry into asexual identity is important as those researchers who have explored asexuality have primarily approached it as either a behavior (lack of sexual acts) or a desire (lack of desire for sexual acts). Much of the research on a lack of sexual desire or behavior examines it as either a bodily dysfunction that requires health intervention (i.e. through hormone therapy) or as a psychological diagnosis that should be treated through therapeutic means (such as Sexual Aversion Disorder and Hyposexual Desire Disorder [APA, 2000]). A focus on asexual *identity* is largely missing from the scholarly literature.

Research on identity is important since, as sexuality researcher Paula Rust argues, 'While the production of identity is a social-psychological process, the consequences of identity are both social and political' (Rust, 1992: 366). Identity is not only an introspective process, but is given meaning by the broader cultural understandings of that identity and connects one's self with others. As Rust (1992: 367) says, 'lesbian and gay identities are examples of communities based on shared identity'. Rust theorizes that coming to an LGBTQ identity connects an individual to a social experience of that identity, which for sexual minorities is often marked by discrimination. For both LGBTQ and asexual people, one of the locations of discrimination is its historical and contemporary connection to institutions of mental and physical health (Conrad and Schneider, 1994). Asexual identity not only reflects an introspective process, but also connects the internal experience of coming to an asexual identity to others, which may in turn motivate social and political action similar to other marginalized sexualities.

[...]

Findings

Three main themes emerged in my analysis: the meaning of the sexual, essentially asexual, and the romantic dimension. The first section describes how asexual individuals give meaning to their identities and behaviors, often drawing on a penetrative conception of sex. The second theme explores how asexual individuals experience their asexuality as an innate aspect of themselves, engaging social constructivist and essentialist debates about sexuality. The last section describes how asexual identities illuminate another dimension of sexuality: interest in romantic partnerships. While each of these sections explore unique aspects of asexuality, they all focus on what asexual identities are, how individuals come to identify as asexual, and what this identity means to them.

The Meaning of the Sexual

As with other sexual identities, the meaning of an asexual identity varies. The most common description of an asexual identity closely mirrors the definition given on AVEN's website, of asexuality as 'a person who does not experience sexual attraction' (AVEN, 2007). Of the 89 participants who responded to the question 'what does this identity mean to you?', 39 (44 %) of participants said that their asexual identity means that they do not experience sexual attraction or sexual desire. AVEN's role in providing one possible meaning of an asexual identity is evidenced by Natalie, a 26-year-old white woman who describes what her asexuality means to her by saying, 'I follow AVEN's description of asexuality'. For Natalie, her internalized meaning of asexuality is hard to separate from AVEN's own conception of asexuality. Another participant, Jenn, an 18-year-old white woman, elaborates on this lack of sexual attraction:

> I just don't feel sexual attraction to people. I love the human form and can regard individuals as works of art and find people aesthetically pleasing, but I don't ever want to come into sexual contact with even the most beautiful of people.

While lack of sexual attraction and desire was a highly common feature of participants' descriptions of their asexuality, it was by no means a universally shared definition of asexuality.

The most common description of asexuality used the same language as the AVEN website, however the remaining 50 participants put forth alternative understandings of their asexual identity. Of these 50, 13 participants offered definitions of their asexuality that continaed relatively limited information about the meaning of their asexual identity. For instance, Barry, a 29-year-old white male characterized his asexuality: 'It's just who I am, romantically and sexually speaking'. Of the remaining 37 participants, the most common definition of asexuality centered on a lack of interest in sexual behavior that was described as not necessarily associated with sexual attraction. For instance, Jodi, a 32-year-old Asian woman describes her asexuality: 'I am sexually attracted to men but have no desire or need to engage in sexual or even non-sexual activity (cuddling, hand-holding, etc.) with them'. Similarly, Sarah, a 22-year-old white woman, says that for her asexuality means that 'I don't have sex and don't understand why people would want to have sex'. For both Jodi and Sarah, an asexual identity is *not* about attraction, but rather intent to participate in sexual behaviors. In addition to the wide variation in the definition of an asexual identity, there was also variation as to what behaviors 'count' as sexual.

Despite describing themselves as not experiencing sexual desire or attraction, 13 participants described interest in some sort of physical intimacy with another or others when describing an 'ideal relationship'. For Mark, a 36-year-old multi-racial male who identifies as a romantic hetero-asexual, 'I'm romantically attracted to the opposite sex, but don't desire sexual contact. I enjoy cuddling, and kissing and even pleasing my wife, but I don't desire sexual intercourse.' Callie, a 28-year-old white woman, said physical affection is fine, 'so long as the physical contact does not become sexual in nature'. This is similar to Dan, a 21-year-old white male, a self-identified hetero-romantic asexual, who says, 'certain things that might be considered sexual behavior—hugging, cuddling, kissing—I would be interested in, but nothing explicitly sexual.' As these participants illustrate, defining the boundaries between physical affection and sexual interactions is important to an asexual identity.

These accounts demonstrate that the boundaries between sexual and not sexual are largely based on an androcentric understanding of sex, where behaviors other than penile-vaginal intercourse are generally delineated as not sexual. According to Maines (1999: 5) an androcentric conception of sex involves 'preparation for penetration ("foreplay"), penetration and male orgasm'. A prime example of this is Mark, who describes himself as a romantic hetero-asexual and his wife as a sexual person. Recall that Mark says that he enjoys 'pleasing his wife' but does not desire sexual intercourse. While we can only guess what was meant by Mark's interest in pleasing his wife, if we assume that 'pleasing his wife' is widely considered a sexual act, then Mark is working to separate what is commonly understood as sexual from what is understood as non-sexual. Yet Mark's interpretation is similar to androcentric understandings of this participant's actions, as both characterize it as non-sexual because of the lack of penile penetration and (presumably) male orgasm.

This negotiation between the sexual and the non-sexual is especially relevant when considering the issue of masturbation. While I did not explicitly ask about masturbation in this survey, 10 of the participants mentioned it while describing their asexual identity. For Farina, a 25-year-old white woman who described herself as a bi-curious asexual, asexuality means, 'I don't need, want, or like sex, including any activities that seem to be leading to sex. For me this includes masturbation. [I experience] no desire for sex with another person or with myself.' Farina and others make the distinction between sex in relation to others and the sexual encounter with the self, or masturbation. Yet despite this distinction, Farina still considers masturbation to be an expression of sexual desire that she is not interested in.

While Farina described masturbation as 'sexual' and something she was not interested in, others describe masturbation as congruent with their asexual identity. For Gloria, a 20-year-old white female who self identifies as asexual,

I do not have any desire to have sex with another person. I masturbate at times but I don't connect it with anything sexual. I know it sounds like a contradiction but it's just something I do every now and then and it seems to help me relax when I am stressed.

For this person, masturbation was a bodily activity, unconnected with sex. Another participant, Carlos, a 21-year-old, self-identified Hispanic and Northern European male, who describes himself as an aromantic asexual, 'occasionally gets the urge to masturbate (which I will occasionally do), but I still do not experience attraction and have no real desire to engage in sexual activity with anyone'. This disconnection between masturbation and sexuality is an interesting divorce, especially given masturbation's historical connection to sex (Laqueur, 2003). These descriptions reinforce findings by Prause and Graham (2007), who found that two of the four self-identified asexual people in their sample did engage in masturbation while defining it as nonsexual. According to Prause and Graham, 'The interviews also suggested that asexual individuals interpret fewer behaviors as sexual, as compared to non-asexual individuals, possibly due to the lack of pleasure associated with them' (2007: 6). While lack of pleasure may be one explanation for this, it is also important to consider how social and cultural factors, in addition to individualistic factors, may be important for delineating appropriate behavior understanding.

[...]

Conclusions

As suggested throughout, there are myriad connections between asexuality and other sexual minorities.[2] First, asexuality shares an association both historically and presently to medical institutions with other marginalized sexual desires and behaviors. Yet, while activists and scholars have challenged the connections between medical discourses and same-sex desire (Conrad and Schneider, 1994; Kraft-Ebbing, 1886 [1959]; Rubin, 1984), diagnoses associated with asexuality (such as Sexual Aversion Disorder and Hyposexual Desire Disorder) are relatively unexplored. These similarities motivate collaboration in political strategy, as both asexual people and other sexual minorities who are in conversation with medical discourses might collaborate for a more complete transformation of these discourses. The lack of visibility and awareness of asexuality is a barrier to its inclusion in other sexuality-based political action groups.

While a historical and contemporary relationship with discourses of medicine are shared, LGBTQ identities also have a historical relationship with legal institutions as gender presentation and same-sex behaviors have been prosecuted by legal institutions (D'Emilio, 1983; Rubin, 1984). Asexuality, on the other hand, has been largely unnoticed by legal institutions, perhaps in part because of its *lack* of behavior and desire. In some ways, because asexuality is defined as a *lack* of behavior or desire, it has escaped attention, which is a clear departure from the experiences of other marginalized sexualities.

Asexual and LGBTQ groups also share similarities as both have created identity-based communities. As research documents, gay, lesbian, trans-gender and BDSM individuals use sexual identity communities to find support, relationships and to engage politically (D'Emilio, 1998; Rust, 1992). This is similar to how asexual individuals describe the functions of asexual communities. These communities not only serve similar functions, but both asexual and LGBTQ people are using internet technologies to form community (Jay, 2003; McKenna and Bargh, 1998; Turkle, 1995). While both utilize the networking possibilities of the internet, queer communities have additional visibility in physical spaces such as bars, bookstores and social service organizations that cater to LGBTQ identities. Furthermore, there are cultural symbols that represent the desires, identities and behaviors of LGBTQ identities and subcultures (such as rainbows or pink triangles), whereas symbols of asexual identities and subcultures are not yet generally recognizable.[3] Thus, while both asexual and LGBTQ identities have identity-based communities, the forms and functions of these communities are distinct.

While the aforementioned aspects are more social-structural, asexuality shares a similar social-psychological process of coming to an identity as other marginalized sexual identities. As Paula Rust says, sexual identity is 'a description of the location of the self in relation to other individuals, groups and institutions' (Rust, 1996: 78). Given this understanding of sexual identity, bisexual, asexual, gay and pan-sexual individuals all draw on existing language, their current social situation and the social and cultural meanings associated with these identities to place themselves in relation to other individuals and institutions and to accurately describe their internal sense of self. Additionally, asexual individuals, as well as gay, bisexual or queer individuals, often share a sense of their sexuality as biological and innate, despite descriptions of coming to these identities that reveal profoundly social experiences.

Notes

1. Notable exceptions include Bogaert, 2004 and 2006; Prause and Graham, 2007 and Rothblum and Brehony, 1993.

2. While I am speaking broadly about sexual minorities and marginalized sexualities, I by no means wish to minimize the differences between these sexualities. Yet in order to make generalizations, for the purposes of this article I am collapsing differences to draw attention to the broader similarities and differences associated with asexuality. Future research may wish to explore distinctions between asexuality and other marginalized sexualities.

3. For symbols of asexuality I invite you to explore the AVEN website at www.asexuality.org.

About the Author

Kristin S. Scherrer, PhD, LCSW
Assistant Professor
School of Social Work
Rutgers, the State University of New Jersey Mailing address: 536 George St. New Brunswick, NJ 08901 Office address: 502 George St. New Brunswick, NJ 08901, Room 309
(848)932-4492
kscherrer@ssw.rutgers.edu

WHOSE FEMINISM IS IT ANYWAY?

The Unspoken Racism of the Trans Inclusion Debate

By Emi Koyama

Emi Koyami, a grass-roots activist, author, and academic in Portland, Oregon, works on transgender and intersex issues, sex-worker rights, queer domestic violence, and anti-racism. In this article she delivers a stinging rebuke of both lesbian-feminists and transgender activists who have participated in the heated debates about the inclusion of transgender women in women's only space. Both groups, she contends, historically have predicated their arguments on racist practices and assumptions.

Koyami pays particular attention to the controversy surrounding transsexual attendance at the Michigan Women's Music Festival, which has played an influential role in shaping the debate on the status of transsexualism within feminist politics in the United States. She is sharply critical of a group of white, middle-class post-operative transsexual women who issued a statement in 2000 that supported a "no-penises" policy at the festival. This policy would allow these women to attend the festival, while barring their transsexual sisters who could not afford expensive genital surgeries not covered by health insurance. This group specifically noted that their proposed policy was disadvantageous to transgender women of color and poor people, but nevertheless considered their proposal the best compromise position available. Koyami has equally harsh words for the lesbian-feminists whose rationale for excluding transsexual women from women-only space recapitulated the logic of similar justifications within identity-based political movements for the exclusion or marginalization of women of color and the poor.

Koyami concludes her article by calling attention to the assimilationist argument for transsexual inclusion in feminist and women's movements espoused by many middle-class white transsexuals, that is, that "except for our history of embodiment we're just like you." She claims this argument, which parallels the liberal movement for gay and lesbian social inclusion, necessarily whitewashes the crucial question of difference within identity-based political communities. It is precisely by denying the importance—or even the very existence—of difference within an identity group that people in unmarked positions of privilege (such as white or middle-class status) gain the ability to falsely universalize from their own experience, and marginalize and exclude those in less privileged circumstances.

I

I have never been interested in getting myself into the mud wrestling of the whole "Michigan" situation (i.e. the debate over the inclusion of trans people in Michigan Womyn's Music Festival). But I have become increasingly alarmed in the recent months by the pattern of "debate" between white middle-class women who run "women's communities" and white middle-class trans activists who run trans movement. It is about time someone challenged the unspoken racism, which this whole discourse is founded upon.

The controversy publicly erupted in 1991, when organizers of the Michigan Womyn's Music Festival expelled a transsexual woman from the campground, or "the Land," announcing that the festival is open only to "womyn-born-womyn" a category designed to exclude transsexual women. Next year, a small group of transsexual activists gathered in front of the Festival entrance to protest the policy. According to Davina Anne Gabriel, then the editor of *TransSisters: The Journal of Transsexual Feminism,* the "stated intent [of the protest] from the very beginning was to persuade the organizers to change the festival policy to allow postoperative—'but not preoperative—'male-to-female transsexuals to attend."[1] Based on the survey Gabriel and others conducted in 1992, they argued that majority of festival participants would support such a policy change, while the same majority would oppose inclusion of "pre-operative" transsexual women.[2]

If that was the case in 1992, the debate certainly expanded by 1994, when the protest came to be known as "Camp Trans." "In the first Camp Trans, the argument wasn't just between us and the festival telling us we weren't really women. It was also between the post-ops in camp telling the pre-ops they weren't real women!" says Riki Anne Wilchins, the executive director of GenderPAC. According to an interview, Wilchins advocates the inclusion of "anyone who lives, or has lived, their normal daily life as a woman" including female-to-male trans people and many "pre-operative" transsexual women,[3] Or, as Gabriel alleged, Wilchins made a "concerted effort" to "put herself in charge" of the protest and to "force us ['post-operative' transsexual women] to advocate for the admission of preoperative [male-to-female] transsexuals." Gabriel reported that she "dropped out of all involvement in the 'transgender movement' in disgust" as she felt it was taking the "hostile and belligerent direction" as symbolized by Wilchins.[4]

For several years since its founding in 1994, GenderPAC and its executive director Wilchins were the dominant voice within the trans movement. "Diverse and feuding factions of the transgender community were brought together and disagreements set aside for the common good," JoAnn Roberts describes of the formation of the organization. But like Gabriel, many initial supporters of GenderPAC became critical of it as Wilchins shifted its focus from advocating for rights of transgender people to fighting all oppressions based on genders including sexism and heterosexism. Dissenters founded alternative political organizations specifically working for trans people's rights.[5]

Similarly, five transsexual women including Gabriel released a joint statement just few days before the Michigan Womyn's Music Festival 2000 criticizing both festival organizers and Wilchins as "untenable, anti-feminist, and ultimately oppressive of women, both transsexual and non-transsexual." Wilchins' tactics were too adversarial, confrontational and disrespectful to women, they argued. Non-transsexual and "post-op" transsexual women alike "deserve the opportunity to gather together in a safe space, free of male genitals," because "male genitals can be so emblematic of male power and sexual dominance that their presence at a festival … is inappropriate." They further stated that "people with male genitals who enter the Festival risk offending and oppressing other attendees."[6]

"We acknowledge that a post-op only/no-penis policy is not perfect," admitted the writers of the statement. "This policy cannot address issues of race and class: specifically, the exclusion of women, especially women of color, who are not able to afford sex reassignment surgery." But it nonetheless is "the best and fairest policy possible," they argue, because it "balances inclusion of transsexual women with legitimate concerns for the integrity of women's culture and safe women's space."[7] Their pretence of being concerned about racism and classism betrayed itself clearly when they used it as a preemptive shield against criticisms they knew they would encounter.

[…]

The kind of threat I am talking about is obviously not physical, but social, political and psychological. It is the same kind of threat bisexual and pansexual politics present to gay identity politics and mixed-race people present to Black Nationalism. Much has been written about the transformative potential of transsexual existence—how it destabilizes the essentialist definitions of gender by exposing the constructedness of essentialism.[8]

In the "women's communities," transsexual existence is particularly threatening to white middle-class lesbian-feminists because it exposes not only the unrealiableness of the body as a source of their identities and politics, but also the fallacy of women's universal experiences and oppressions. These valid criticisms against feminist identity politics have been made by women of color and working class women all along, and white middle-class women have traditionally dismissed them by arguing that they are patriarchal attempts to trivialize women's oppression and bring down feminism as Dobkin did. The question of transsexual inclusion has pushed them to the position of having to defend the reliableness of such absurd body elements as chromosomes as the source of political affiliation as well as the universal differences between transsexual women and non-transsexual women, a nonsensical position fraught with many bizarre contradictions.

It is my feeling that transsexual women know this intrinsically, and that is why they feel it is necessary to repeatedly stress how non-threatening they really are. By pretending that they are "just like" other women, however, they are leaving intact the flawed and unspoken lesbian-feminist assumption that *continuation of struggle against sexism requires silent compliance with all other oppressions.*

Like Gloria Anzaldúa's "New Mestiza," transsexual people occupy the borderland where notions of masculinity and femininity collide. "It is not a comfortable territory to live in, this place of contradictions." But speaking from the borderland, from its unique "shifting and multiple identity and integrity," is where transsexual activists will find the most authentic strength.

The borderland analogy is not meant to suggest that transsexual people are somewhere between male and female. Rather, the space they occupy is naturally and rightfully theirs, as the actual Texas-Mexico borderlands belong to Chicano/as, and I am merely calling attention to the unnaturalness of the boundary that was designed to keep them out. "A borderland is a vague and undetermined place created by the emotional residue of an unnatural boundary," Anzaldúa wrote, "it is in a constant state of transition. The prohibited and forbidden are its inhabitants."[9] The fact that many transsexual women have experienced some form of male privilege is not a burden to their feminist consciousness and credibility, but an asset—that is, provided they have the integrity and conscience to recognize and confront this and other privileges they may have received.

In her piece about racism and feminist identity politics, Elliott Femyne bat Tzedek discusses how threatening boundary-crossings are to those in the position of power and privilege. "Think about the phrase ... 'You people make me sick.' Think of how the person screaming this phrase may commit physical violence against what so disturbs him/her ... those in power do actually feel sick, feel their lives being threatened ... Men protecting male power have a much clearer view than Feminists do of exactly how threatening crossing gender is."[10]

By the same token, feminists who are vehemently anti-transsexual have much better understanding of how threatening transsexual existence is to their flawed ideology than do transsexual people themselves. The power is in consciously recognizing this unique positionality and making connections to the contributions of women of color and other groups of women who have been marginalized within the feminist movement. With this approach, I am hopeful that transsexual women, along with all other women who live complex lives, will be able to advance the feminist discussions about power, privilege and oppression.

Notes

1. Davina Anne Gabriel, from an open letter to *Lesbian Connection* dated Jan. 27, 2000. Distributed on-line.

2. Phrases "pre-operative" and "post-operative" are put inside quotation marks (except when it is part of someone else's quote) because it is my belief that such distinction is irrelevant, classist and MtF-centric (i.e. disregards experiences of FtM trans people). I believe that such over-emphasis on genital shape is deeply oppressive to trans people and contributes to the suppression and erasure of intersex people.

3. *In Your Face* Interview of Riki Anne Wilchins. Distributed as a press release from GenderPAC on Aug. 18, 1999.

4. Gabriel, from the open letter.

5. JoAnn Roberts, *The Next Wave: Post-Reform Transgender Activism* (2000), distributed on-line.

6. Beth Elliott et al., *The Michigan Women's Music Festival and Transsexual Women: A Statement by Transsexual Women* (2000). Distributed on-line.

7. Ibid.

8. For example, *see* Marjorie Garber, *Spare Parts: The Surgical Construction of Gender,* from *Differences: A Journal of Feminist Cultural Studies,* no. 3, 1989.

9. Gloria Anzaldúa, *Borderlands/La Frontera: The New Mestiza* (1987).

10. Elliott Femyne bat Tzedek, *Identity Politics and Racism: Some Thoughts and Questions,* from *Rain and Thunder: A Radical Feminist Journal of Discussion and Activism,* issue 5, 1999. Personally, I was surprised to find this article in a radical feminist publication, especially since the same issue of *Rain and Thunder* also published a very hurtful column by Alix Dobkin that appear to endorse violence against transsexual women in women's restrooms.

BISEXUAL INVISIBILITY: IMPACTS AND RECOMMENDATIONS

By San Francisco Human Rights Commission LGBT Advisory Committee

Bisexuality is the capacity for emotional, romantic, and/or physical attraction to more than one sex or gender. A bisexual orientation speaks to the potential for, but not requirement of, involvement with more than one sex/gender.[1]

Bisexuals experience high rates of being ignored, discriminated against, demonized, or rendered invisible by both the heterosexual world and the lesbian and gay communities.[2] Often, the entire sexual orientation is branded as invalid, immoral, or irrelevant. Despite years of activism and the largest population within the LGBT community, the needs of bisexuals still go unaddressed and their very existence is still called into question. This erasure has serious consequences on bisexuals' health, economic well-being, and funding for bi organizations and programs.

As the authors of one study put it, "Bi-invisibility refers to a lack of acknowledgment and ignoring of the clear evidence that bisexuals exist."[3]

An Invisible Majority

According to several studies, self-identified bisexuals make up the largest single population within the LGBT community in the United States. In each study, more women identified as bisexual than lesbian, and fewer men identified as bisexual than gay.[4]

In 2010, a study published in the Journal of Sexual Medicine[5], based on a nationally representative probability sample of women and men in the U.S., found that among adults (5,042 respondents), 3.1% self-identified as bisexual, compared to 2.5% as gay/lesbian (Table 1).

While the sample size was smaller for adolescents (818 respondents), the split was even more striking: 4.9% self-identified as bisexual compared to just 1.0% gay/lesbian (Table 2).

Data from the 2002 National Survey of Family Growth[6]—based on in-person interviews with 7,643 women and 4,928 men—found that 2.8% of women and 1.8% of men identify as bisexual. By comparison, 1.3% of women describe themselves as lesbian and 2.3% of men as gay. It is also

Table 1: Sexual orientation in adults (Herbenick et al., 2010)

Sexual Orientation	Adult Males (N = 2,521)		Adult Females (N = 2,521)		ALL ADULTS (N = 5,042)	
	Number	%	Number	%	Number	%
Heterosexual	2,325	92.2	2,348	93.1	4,673	92.7
Gay or lesbian	105	4.2	23	0.9	128	2.5
Bisexual	66	2.6	92	3.6	158	3.1
Other	25	1.0	58	2.3	83	1.6

Table 2: Sexual orientation in adolescents (Herbenick et al., 2010)

Sexual Orientation	Adolescent Males (N = 413)		Adolescent Females (N = 405)		ALL ADOLESCENTS (N = 818)	
	Number	%	Number	%	Number	%
Heterosexual	398	96.1	367	90.5	765	93.5
Gay or lesbian	7	1.8	1	0.2	8	1.0
Bisexual	6	1.5	34	8.4	40	4.9
Other	2	0.1	3	0.9	5	0.6

Table 3: Proportion of lesbians, gays, and bisexuals (Egan et al., 2007)

Which of the following best describes your sexual orientation?	TOTAL	Males	Females
Lesbian, gay, or homosexual	51.1%	68.4%	34.7%
Bisexual	48.9%	31.6%	65.3%
TOTAL	100.0%	100.0%	100.0%

interesting to note that while behavior is distinct from identity—not everyone who is attracted to more than one gender identifies as bisexual—the study also found that about 13% of women and 6% of men reported attractions to both women and men.

A 2007 survey of 768 self-identified lesbians, gays, and bisexuals drawn from a nationally representative sample of respondents found similar proportions: approximately half of LGB people self-identified as bisexual, including about one-third of the men and two-thirds of the women (Table 3).[7]

An "Eclipsed and Conflated" Identity

Despite the overwhelming data that bisexuals exist, other people's assumptions often render bisexuals invisible. Two women holding hands are read as "lesbian," two men as "gay," and a man and a woman as "straight." In reality, any of these people might be bi—perhaps all of them.

The majority of research lumps data on bisexuals under "gay" or "lesbian," which makes it difficult to draw any conclusions about bisexuals and skews the data about lesbians and gay men. "Thus any particular needs of bisexuals are eclipsed and conflated. Only a handful of studies separate out bisexuals and/or report on their bisexual-specific findings. Fewer compare bisexuals to people who are not bisexual."[8]

Inconsistent terminology, even within a single study, makes it hard to decipher the findings accurately. The NGLTF Policy Institute's report on bisexual health recommends that researchers use standardized definitions of sexual orientation labels and remain clear about them throughout the course of their work, both in conducting studies and in reporting findings. A good set of guidelines is to allow participants to self-report their own gender and sexual orientation labels and to describe the gender(s) and sexual identity(ies) of their sexual partner(s). Reported analyses should reflect these identities.[9]

Not Just a Phase

While bisexuality has often been considered merely a "phase" en route to a stable gay or lesbian orientation, it is also a stable sexual orientation in itself. A longitudinal study[10] of sexual minority women (lesbian, bisexual, or unlabeled) found that over 10 years, "more women *adopted* bisexual/unlabeled identities than *relinquished* them" [emphasis in original]. Of those who began the study identifying as bisexual, 92% identified as bisexual or unlabeled 10 years later, and 61% those who began as unlabeled identified as bisexual or unlabeled 10 years later. While no similar long-term study has been done with bisexual men, at least one study suggests that bisexuality can be a stable sexual orientation for men as well.[11]

An Invisible Place in History

Bisexuals find themselves erased in history. Many famous people—such as Marlene Dietrich, June Jordan, Freddie Mercury, Eleanor Roosevelt, and Walt Whitman—have been labeled as lesbian or gay for their same-sex relationships, yet their long-term relationships with different-sex partners are ignored or their importance minimized. This disrespects the truth of their lives for the sake of a binary conception of sexual orientation. It also makes it more difficult for bisexuals just coming out to find role models.

This historical erasure also extends to activists. Rather than acknowledging the decades of hard work bisexuals have done in the LGBT movement, many gays and lesbians have accused bisexuals of trying to "ride their coattails." In fact, bisexuals have often been leaders in the movement. In just one example, it was a bi woman, Brenda Howard, who organized the one-month anniversary rally in honor of the Stonewall uprising (which in turn was led by transsexuals and drag queens). Then a year later, she organized a march and celebration that turned into New York's annual pride parade and inspired countless other pride celebrations around the world. Yet it wasn't that long ago that bisexuals and transgender people had to fight for inclusion in the name of San Francisco Pride, one of the last major U.S. cities to do so.[12]

[...]

"The only thing I would change about my sexuality is how others treat me for it."

My coming out as bi has been both extremely satisfying and saddening. I came out as gay in high school when I was 16. While I thought occasionally about women, I largely discounted these feelings as random daydreams. I had heard that bisexuality was a farce so many times from gay friends, that people who were bisexual were just afraid to come all the way out of the closet, that I never thought of coming out as bisexual when I was younger. I was attracted to men, I didn't have any shame about this, and I wanted to be recognized.

Despite San Francisco's reputation as a gay mecca, it is where I first came to recognize my opposite-sex attractions. Being single at college parties, I often found myself in situations where women were hitting on me. I was interested but at the same time befuddled. The idea that my same-sex attractions represented an inflexible and absolute sexuality had become entrenched in my thinking, and I wasn't prepared to question this. Despite this lack of mental readiness, my desire and curiosity were far greater, and I eventually began sleeping with women. I kept my opposite-sex attractions subordinated, leaving them out of discussions with friends back home and rationalizing them away as mistakes to myself.

After roughly a year, stories began to trickle back to friends and family. As questions and underhanded comments started coming in, I found myself constantly being put on trial. Why was I doing this? Was I closeting myself? Why wasn't I being "normal," gay how I should be? In the process of trying to answer these questions for myself and others, I realized how long I had been cheating myself and sublimating my desires to others' ideas about sexuality.

I came out as bi when I was 19 and have remained so since. Rather than quieting the doubts of others, animosity only intensified. Aggressive queries about when I was going to focus on guys full-time again became a standard part of trips home. On top of this, I noticed a change in how sexual partners treated me. Women I was with, no longer with the safety of presuming me straight, would question my real orientation and complain that my sexuality made them anxious that I would one day vanish into a relationship with a man. Men I was with wouldn't acknowledge my sexuality, referring to me as gay despite my protest. I found myself in relationships waiting for accusations and dismissive comments, ready from the start to move along to someone new.

I am happy with my sexuality, and very grateful that I was finally able to fully realize my desires. The only thing I would change about my sexuality is how others treat me for it. Finding my sexuality has been wonderful. I only wish I didn't have to sacrifice feeling safe, feeling part of a community, and feeling like I have anyone to confide in but myself.

—Jack M., 21, male

Bisexual and Transgender Allies in Invisibility

"From the earliest years of the bi community, significant numbers of [transgender people] have always been involved in it. The bi community served as a kind of refuge for people who felt excluded from the established lesbian and gay communities."

—Kevin Lano[13]

In San Francisco, the bisexual and transgender communities have long worked together as allies. This was especially important when both groups lobbied gay and lesbian groups for more inclusion of their issues.

For example, the Human Rights Commission first formed a "Gay Advisory Committee" in 1979, in response to a call for the city to create a Lesbian/Gay Commission in the wake of Harvey Milk's assassination. According to long-time bi activist and former LGBTAC member Lani Ka'ahumanu, it took a lot of education and discussion before "bisexual" was added to the name in January 1993, and she found an ally in Kiki Whitlock, the first self-identified transgender person appointed to the Advisory Committee. Both recognized that together they could push for broader recognition of their communities' concerns and needs. Panels on bisexual issues were transgender-inclusive and vice versa.

By February 1994, the Commission had voted to change the name to the Lesbian Gay Bisexual Transgender Advisory Committee, and in May 1994, held a public hearing on discrimination against transgender people. The recommendations that came out of that hearing paved the way for the Board of Supervisors to pass groundbreaking legislation adding gender identity as a protected category in San Francisco.

Other Forms of Biphobia[14]

Bisexual invisibility is one of many manifestations of biphobia. Others include:

- Assuming that everyone you meet is either heterosexual or homosexual.
- Supporting and understanding a bisexual identity for young people because you identified "that way" before you came to your "real" lesbian/gay/heterosexual identity.
- Automatically assuming romantic couplings of two women are lesbian, or two men are gay, or a man and a woman are heterosexual.
- Expecting a bisexual to identify as gay or lesbian when coupled with the "same" sex/gender.
- Expecting a bisexual to identify as heterosexual when coupled with the "opposite" sex/gender.
- Believing that bisexual men spread HIV/AIDS to heterosexuals.
- Believing that bisexual women spread HIV/AIDS to lesbians.
- Thinking bisexual people haven't made up their minds.
- Refusing to accept someone's self-identification as bisexual if the person hasn't had sex with both men and women.
- Expecting bisexual people to get services, information, and education from heterosexual service agencies for their "heterosexual side" and then go to gay and/or lesbian service agencies for their "homosexual side."
- Feeling bisexuals just want to have their cake and eat it too.
- Assuming a bisexual person would want to fulfill your sexual fantasies or curiosities.
- Thinking bisexuals only have committed relationships with "opposite" sex/gender partners.
- Being gay or lesbian and asking your bisexual friends about their lovers or whom they are dating only when that person is the "same" sex/gender.
- Assuming that bisexuals, if given the choice, would prefer to be in an "opposite" gender/sex coupling to reap the social benefits of a "heterosexual" pairing.
- Assuming bisexuals would be willing to "pass" as anything other than bisexual.
- Believing bisexuals are confused about their sexuality.

- Feeling that you can't trust a bisexual because they aren't really gay or lesbian, or aren't really heterosexual.
- Refusing to use the word bisexual in the media when reporting on people attracted to more than one gender, instead substituting made-up terms such as "gay-ish."
- Using the terms *phase* or *stage* or *confused* or *fence-sitter* or *bisexual* or *AC/DC* or *switch-hitter* as slurs or in an accusatory way.
- Assuming bisexuals are incapable of monogamy.
- Feeling that bisexual people are too outspoken and pushy about their visibility and rights.
- Looking at a bisexual person and automatically thinking of her/his sexuality rather than seeing her/him as a whole, complete person.
- Not confronting a biphobic remark or joke for fear of being identified as bisexual.
- Assuming bisexual means "available."
- Thinking that bisexual people will have their rights when lesbian and gay people win theirs.
- Expecting bisexual activists and organizers to minimize bisexual issues (such as HIV/AIDS, violence, basic civil rights, military service, same-sex marriage, child custody, adoption, etc.) and to prioritize the visibility of "lesbian and/or gay" issues.
- Avoiding mentioning to friends that you are involved with a bisexual or working with a bisexual group because you are afraid they will think you are a bisexual.

As an example of the extent and depth of biphobia, a study published in the *Journal of Sex Research* reported that heterosexuals rate bisexuals as a group less favorably than any of a number of groups (including Catholics, lesbians, people with AIDS, and people who are pro-life), except for the category of people who inject illegal drugs.[15]

[...]

IMPACT OF BISEXUAL INVISIBILITY ON HEALTH

The implications of bi invisibility go far beyond bisexuals wanting to feel welcome at the table. It also has a significant impact on bisexuals' health. Here are just a few examples from recent large-scale studies[16]:

- Bisexual people experience greater health disparities than the broader population, including a greater likelihood of suffering from depression and other mood or anxiety disorders.
- Bisexuals report higher rates of hypertension, poor or fair physical health, smoking, and risky drinking than heterosexuals or lesbians/gays.
- Many, if not most, bisexual people don't come out to their healthcare providers. This means they are getting incomplete information (for example, about safer sex practices).
- Most HIV and STI prevention programs don't adequately address the health needs of bisexuals, much less those who have sex with both men and women but do not identify as bisexual.
- Bisexual women in relationships with monosexual partners have an increased rate of domestic violence compared to women in other demographic categories.

In the 1980s and 1990s, bisexuals were vociferously blamed for the spread of HIV (even though the virus is spread by unprotected sex, not a bisexual identity). However, a 1994 study of data from San Francisco is also worth noting: it found that at that time, bisexually identified MSMW (men who have sex with men and women) weren't a "common vector or 'bridge' for spreading HIV from male partners to female partners due to high rates of using barrier protection and extremely low rates of risky behavior."[17]

Yet scapegoating continues. Sometimes it is explicit, as in the misleading hysteria about men on the "down low" infecting unsuspecting female partners, particularly in the African-American community. Other times, the negative message is communicated in subtle ways. For example, in the 2008 San Francisco Department of Public Health HIV/AIDS Epidemiology Annual Report, MSMWs are not mentioned at all, their data most likely absorbed into information about MSMs. The only time the word "bisexual" appears is as an infection source for heterosexual women.[18]

In a 2010 study using Behavioral Risk Factor Surveillance System data from Washington State—collected between 2003 and 2007 through a telephone interview survey of randomly selected adults aged 18 or older—the researchers looked at health disparities between lesbians and bisexual women.[19] They found many commonalities among their sample of 1,496 sexual minority women, but also a wide array of differences. Compared to lesbians:

- Bisexual women had significantly lower levels of education, were more likely to be living with income below 200% of the federal poverty level, and had more children living in the household.
- Bisexual women were significantly less likely to have health insurance coverage and more likely to experience financial barriers to receiving healthcare services.
- Bisexual women were more likely to be current smokers and acute drinkers.
- Bisexual women showed significantly higher rates of poor general health and frequent mental distress, even after controlling for confounding variables.

Of particular interest for San Francisco is the comparison of frequent mental distress for sexual minority women living in urban versus nonurban areas. In nonurban areas, lesbians and bisexual women experience similar levels of frequent mental distress. However, while the odds of frequent mental distress *decrease* significantly for lesbians in urban areas, the odds *nearly double* for bisexual women. The researchers theorize, "In addition to the minority stressors encountered by lesbians, bisexual women may face stressors which may be associated with poor health outcomes, such as lack of support by lesbian and gay communities as well as the larger community. Urban environments are typically characterized as having more well-organized gay and lesbian

Table 4: Suicidality among bisexuals, lesbians/gays, and heterosexuals

Sexual Orientation	Suicidality Among Women		Suicidality Among Men	
	Percentage	Adjusted rate (compared to heterosexual)	Percentage	Adjusted rate (compared to heterosexual)
Bisexual	45.4%	5.9	34.8%	6.3
Lesbian/Gay	29.5%	3.5	25.2%	4.1
Heterosexual	9.6%	–	7.4%	–

communities; bisexual women in such environments may feel even more isolated because they do not have access to a defined community."[20]

Alarmingly, bisexuals are also far more likely to feel suicidal than their heterosexual, gay, and lesbian counterparts. In two recent studies on sexual orientation and health, based on the Canadian Community Health Survey (a national population-based survey using a representative sample), *nearly half of bisexual women* and *more than a third of bisexual men* had seriously considered (or attempted) taking their own lives (see Table 4).[21]

When controlled for potentially confounding factors, bisexual men were 6.3 times more likely and gay men 4.1 times more likely than heterosexual men to report lifetime suicidality. Among women, bisexuals were 5.9 times more likely and lesbians 3.5 times more likely to report lifetime suicidality than their heterosexual counterparts.

A Hidden Effect of Conflated Data

As noted earlier, when researchers conflate data about bisexuals with data about gay men or lesbians, it may significantly skew the findings. It may also result in interventions not reaching or not being effective for key populations. For example, because bisexuals have worse outcomes in most areas of health where specific data are available, conflating the data will generally make the picture look more urgent. Yet few public health programs specifically reach out to bisexuals. This means that even though bisexuals may have greater need, the resources primarily wind up benefitting lesbians and gay men.

Why Focus on Bisexual Health?[22]

One area where we see the effects of biphobia and bi-invisibility is in the health and well-being of bisexuals, MSMW, and WSMW. This is because, as confirmed by the available research, these groups experience greater health disparities compared to the broader population, and they continue to experience biphobia and bi-invisibility from healthcare providers, including providers who may be gay or lesbian, or are knowledgeable about homosexuality and accepting of their gay and lesbian clients.

Although we have some information about the health of bisexual people and of men and women who have sex with more than one gender, there is still much that we do not know. It is important for researchers to employ methodologies that group bisexuals together, or that group together people who have sex with partners of more than one gender; rather than only the more common practice of grouping gay and bisexual men or lesbian and bisexual women together, never separately examining attributes of and needs of the latter. Why? Because bisexual women's issues are not always the same as lesbian issues, even for bisexual women who only have sex with partners of the same gender or for lesbian-identified women who have sex with men as well as women. Bisexual men's issues are not always the same as gay male issues, even for bisexual men who only have sex with partners of the same gender or for gay-identified men who have sex with women as well as men. Likewise, heterosexuals' issues are different from those of bisexuals, even among heterosexually-identified MSMW and WSMW.

[...]

INVISIBLE RESOURCES

Economic Discrimination

Biphobia affects how much bisexuals earn in the workplace. There are no studies that look specifically at income data for San Francisco, but a literature review done by researchers at UCLA's Williams Institute, one of the leading institutions for research on LGBT issues, examined 12 studies on the subject.[23] It was clear from the body of research that no LGBT people fared well when their wages were compared to straight men's. One study of California data was striking, though: it found that while gay men earned 2-3% less than straight men and lesbians 2.7% less, bisexual men earned 10-15% less and bisexual women nearly 11% less.

Another 2009 study from the Williams Institute analyzed data from three surveys to compare poverty (as defined by the federal poverty line) between LGB and heterosexual people.[24] Two of the surveys—the 2003 and 2005 California Health Interview Surveys, the only data that included separate numbers for bisexuals—found that bisexual women are more than *twice* as likely as lesbians to live in poverty (17.7% compared to 7.8%), and bisexual men are over 50% more likely to live in poverty than gay men (9.7% compared to 6.2%).

Economic health is one strong indicator of someone's place in society. While the full pictures of income disparities and poverty contain many subtleties, the data certainly undermine the oft-repeated stereotype that bisexuals hide within straight privilege. In the meantime, the very real effects of biphobia get overlooked.

Lack of Institutional Support

The stark reality is that the bisexual community also has few resources to address its needs and educate the public about bisexuals' lives.

For many years, Funders for LGBTQ Issues has tracked data on grants made by U.S. foundations to LGBT organizations. Although LGBT funding has risen in terms of dollars, it still represents a tiny fraction of the total grantmaking, with bi issues among the least supported every year. In 2008, while total foundation giving to LGBT issues increased compared to the previous year (from $77 million in 2007 to $107 million in 2008) and the percentage of dollars increased (from 0.18% to 0.24%), funding for bi organizations or programs went down; it was the lowest of all two dozen demographic groups they tracked.[25] In fact, during all of 2008, *not a single grant in the entire country* explicitly addressed bisexual issues.

Notes

1. Miller, M., André, A., Ebin, J., & Bessonova, L. (2007). *Bisexual health: An introduction and model practices for HIV/STI prevention programming.* National Gay and Lesbian Task Force Policy Institute, the Fenway Institute at Fenway Community Health, and BiNet USA.

2. In San Francisco, the bisexual and transgender communities have generally been strong allies for each other; page 8 of this report gives one example. (Note: Sexual orientation and gender identity are independent; transgender people may have any sexual orientation.)

3. Miller et al. (2007).

4. While few large-scale demographic data sets ask directly about sexual orientation, the studies found for this report show a high level of consistency in their overall findings.

5. Herbenick, D., Reece, M., Schick, V., Sanders, S.A., Dodge, B., & Fortenberry J.D. (2010). Sexual behavior in the United States: Results from a national probability sample of men and women aged 14–94. *Journal of Sexual Medicine,* 7(suppl 5): 255–265.

6. Mosher, W.D., Chandra, A., & Jones, J. (2005). Sexual Behavior and Selected Health Measures: Men and Women 15– 44 Years of Age, United States, 2002. *Advance data from vital and health statistics; no 362.* Hyattsville, MD: National Center for Health Statistics.

7. Egan, P.J., Edelman, M.S., & Sherrill, K. (2007). *Findings from the Hunter College Poll of Lesbians, Gays, and Bisexuals: New Discoveries about Identity, Political Attitudes, and Civic Engagement.* Hunter College, CUNY. The poll was not able to obtain a representative sample of the transgender population.

8. Miller et al. (2007).

9. Miller et al. (2007).

10. Diamond, Lisa M. (2008). Female Bisexuality From Adolescence to Adulthood: Results From a 10-Year Longitudinal Study. *Developmental Psychology,* 44:1, 5–14.

11. For example, in one study, approximately half of bisexual men retained a bisexual identity at the end of a one-year period, while about a third moved toward a more homosexual identity and 17% toward a more heterosexual direction. Stokes, J.P., Damon, W., and McKirnan, D.J. (1997). Predictors of movement toward homosexuality: A longitudinal study of bisexual men. *Journal of Sex Research,* 34, 304–312.

12. 1995 was the first time "LGBT" appeared in the official event name.

13. Alexander, J. & Yescavage, K. (2003). Bisexuality and transgenderism: InterSEXions of the others. *Journal of Bisexuality, 3*(3/4). p. 8, as quoted in Miller et al. (2007).

14. Drawn mainly from *What Does Biphobia Look Like?*, a resource adapted by Lani Ka'ahumanu and Rob Yaeger/BiNet USA (1996) from Rape Crisis Center of West Contra Costa County, CA, and from *Lesbians: A Consciousness Raising Kit* by the Boston Lesbian Task Force and Building Bridges (March 1995). "Sexuality, biological sex, and gender are not binary. The [English] language is inadequate to express our new understandings. Therefore, in some instances quotes are used with certain words (i.e. 'opposite,' 'same') to highlight problematic areas" (Ka'ahumanu and Yaeger, 1996).

15. Herek, G. M. (2002). Heterosexuals' attitudes toward bisexual men and women in the United States. *The Journal of Sex Research, 39*(4), as quoted in Miller et al. (2007).

16. Miller et al. (2007); Brennan, D.J., Ross, L.E., Dobinson, C., Veldhuizen, S., & Steele, L.S. (2010). Men's sexual orientation and health in Canada. *Canadian Journal of Public Health,* 101:3, 255–258; Steele, L.S., Ross, L.E., Dobinson, C., Veldhuizen, S., & Tinmouth, J.M. (2009). Women's Sexual Orientation and Health: Results from a Canadian Population-Based Survey. *Women & Health,* 49:5, 353–367.

17. Ekstrand, M. L., Coates, T.J., Guydish, J.R., Hauck, W.W., Collette, L. & Hulley, S.B. (1994). Are bisexually identified men in San Francisco a common vector for spreading HIV infection to women? *American Journal of Public Health,* 84(6), as quoted in Miller et al.

18. San Francisco Department of Public Health HIV Epidemiology Section. (2009). *HIV/AIDS Epidemiology Annual Report: 2008.*

19. Fredriksen-Goldsen, K.I., Kim, H., Barkan, S.E., Balsam, K.F., & Mincer, S.L. (2010). Disparities in Health-Related Quality of Life: A Comparison of Lesbians and Bisexual Women. *American Journal of Public Health,* 100(11), 2255–2261.

20. Fredriksen-Goldsen et al. (2010).

21. Brennan et al. (2010); Steele et al. (2010). While these rates are based on Canadian population data, they are still highly useful here because they distinguish the findings for bisexuals from those for gays or lesbians. Far more commonly, the literature on suicide among LGBT people breaks down the data by gender (that is, gay/bisexual men or lesbian/bisexual women; there are also some studies on transgender people) or looks at the LGBT community as a whole.

22. The remainder of this chapter excerpted with permission from Miller et al. (2007).

23. Badgett, M.V.L., Lau, H., Sears, B. & Ho, D. (2007). *Bias in the Workplace: Consistent Evidence of Sexual Orientation and Gender Identity Discrimination.* The Williams Institute, UCLA.

24. Albelda, R., Badgett, M.V.L., Schneebaum, A. & Gates, G.J. (2009). *Poverty in the Lesbian, Gay, and Bisexual Community.* The Williams Institute, UCLA. No data about transgender people were collected in these surveys.

25. Funders for LGBTQ Issues. (2010). *Lesbian, Gay, Bisexual, Transgender, and Queer Grantmaking by U.S. Foundations (Calendar Year 2008).*

BIPHOBIA, QUEER COMMUNITIES, AND "CONVERSION THERAPY"

By Cabell Gathman

I.

There are so many places I could begin.

I am 14 and I think I might like girls. Then I think I'm just trying too hard to be interesting, because I know I like boys. It is months before I settle on "bisexual." I search the nascent internet desperately for images of people like myself, but I barely find any. I read all the *Dykes to Watch Out For* I can get my hands on; at least it's something.

I am 15 and the whole school knows that I'm bi, even if I get called "dyke" a lot. Other girls find me after school, on weekends; they whisper to me about the girls they want to kiss but can't. None of them want to kiss me, though.

I am 16 and a senior in high school. I tell my parents, who have been telling me for the past five years that they don't care if I bring home boyfriends or girlfriends, that I'm bi. At graduation I'm excited to be seated next to one of the hottest guys in my class. My mom tells her best friend: "I knew she was really straight."

I am 17 and a freshman in college. I wear my Pride rings everywhere and all the other queer[1] kids want to talk to me—until I start dating a guy. I'm not one of them.

I am 18 and working on a campus women's event. One of the other participants comments on my shaved head: "If you weren't dating that big guy, people might think you were a lesbian." I tell her that I'm bi. She says: "Oh." She stops talking to me.

I am 22 and a graduate student in Wisconsin. All winter I wear a giant rainbow scarf that I crocheted myself. A lesbian classmate stops me in the hall and jokes: "What are you wearing?!

---

1   I use the term "queer" here as an umbrella term and because I have often felt most comfortable with it myself. I recognize that not everyone under the LGBT umbrella feels comfortable with the word or would self-identify with it.

You straight people can't just steal all our queer symbols!" I tell her that I'm bi. She laughs: "Whatever."

I am 25 and teaching Intro to LGBTQ Studies for the first time. I notice that students talk about being gay or lesbian, but they never talk about being bi, even when they write about it in the papers that only I see.

I am 26 and I say something in casual conversation with a faculty member about my ex-girlfriend from college (the first person to ever truly break my heart, but I don't say that, because it's not very casual). She blinks: "But you date men!" I tell her that I'm bi. She changes the subject.

I am 27 and teaching Intro to LGBTQ Studies for the third time. I start telling my students that I am a bisexual woman on the first day. Some of them start openly identifying as bisexual or pansexual in class.

I am 28 and I marry a straight man, because I love him and I want to. People call our relationship "straight," as if its very existence trumps mine.

I am 31 and I am tired of people posting links on Facebook to an article by a lesbian complaining about straight women invading queer spaces like bars—she doesn't allow for even the possibility that some people aren't straight OR gay. I make my own post about the problem of bisexual erasure, because I don't want to hijack anyone else's discussion about the real problems of appropriation and identity tourism. A gay man with whom I have worked and socialized for years is outraged. Why am I making a big deal about this, he demands: "**You** wouldn't try to do this! **You** know you don't **belong** in queer spaces!" Of course, he's right. It has been a very long time since I thought there was any room for me in "queer" spaces.

I am 31 and I get mad. Really mad.

I am 31 and a bisexual man with whom I've been friends for years asks me if I want to start an organization for bisexual, pansexual, and otherwise non-monosexual people[2] in the state of Wisconsin. I say: "Yes. Count me in." People have been pushing me into closets for 17 years now and I am **pissed**.

I am 32 and I want more than just the right to exist, although that would certainly be nice. I want my queer family: the one I was promised by *Dykes to Watch Out For*, the one I never got because there was never a "queer space" that welcomed us, the one I couldn't build because we couldn't find each other. **We are looking for you now.**

II.

Many people have produced relevant criticisms of "It Gets Better" as a flagship campaign for mainstream LGBTQ activism, and the root problem for many of them is that the adult "LGBTQ community" welcomes some people much more than it does others. If you're bisexual or pansexual, or if you are poor, a person of color, disabled, or otherwise marginalized on multiple axes, that "community" that you're supposed to seek out in the magical Some Day often turns out to be a mirage. (This is not to equate those experiences, but to note that there are some similarities.) Pride parades are pretty until you realize that in ten blocks you haven't seen a single person claiming an identity like yours.

---

2   While it pains me to use language centered around non-membership in another group, there's little agreement on a good blanket term at the present time.

Not everyone wants to move to urban areas, or can. But when bisexual women do,[3] many of us operating under the assumption that finally we're going to belong, it's not just that things don't really improve. They actually get worse.

Lesbian and bisexual women experience similar levels of mental distress in nonurban areas, but when they move to urban areas, while lesbian women's distress goes down, bisexual women's distress actually **increases** (Fredriksen-Goldsen et al. 2010). These places with, presumably, relatively large "LGBTQ communities" don't help bisexual women. They hurt us.

When I present this research finding in lectures and talks, many people are astonished. They can't figure out why this would happen. A large proportion of them think that bisexual and pansexual people are just Lesbian Gay Lite, with all the same problems and issues except 50% less intense. Or they think we're just "basically straight," with no problems or issues at all. Either way, we obviously have nothing to complain about when lesbian and gay people have it worse—except they don't.

Like trans people, bisexual and pansexual people actually make "average outcomes" of various kinds for the "LGBTQ community" worse. Our rates of mental illness, substance abuse (Green & Feinstein 2012), and suicidal ideation are all higher than those of lesbian and gay people (Kerr et al. 2013; Fredriksen-Goldsen et al. 2010), which are higher than those of straight people (trans people, who can of course also be bi or pan, have higher rates than we do). Bisexual women with monosexual partners—whether they are straight men or lesbian women—experience domestic violence at higher rates than lesbian or straight women (Walters et al. 2013; San Francisco Human Rights Commission 2011).

Bisexual people earn less than lesbian and gay people of the same gender, and we are more likely to live in poverty (Badgett et al. 2013; Albelda et al. 2009; Badgett et al. 2007), despite being less likely to be out at work—though it's hard to say exactly what that means, when people routinely ignore or deny our own identity claims. By the same token, we are less likely to be out to our healthcare providers (San Francisco Human Rights Commission 2011).

All the scary numbers that LGBTQ groups use to drum up support include bisexual and pansexual people.[4] But those groups rarely direct any of that support towards us, even though bisexual and pansexual and otherwise non-monosexual people make up a majority of the US LGB community (Herbenick et al. 2010). They very rarely acknowledge that on more and more measures, as researchers begin to distinguish in data collection and analysis between lesbian and gay people and non-monosexual people, it is becoming apparent that bisexual and pansexual people are doing worse than lesbian and gay people.

To add insult to injury, when we're in different-gender relationships, many people call those relationships "straight." They tell us that we may be queer (**maybe**), but we have straight privilege so we shouldn't start thinking we have problems.

There are certainly social and institutional advantages to being in (perceived) different-gender relationships, particularly those that are legally recognized as marriage by the state. But of course, there are also advantages and privileges conferred by being White, cisgender, middle- or upper-class, abled, thin... For some reason, though, few people in the mainstream "LGBTQ

---

3   Please note that when I reference specific research studies, I often restrict my claims to bisexual people, or only bisexual women; this is because the limits of these studies require it. "Pansexual" and other non-monosexual identity labels are not typically used by researchers, just as for a long time, bisexual people were not analyzed separately from lesbian and gay people.

4   They also include trans people, and similarly often fail to provide any resources or support to actual trans people. I hesitate to draw too many comparisons here because I don't want to equate bi/pan experiences with trans experiences.

community" would suggest that White cisgender middle-class gay men's queerness somehow counts less because they have race, cisgender, class, and gender privilege. (I owe this general line of analysis to Emi Koyama, who breaks it down brilliantly in reference to racism and trans exclusion in feminist and LGB communities.)

Nobody says that closeted lesbian and gay people have "straight privilege." In some cases, they may suffer from internalized homophobia, but the key word there is "suffer." Most of us would accept that even closeted conservative politicians, who may hurt more vulnerable queer people very badly indeed, are to some degree hurting themselves, too–not to excuse their actions, but to understand them as including self-harm.

Bisexual and pansexual people, so often forced into closets whether we like it or not, do not have "straight privilege." We may occupy a lot of privileged positions in our lives, but that isn't one of them. **Biphobia does not benefit us.** Erasure is never a privilege.

III.

When I teach Intro to LGBTQ Studies, we talk about identity, community, and how social context necessarily shapes these things. We also talk about what it means to say that something is "socially constructed," and perhaps more importantly, what it **doesn't** mean—in the words of Imogen Binnie, discussing gender as a trans woman:

"Eventually you can't help but figure out that, while gender is a construct, so is a traffic light, and if you ignore either of them, you get hit by cars. Which, also, are constructs." (Nevada, p. 26)

So identity is a construct, but that doesn't make it any less real. Once you figure out how who you are, you can't change it just because you'd rather be someone else.

We talk about "conversion therapy" and the "ex-gay" movement, and how harmful they are. There's a reason that virtually every major professional organization related to psychology and counseling, as well as the World Health Organization, has denounced them: "conversion therapy" does not change sexual orientation, but it does cause increased rates of depression, anxiety, and suicide. The Southern Poverty Law Center tracks "conversion therapists" just as it does other prominent hate groups.

This isn't news to most of my 18-22-year-old students, regardless of how they personally identify. It makes sense to them that trying to force a person to fit a particular community's idea of acceptable consensual sexuality—of acceptable **personal identity**—is ultimately ineffective and extremely damaging to the person in question in the meantime.

And yet, while my students find this intuitive and the evidence is in fact so compelling that some states have now criminalized "conversion therapy" when practiced on minors, I still hear from people like the woman who attended one of my talks about bisexual/pansexual inclusion in the classroom and approached me later to tell me, her voice never rising above a whisper, how she has hidden her current romantic relationship with a man because she knows that her "community," made up primarily of lesbian women, would ostracize her if it were known that she is dating a man. She knows because she has seen what happens when women who openly identify as bisexual or pansexual try to find a place for themselves there. The community doesn't want them.

We know that attempts to force lesbian and gay people, even those who may seek out such attempts, to identify as straight are doomed to failure and that their mental health effects are negative and severe. And yet, when I talk about how bisexual women experience an increase in mental distress when they move to areas with a relatively large "LGBTQ community," many people are shocked. They ask how and why that could possibly be.

If we know that "conversion therapy" is violence against lesbian and gay people, then we have to understand that the rejection of bisexual and pansexual people, the assumption that we are "really straight" or "really gay," the conditional lesbian and gay acceptance of us only as long as we don't actually have significant, visible different-gender relationships—**all of that is violence, too.**

We often lack community because the community that was supposed to be ours rejects and denies us—has in fact convinced many of us, just as I feared at 14, that what and who we are isn't real. Bisexuality and pansexuality are often rejected as fake or inadequate queerness: something we have to "grow out of" or "get over." Straight people tell us the same thing, certainly, but we've been taught to expect straight resistance to queer identities. Many of us have had to learn on our own, painfully, that other queer people may resist our existence just as much.

That withholding of community, that refusal to acknowledge our identities as something other than veiled straightness or gayness, that ultimate understanding of us as, for one reason or another, not to be trusted on even our own selves, isn't so different from "conversion therapy" and the worldview that embraces it. It breaks us down and leaves us more vulnerable to institutional and personal abuse. It teaches us that we are fundamentally unlovable, unacceptable, unworthy.

We are real. And we need our queer family, too.

[This piece originally published at http://cabell.info/4/ with hyperlinks to relevant sources.]

LED BY THE CHILD WHO SIMPLY KNEW

By Bella English

The twin boys were identical in every way but one. Wyatt was a girl to the core, and now lives as one, with the help of a brave, loving family and a path-breaking doctor's care.

Jonas and Wyatt Maines were born identical twins, but from the start each had a distinct personality.

Jonas was all boy. He loved Spiderman, action figures, pirates, and swords.

Wyatt favored pink tutus and beads. At 4, he insisted on a Barbie birthday cake and had a thing for mermaids. On Halloween, Jonas was Buzz Lightyear. Wyatt wanted to be a princess; his mother compromised on a prince costume.

Once, when Wyatt appeared in a sequin shirt and his mother's heels, his father said: "You don't want to wear that."

"Yes, I do," Wyatt replied.

"Dad, you might as well face it," Wayne recalls Jonas saying. "You have a son and a daughter."

That early declaration marked, as much as any one moment could, the beginning of a journey that few have taken, one the Maineses themselves couldn't have imagined until it was theirs. The process of remaking a family of identical twin boys into a family with one boy and one girl has been heartbreaking and harrowing and, in the end, inspiring—a lesson in the courage of a child, a child who led them, and in the transformational power of love.

Wayne and Kelly Maines have struggled to know whether they are doing the right things for their children, especially for Wyatt, who now goes by the name Nicole. Was he merely expressing a softer side of his personality, or was he really what he kept saying: a girl in a boy's body? Was he exhibiting early signs that he might be gay? Was it even possible, at such a young age, to determine what exactly was going on?

Until recently, there was little help for children in such situations. But now a groundbreaking clinic at Children's Hospital in Boston—one of the few of its kind in the world—helps families deal with the issues, both emotional and medical, that arise from having a transgender child—one who doesn't identify with the gender he or she was born into.

Identical 14-year-old twins, Nicole and Jonas Maines, started out life as brothers Wyatt and Jonas. Nicole is transgender.

The Children's Hospital Gender Management Services Clinic can, using hormone therapies, halt puberty in transgender children, blocking the development of secondary sexual characteristics—a beard, say, or breasts—that can make the eventual transition to the other gender more difficult, painful, and costly.

Founded in 2007 by endocrinologist Norman Spack and urologist David Diamond, the clinic—known as GeMS and modeled on a Dutch program—is the first pediatric academic program in the Western Hemisphere that evaluates and treats pubescent transgenders. A handful of other pediatric centers in the United States are developing similar programs, some started by former staffers at GeMS.

It was in that clinic, under Spack's care, that Nicole and her family finally began to have hope for her future.

The Maineses decided to tell their story, they say, in order to help fight the deep stigma against transgender youth, and to ease the path for other such children who, without help, often suffer from depression, anxiety, and isolation.

"We told our kids you can't create change if you don't get involved," says Wayne, 53, sitting in the living room of their comfortable home in a southern Maine community they do not want identified.

They have good reason for caution. Their journey has included a lawsuit to protect their daughter's rights, and a battle against bullying and insensitivity that led them to move to a new place and new schools.

It has been a hard road, but nothing that compares with the physical transformation of Wyatt into Nicole.

"I have always known I was a girl," says Nicole, now 14. "I think what I'm aiming for is to undergo surgery to get a physical female body that matches up to my image of myself."

Early Confusion

When Wyatt and Jonas were born, their father was thrilled. Wayne looked forward to the day when he could hunt deer with his boys in the Maine woods. The family lived in Orono, near the University of Maine campus, where Wayne is the director of safety and environmental management.

They had no preparation for what would come next.

When Wyatt was 4, he asked his mother: "When do I get to be a girl?" He told his father that he hated his penis and asked when he could be rid of it. Both father and son cried. When first grade started, Wyatt carried a pink backpack and a Kim Possible lunchbox.

His parents had no idea what was going on. They had barely heard the term "transgender." Baffled, they tried to deflect Wyatt's girlish impulses by buying him action figures like his brother's and steering him toward Cub Scouts, soccer, and baseball.

When the boys were 5, Kelly and Wayne threw a "get-to-know-me" party for classmates and parents. Wyatt appeared beaming at the top of the stairs in a princess gown, a gift from his grandmother.

Kelly whisked him off and made him put on pants. Though she and Wayne were accustomed to his girly antics, they were afraid of what others might think.

To this day, she feels guilty about it. "I know she was totally confused and felt like she had done something wrong," says Kelly, 50, who works in law enforcement.

"Even when we did all the boy events to see if she would 'conform,' she would just put her shirt on her head as hair, strap on some heels and join in," Kelly says. "It wasn't really a matter of encouraging her to be a boy or a girl. That came about naturally."

Kelly and Wayne didn't look at it as a choice their child was making.

"She really is a girl," Kelly says, "a girl born with a birth defect. That's how she looks at it."

Fear of the Unknown

After Wyatt began to openly object to being a boy, his mother started doing research on transgender children. There was little out there; it seemed they would have to find their way largely on their own.

During those early years, while Kelly was doing her research, Wayne was hoping that this was no big deal, that this was a stage Wyatt just had to go through.

"I felt it had nothing to do with how they would grow up," he says.

But as they grew older, his concern grew. "I feared the unknown," he says.

Even the family Christmas card became a challenge. They would write about Jonas's affinity for sports and Wyatt's "flair for the dramatic."

Their elderly pediatrician, nearing retirement, did not want to discuss the matter with them. Finally, Kelly picked another pediatrician out of the phone book. "I told her how it was, and it turned out that she understood and was very supportive."

When the twins were in the first grade, their parents found a therapist for Wyatt, who was starting to act out. In the third grade, before the GeMS Clinic was even open, Kelly heard about Dr. Spack and made an appointment with him.

"He told us everything," Wayne says, recalling that first meeting. "I didn't understand it all, but I saw the weight lift off Kelly's shoulders and a smile in Nicole's eyes. That was it for me. There were tons of challenges for us after that, but I knew my daughter was going to be OK, medically."

Jonas and Wyatt during their second birthday party.

Elementary School Changes

In elementary school, Wyatt told classmates that he was a "girl-boy." In the fourth grade, he grew his hair longer and started talking about a name change. That same year, he drew a self-portrait as a girl, and in a class essay, wrote: "Wyatt needs hair accessories, clothes, shoes … likes to wear bikinis, high heels, mini-skirts."

Emma Peterson of Orono, a close friend from the elementary years at the Asa Adams School, recalls playing dolls with Nicole's giant dollhouse, and the two of them putting on makeup. "Before Nikki started growing her hair out, she looked exactly like Jonas," Emma says.

In fourth grade, Wyatt started using "Nicole" as a name, and many classmates were calling him "Nikki." The next year, the family went to court and had the name legally changed to Nicole.

To Kelly, it seemed the next logical step. Family discussions merely centered around what the name would be. In the end, Nicole chose it. "I believed in Nicole," her mother says. "She always knew who she was."

Wayne was nervous. Could he call his son Nicole? As usual, he relied on his wife's instincts. "I have to tell you, Kelly's the leader in our family," he says. "Both she and Nicole are extremely strong-willed, and I went with the flow."

At first, though, he couldn't bring himself to use the new name. An Air Force veteran and former Republican, he realizes now he was grieving the loss of a son. "But once you get past that, I realize I never had a son," he says.

When he was 4, Wyatt asked his mother: "When do I get to be a girl?" In the fifth grade, Wyatt's name was legally changed to Nicole.

Legal Battles

When fifth grade started, Wyatt was gone. Nicole showed up for school, sometimes wearing a dress and sporting shoulder-length hair. She began using the girls' bathroom. Nikki's friends didn't have a problem with the transformation; there were playdates and sleepovers.

"They said, 'It was about time!'" Nicole says. She was elected vice president of her class and excelled academically.

But one day a boy called her a "faggot," objected to her using the girls' bathroom, and reported the matter to his grandfather, who is his legal guardian. The grandfather complained to the Orono School Committee, with the Christian Civic League of Maine backing him. The superintendent of schools then decided Nicole should use a staff bathroom.

"It was like a switch had been turned on, saying it is now OK to question Nicole's choice to be transgender and it was OK to pursue behavior that was not OK before," Wayne says. "Every day she was reminded that she was different, and the other kids picked up on it."

According to a 2009 study by the Gay, Lesbian and Straight Education Network, 90 percent of transgender youth report being verbally harassed and more than half physically harassed. Two-thirds of them said they felt unsafe in school.

To protect her from bullying at school, Nicole was assigned an adult to watch her at all times between classes, following her to the cafeteria, to the bathroom. She found it intrusive and stressful. It made her feel like even more of an outsider.

"Separate but equal does not work," she says.

Wyatt often liked to dress in girl's clothes and identified more as a girl than a boy.

It was a burden that Jonas shouldered as well. The same boy who in fifth grade objected to her using the girls bathroom made the mistake of saying to Jonas in sixth grade that "freaking gay people" shouldn't be allowed in the school. Jonas jumped on him and a scuffle ensued.

"He's taken on a lot," Wayne says. "Middle school boys and sexuality, you know … boys can get picked on."

Nicole and her parents filed a complaint with the Maine Humans Right Commission over her right to use the girls bathroom. The commission found that she had been discriminated against and, along with the Maines family, filed a lawsuit against the Orono School District. The suit is pending in Penobscot County Superior Court, and the Maines family is represented by lawyers from the Gay & Lesbian Advocates & Defenders (GLAD) in Boston and by Jodi Nofsinger, who serves on the Maine ACLU board.

"What Nicole and Jonas both went through in school was unconscionable," says Jennifer Levi, one of the GLAD lawyers on the case. "Their one huge stroke of luck was having Kelly and Wayne as parents."

A Huge Relief

Since that first visit to Spack when Nicole was 9, her parents discussed putting her into the GeMS Clinic when the right time came. They were glad there was time to adjust to the idea. "Baby steps," Kelly calls their path toward treatment.

"I wasn't always on board," Wayne says. "Kelly and I were not on the same page. My question was, what is this doctor doing? It scared me. I was grieving. I was losing my son."

But the more he watched his child struggle, the better he felt about going to Spack. And once he got there, he says, it was a huge relief. "Not only does he know what he's doing, he's extremely comforting. He's got to deal with a ton of dads who are just freaking out, and he made me feel good."

Spack's experience runs deep; before the clinic was established, he had long worked with transgender youth, as well as with adults. "The most striking thing about these kids was the

Jonas, Nicole and their parents, Kelly and Wayne Maines.

fact that they were just normal young people who had this incredibly unusual and problematic situation," says Spack, 68.

He believes it is crucial to intervene with such children before adolescent changes begin in earnest.

"Most of us look pretty similar until we hit puberty," he says. "I bet I could go to any fourth or fifth-grade class, cut the hair of the boys, put earrings on various kids, change their clothing, and we could send all those kids off to the opposite-gender bathrooms and nobody would say boo."

He adds: "We can do wonders if we can get them early."

Second-Guessing

Not everyone agrees that they should, of course, and Spack has heard the arguments: Man should not interfere with what God has wrought. Early adolescents are too young for such huge decisions, much less life-altering treatment.

Though GeMS treatment is now considered the standard of care by mainstream medical groups, some have their doubts. Dr. Kenneth Zucker, a psychologist and head of the gender-identity service at the Center for Addiction and Mental Health in Toronto, says he worries about putting youngsters on puberty blockers, drugs that suppress the release of testosterone in boys and estrogen in girls.

"One controversy is, how low does one go in starting blockers?" Zucker says. "Should you start at 11? At 10? What if someone starts their period at 9?" Nicole started on the blockers at age 11.

He also questions the role the parents have played; have they simply followed the child's lead? "Say a 5-year-old says repeatedly that he wants to be a girl," Zucker says. "The parents deduce this must mean the child is transgender, so they socially transition him to living in the other gender."

Spack and others, however, say the issue is a medical one and that early intervention makes sense. "We're talking about a population that has the highest rate of suicide attempts in the world, and it's strongly linked to nontreatment, especially if they are rejected within their family for being who they think they are," says Spack, who adds that nearly a quarter of his patients admitted to "serious self-harm" before coming to him.

As for the criticisms about "playing God," Spack quotes from the Old Testament: "Leviticus says, 'If thy neighbor is bleeding by the side of the road, you shall not stand idly by the blood of thy neighbor.' It's a mandate. I think these kids have been bleeding."

The Next Step

The clinic, which includes geneticists, social workers, psychiatrists, psychologists, and nurses, has so far treated 95 patients for disorders that range from babies born with ambiguous genitalia to cases where normal sexual development does not occur.

About a third of the patients have undergone puberty suppression.

Each patient must have been in therapy with someone familiar with transgender issues and who writes a letter recommending the treatment. The child's family also must undergo extensive psychological testing before and during treatment. And the patient must be in the early stage of puberty, before bodily changes are noticeable.

Jonas and Wyatt Maines at age 9. Wyatt started growing his hair longer and started talking about a name change in fourth grade.

Nicole and Jonas are the first set of identical twins the program has seen, and they have provided critical comparative data, Spack says.

The effects of the blockers—an injection given monthly to prevent the gonads from releasing the unwanted hormones—are reversible; patients can stop taking them and go through puberty as their biological sex. This is critical, Spack says, because a "very significant number of children who exhibit cross-gender behavior" before puberty "do not end up being transgender."

Since the 1970s, the blockers have been used for the rare condition of precocious puberty, when children as young as 3 can hit puberty. They are kept on the blockers until they are of appropriate age. "The drugs have a great track record; we already know that these kids do fine," says Spack. "There are no ill consequences."

It is the next big step—taking sex hormones of the opposite gender—that creates permanent changes, such as breasts and broadened hips, that cannot be hormonally reversed.

"In puberty,'" Spack says, "when your body starts making a statement, you either have to accept it or reject it."

There is no definitive answer to the question of what causes gender identity disorder, though studies suggest a genetic contribution. "It's still a very open question," Zucker says. And how could it affect just one of two identical twins? "There can be genetic changes during fetal development that maybe hit one twin but not the other."

Changed Atmosphere

After the family's lawsuit against the Orono schools was publicized, the atmosphere in town changed. When they went to the movies, people pointed and whispered. There were fewer party invitations, fewer sleepovers.

In the sixth grade, the twins joined the school's Outing Club. All year they attended meetings to prepare for the crowning event: a whitewater rafting trip. Wayne went to several meetings, too, so he could serve as a chaperone.

Wayne thought he had a good relationship with the club leader. But then the man informed him that Nicole would not be allowed to sleep in the tent with the girls—the same girls who had slept over her house several times. She and her father could have a separate tent.

A difficult family conversation followed. Jonas and Wayne went on the trip. Nicole stayed home.

After that episode, Kelly and Wayne decided a new start would be good for the family. The summer after the sixth grade, they moved to a larger, more diverse community in southern Maine, and the twins enrolled in public school. Wayne still works at UMaine and stays in Orono during the week, spending weekends with his family.

For two years, in seventh and eighth grade, Nicole went "stealth," as she calls it: passing as a girl. She did not tell anyone that she was biologically male. Though she made friends at school, she never brought them to the house. After that hard last year in Orono, the family was afraid to come out.

This fall the twins entered high school, transferring to a smaller, private school known for open-mindedness. Before they arrived, the school changed its bathrooms to unisex. And before classes started, the family met with members of the school's Gay Straight Alliance—"so she'd have older kids watching her back," says Wayne. After the meeting, the group changed its name to include transgender; it is now the Gay Straight Transgender Alliance.

"It made me a lot more comfortable," Nicole says. "I thought, this is OK. I can do this."

She recently started telling some of her new friends her story. One girl replied: "Does this mean you're going to start wearing boys' clothes to school?"

"No," replied Nicole. "I'm male to female."

The girl's reaction? "She was like, 'Ohhhhhhhhhhhhhhh.'"

Concerns about Safety

The male hormone suppressors have done their job, and the next step is to add female hormones so that Nicole will undergo puberty as a girl and develop as a woman, with breasts and curvy hips. She is due to see Spack in January, and a date may then be set for adding estrogen, which she will take every day for the rest of her life. Though she will have a higher risk of breast cancer than if she were a male, she will have a lower risk of prostate cancer, Spack says. The treatment will leave her infertile.

But before the estrogen is administered, the GeMS clinic will reevaluate Nicole to make sure that she still identifies as a female and wants to continue.

"In my experience, the patients just blossom physically and mentally when they get the hormones of the gender they affirm," Spack says. "It's quite amazing. I feel good about Nicole and who she is and where she's going."

An endocrinologist in Maine now administers the blockers Nicole needs, but Spack still sees her in Boston every four to six months. The Maines family has grown close to him and others in the clinic. "I love going to see him," says Wayne, who has thanked Spack for "saving my daughter's life." The Maines family declined to talk about the cost of the treatment but said insurance has covered much of it.

But as well as things are going, the Maines family still worries about Nicole's safety. Last year Wayne and Nicole attended Transgender Day of Remembrance in Maine, which honors those who have been killed in hate crimes.

Wayne spoke to the crowd, telling them that as much as Nicole is loved at home, her family cannot always protect her.

"I remind her that she needs to always be aware of her surroundings, to stay close to friends and her brother if she feels uncomfortable, and to call me anytime she feels threatened," he said.

Nicole is part of the groundbreaking clinic at Children's Hospital founded by Dr. Norman Spack, that helps families deal with emotional and medical issues that arise from having a transgender child. The Maines are the first identical twins the program has seen.

Lobbying the Legislature

Last winter, Maine state representative Kenneth Fredette, a Republican from Penobscot County, sponsored a bill that would have repealed protections for transgender people in public restrooms, instead allowing schools and businesses to adopt their own policies. The bill was a response to the Maines' 2009 lawsuit against the Orono School District.

Last spring Wayne and Nicole roamed the halls of the State House, button-holing legislators and testifying against the bill. "I'd be in more danger if I went into the boys bathroom," Nicole told the lawmakers, who ultimately rejected the bill.

"She knows how to work a room," her father says proudly. "She even convinced a cosponsor to vote the other way."

In October, the family was honored for its activism in helping defeat the transgender bathroom bill. The Maineses received the Roger Baldwin Award, named for a founder of the American Civil Liberties Union, from the Maine chapter of the ACLU.

Surrounded by Kelly and the kids, Wayne told the audience that he and his wife have had top-notch guides as they confronted the unknown.

"As a conventional dad, hunter, and former Republican, it took me longer to understand that I never had two sons," he told them. "My children taught me who Nicole is and who she needed to be."

Typical Teens

In some respects, Jonas has had as tough a time as Nicole. For one thing, there's the personality difference: Nicole is the dominant twin, talkative and tough, while Jonas is cautious and reserved.

"If this had been Jonas, I would have had to home school him," his mother says.

The twins have always been close. During an interview, Nicole sits next to her brother on the couch and occasionally lays her head on his shoulder. At one point, when Jonas goes silent as the twins talk of their lives, she whispers words of encouragement into his ear.

But the next minute, like typical teenage siblings, they're teasing and tussling. Jonas displays a faint scar on his arm where Nicole jabbed him with a pencil. Both have black belts in tae kwon do, which they started at age 5.

They often hang out in Jonas's spacious basement room, where they watch TV and play video games.

"I love having a sister," says Jonas, who acknowledges being protective of her. "We have a very strong relationship."

Nicole calls Jonas her closest friend.

"I would say my brother got lucky with me. Because we grew up with only boy neighbors, I developed a liking to shoot-'em-up and military video games," she says. "I could have come out a lot girlier."

At 14, Jonas is handsome, Nicole pretty. Jonas is midway through puberty. His shoulders have broadened, his voice has deepened, and there's a shadow on his upper lip. He's 5 feet 6 and weighs 115 pounds, with a size 11 shoe.

Nicole is petite: 5 feet 1, 100 pounds. She's got long, dark hair and she wears girls' size 14–16. Her closet contains nice shirts and jeans, party dresses, glittery shoes, and a pair of footy pajamas.

"The thought of being a boy makes me cringe," she says. "I just couldn't do it."

Excited, Worried about Surgery

Nicole's final step on her journey to womanhood would be gender reassignment surgery. Doctors generally won't perform it until the age of consent, which is 18. No hospitals in New England perform such surgery, says Spack. The nearest that do are in Montreal and Philadelphia.

Nicole says she's excited about the idea of surgery, though a bit worried about the results— "and maybe the pain, too."

While she's interested in boys, she has expressed fear that "nobody is ever going to love me."

She has gone on weekend retreats sponsored by the Trans Youth Equality Foundation and to summer camp for transgender children, where she developed her first crush on a boy.

Over the years, the family has become close to several adult transsexuals, and Nicole has seen that some have found happy marriages. "She says she does feel better about it," Kelly says, "but still wonders if she ever met a boy who falls for her, and then found out that she was trans, if he would still like her, or say awful things as he skedaddled out the door."

Nicole knows there is a long road ahead, but she feels she's on the right path.

"Obviously my life is not going to be as easy as being gender-conforming, but there are perks like being able to get out there and do things that will benefit the [transgender] community," she says. "I think everything's going to turn out pretty well for me."

For now, at least, life feels more normal to the Maines family.

Wayne recently spoke at GLAD's Spirit of Justice dinner in Boston and was introduced by Nicole. She kept her composure in her brief remarks and thanked GLAD for giving them a rare chance to "safely speak out."

Wayne choked up when thanking the group for its support. He recounted young Wyatt asking him, sadly, "Daddy, why can't boys wear dresses?" Wayne hated to tell his son that society wouldn't accept that.

But today, when Nicole asks her father what he thinks of a certain dress she's wearing, his typical response, he told the audience, is: "That dress is too short. Go change your clothes."

In conversation later, Wayne tells another story of how things have changed, for good and forever. He and the twins were getting out of the car recently, and he grabbed their hands to walk with them.

Jonas, being a teenage boy, shook his father off, while Nicole was happy to walk hand-in-hand, swinging arms.

"She'll do that the rest of her life," Wayne says with a wide grin. "It was an epiphany for me."

SAME-SEX MARRIAGE IN CANADA: THE IMPACT OF LEGAL MARRIAGE ON THE FIRST COHORT OF GAY AND LESBIAN CANADIANS TO WED

By Heather MacIntosh, Elke D. Reissing, and Heather Andruff

INTRODUCTION

In the last three decades, most Western countries have seen important steps in the advancement of equal rights and protection for all citizens. With respect to gay and lesbian individuals, the Trudeau government's removal of homosexuality from Canada's criminal code in 1969 was an early and significant change. However, it was not until 1996 that it became illegal to discriminate against persons on the basis of their sexual orientation. Following a court decision in 1999, both the federal and provincial governments introduced bills amending laws related to family law, adoption, pension benefits, and income tax to give couples in same-sex relationships the same rights and obligations as heterosexual couples in common-law relationships. Equality for Gays and Lesbians Everywhere (Egale) argued that this change was still not sufficient and that legal recognition of same-sex relationships was necessary to achieve equality.

On June 10, 2003, a ruling of the Court of Appeal for Ontario deemed the definition of marriage (a union of a man and a woman) unconstitutional and redefined marriage to include the "voluntary union for life of two persons to the exclusion of all others." City halls across Ontario were quickly flooded with same-sex couples seeking marriage licenses reflecting a fear that the ruling would be appealed and the opportunity to be legally married lost. British Columbia followed suit on July 8, 2003, and Quebec on March 19, 2004. The federal government's passage of the Civil Marriage Act on July 20, 2005, extended the right to marry to same-sex partners across Canada. This legislation created the first cohort of same-sex couples in North America to become

Heather MacIntosh, Elke D. Reissing, and Heather Andruff, "Same-Sex Marriage in Canada: The Impact of Legal Marriage on the First Cohort of Gay and Lesbian Canadians to Wed," The Canadian Journal of Human Sexuality, vol. 19, issue 3, pp. 79-90. Copyright © 2010 by Sex Information and Education Council of Canada. Reprinted with permission. Provided by ProQuest LLC. All rights reserved.

legally married. It also provided a unique opportunity to examine the effects of the legalization of same-sex marriage in Canada.

The present quantitative and qualitative study explored these effects in a sample of 26 lesbian and gay married couples. Themes of interest in the study are reflected in the background literature reviewed below.

The Impact of Marriage on Same-Sex Couples

Practical Benefits

The practical benefits of legal marriage for same-sex couples include those related to family law, pension and health benefits, income tax, inheritance and power of attorney, and immigration law. These rights are afforded immediately to married couples without the waiting period required of common-law couples. Same-sex married couples are bound by the same responsibilities as heterosexual married couples including decision-making in medical or legal emergencies, spousal support, child support, and division of property upon dissolution of marriage. A recent survey of 558 individuals in same-sex marriages in Massachusetts conducted by the Massachusetts Department of Public Health (Ramos, Goldberg, & Badgett, 2009) found that 85% of participants listed legal recognition as one of their top three reasons for getting married. In a phenomenological study of 22 married or soon to be married same-sex couples from Canada and around the world, Alderson (2004) highlighted the importance of practical and legal benefits to the couples interviewed. The legal benefits that these couples identified as having had a particularly significant impact in their relational lives were the opportunities to create families through adoption, to automatically have the right to care for a partner in the case of illness or injury, and to act on other legal matters.

Social Support

Zicklin (1995) hypothesized that public and legal marriage for same-sex couples living in the United States would increase social support for these couples because of the higher social recognition afforded to legally married couples. As Zicklin anticipated, this has now been shown to be the case in several studies (e.g., Ramos et al., 2009; Balsam, Beauchaine, Rothblum, & Solomon, 2008; Lannutti, 2008). Given that many gay and lesbian couples lack family support (e.g., Kurdek, 2005; 2006), legal marriage might challenge families and public opinion to be more accepting. Family members who opposed a couple's cohabiting outside of marriage might be less negative toward gay or lesbian couples who were legally married and more inclined to provide support (Ramos et al., 2009). Social support from family and friends has been shown to influence commitment to the relationship in gay and lesbian couples in that partners with higher levels of social support also demonstrate higher levels of commitment (Kurdek, 2008a).

Prior to the legalization of same-sex marriage in Canada, a national poll found that 49% of Canadians supported the legalization of same-sex marriage and 46% opposed. Among those aged from 18 to 40, that support was 60% (The Strategic Counsel, 2002). A more recent Angus Reid poll conducted in September, 2009 showed that 61% of Canadians supported the legalization of same-sex marriage and an additional 23% were supportive of same-sex unions (Angus Reid Strategies, 2009). Only 11 % felt that same-sex couples should not have any legal recognition.

In some cases, marriage can also have a negative effect on social support for same-sex couples. For example, Lannutti's (2008) qualitative interviews with 26 female couples in Massachusetts in which one partner was bisexual found that some of the bi-women felt that family members (particularly parents) were very unsupportive of their decision to marry. It appeared in some cases that family members may have tolerated the same-sex relationship prior to marriage in the hope that the bisexual partner would once again have relationships with men. Embarrassment at having a lesbian or bisexual daughter was also given as a reason for lack of parental support.

Relationship Satisfaction

Kurdek (2003) has extensively examined the correlates of relationship satisfaction in gay and lesbian couples in the United States. The comparison groups have been both homosexual and heterosexual couples. The findings have consistently indicated that similar factors are correlated with relationship satisfaction in heterosexual, gay and lesbian relationships (e.g., Kurdek, 2005; 2006). These factors include arguing about issues related to power and intimacy, attachment styles and behaviours, commitment, and relationship history. Gottman et al. (2003) have also assessed the correlates of relationship satisfaction and dissolution in gay and lesbian couples and found that similar factors predicted satisfaction in heterosexual and gay/lesbian couples.

In their comparative study of cohabiting, married, and remarried heterosexual couples in the U.S., Skinner, Barh, Crane, and Call (2002) found that the cohabiting couples reported lower relationship happiness and fairness. Moore, McCabe, and Brink (2001) similarly reported that married heterosexual couples in Australia had higher levels of intimacy and relationship satisfaction than cohabiting couples. With respect to relationship quality in unmarried same-sex couples, Balsam et al. (2008) compared 203 same-sex couples in civil unions, 84 same-sex couples who were not in civil unions and 55 heterosexual married couples in Vermont. Whether they were in civil unions or not, the sample-sex couples reported more positive relationship quality and less conflict than the heterosexual married participants. However, same-sex couples not in civil unions were more likely to have ended their relationships on three-year follow-up than those who were in civil unions. Wienke and Hill's (2009) comparative study of 282 partnered gay and lesbian couples and 6,734 legally married heterosexual couples in the U.S. asked about general life happiness rather than relationship happiness or satisfaction in particular. They found that the partnered gay men and lesbian women reported less general happiness with their lives than did the married heterosexual participants.

In another approach to studying relationship quality of partners in different types of cohabiting relationships, Kurdek (2008b) followed 95 lesbian couples, 92 gay male couples, 226 heterosexual couples without children, and 312 heterosexual couples with children. Participants in these cohabiting relationships were contacted every year for 10 years to determine patterns of relationship quality based on the Dyadic Adjustment Scale. Lesbian couples showed the overall highest level of relationship quality and gay male couples showed significantly higher levels of relationship quality compared to heterosexual couples with children. In addition, relationship quality for both gay male and lesbian couples remained constant over the course of the study whereas heterosexual couples showed an accelerated decline in relationship quality at the beginning of cohabitation followed by a second period of accelerated decline if the couple was living with children.

Alderson's (2004) phenomenological exploration provided the first insights into relationship functioning in a predominantly Canadian sample of legally married same-sex couples. Participants in this study noted an increase in commitment and connection, a finding replicated by Ramos et al. (2009) who found that 72% of their sample felt more committed to their partners following marriage and by Lannutti (2008) whose participants expressed greater feelings of love and a closer emotional bond to their partner following legal marriage. With regard to the feeling among some same-sex couples that their relationships seem more egalitarian than they observe in heterosexual couples, Solomon, Rothblum, and Balsam's (2005) study of the division of finances and household tasks among 336 members of same-sex civil unions, 238 members of same-sex couples not in civil unions, and 413 married heterosexual couples in Vermont is of interest. These authors found that lesbian and gay male couples, both those in civil unions and those not, were more egalitarian with respect to money and housework, than heterosexual married couples. Kurdek (2005; 2006) noted similar findings with respect to division of household labour and has also suggested that satisfaction with the division of household labour increases both relationship satisfaction and relationship stability (Kurdek, 2007).

Coming Out

Disclosure of sexual orientation and relationship status has been consistently associated with measures of positive mental health and relationship satisfaction in gay and lesbian persons, and with decreases in internalized homophobia (e.g., Jordan, 2000; Rosario, Hunter, Maguen, Gwadz, & Smith, 2001; Saphira & Glover, 2001). Cabaj and Purcel (1998) hypothesized that legalized marriage would increase disclosure and have a positive impact on relationship satisfaction and internalized homophobia. While this has shown to be the case for some, other individuals have described feelings of anguish when their loved ones respond with anger (e.g., Alderson, 2004; Lannutti, 2008). Same-sex couples who appreciate the formal recognition of a legal marriage may be less hesitant to disclose their same-sex relationship. This was noted in one study where more than 80% of participants indicated that being in a same-sex marriage had caused them to be more likely to come out to coworkers and healthcare providers (Ramos et al., 2009). Further, it has been shown that lesbian women in civil unions demonstrate significantly higher levels of "being out" than lesbian women not in civil unions (Solomon, Rothblum, & Balsam, 200). Finally, level of "being out" has been shown to be a positive predictor of relationship quality in men such that those men who were more likely to be out demonstrated greater relationship quality at follow-up (Balsam et al., 2008).

Rationale for the Current Study

The literature reviewed above indicates that many gay and lesbian couples who have married experience not only the practical benefits related to the laws affecting married couples and the social benefits of acknowledgement and societal acceptance but also the relational benefits of increased relationship satisfaction (e.g., Alderson, 2004). In these respects, legal marriage appears to bring to same-sex couples many of the positive benefits experienced by heterosexual couples when they marry. Since this is a new area of research, the particular ways in which legal marriage has impacted on same-sex couples who were previously in long-term relationships warrants further investigation. The current study thus used both qualitative and quantitative methodology to assess the impact of marriage on members of the first cohort of legally-married, Canadian same-sex couples.

METHODS

Participants

Participants were recruited through gay, lesbian, bisexual and transgendered (GLBT) newspapers (e.g., Capital XTra), GLBT advocacy groups and web sites (e.g., Egale) and pro-same-sex marriage web sites (e.g., Canadians for Equal Marriage). Recruitment began in Ontario in response to the initial legislative change and expanded to British Columbia (B.C.) in response to requests from couples who had seen the call for participants on various web sites and who wanted to participate in the study.

Procedures

Couples who initiated contact through e-mail were e-mailed a package containing information about the study and what participants would be asked to do. Those who contacted us through telephone were provided with this information verbally. Inclusion criteria included (a) being legally married, (b) having lived together for a minimum of one year, and (c) no physical violence in the relationship. Couples who met these criteria and were participating from outside the Ottawa area were e-mailed a questionnaire package, information letter, and consent form. Questionnaires were returned by e-mail through a secured server or mail, and consent forms were sent back by mail to ensure that a signed original was in the file. The first author carried out telephone interviews with both members of the couple on the phone at the same time. Couples in the Ottawa area who were interviewed in person were given the information and consent forms and completed the questionnaires at the time of the interview. This study was approved by the Research Ethics Board of the University of Ottawa.

Measures

In addition to requesting demographic information, the questionnaire included the two research instruments described below.

Relationship Satisfaction

Relationship satisfaction was measured using the Dyadic Adjustment Scale (DAS, Spanier, 1976). This is a widely used self report index of global couple adjustment with well established psychometric properties. Johnson and O'Conner (2001) used the DAS in a study examining parenting in same-sex couples and found that the norms for their study were consistent with published test norms for married heterosexual couples. The DAS may also have utility for comparing same-sex and heterosexual couples because it is somewhat gender neutral in that it primarily uses the terms "partner" and "couple" throughout.

Attachment Security

Security and comfort with closeness in relationships was measured using the Experiences in Close Relationsbips-Revised (ECR-R, Brennan, Clark, & Shaver, 1998). The ECR-R is a 36-item measure of adult attachment in romantic relationships with well established psychometric properties. The measure can be used to measure attachment along two attachment dimensions: avoidance and anxiety. Reliability of the items in both dimensions is high with alphas of .94 for the avoidance dimension and .91 for the anxiety dimension.

Semi-Structured Interview

The semi-structured, open-ended interview was designed to assess the impact of legal marriage on the couple. Three questions were asked in all of the interviews. These questions were used to stimulate discussion and couples were given time to expand upon their responses prior to being asked a successive question. The questions were: "What were your reasons for getting married?", "How did this change your relationship?", and "What impact did legal marriage have on your family?" Other questions were not structured and were emergent based on the content of the discussions. Interviews lasted between half an hour and an hour and both members of the couple were present in the room or on the phone. Couples were allowed to answer the questions with as much or as little detail as they were comfortable and to take the interview off to different topics that were not included in the interviewer's list of questions. All interviews were carried out by the first author.

Thematic Analysis

Thematic analysis is particularly suited to the relatively new study of same-sex marriage because it is an emergent rather than hypothesis driven methodology. It is appropriate for research topics where no established theories exist, and/or the theories are not specific enough or relevant to the area one is investigating, and/or the research questions are difficult to study with traditional research design and methods (e.g., Fereday & Muir-Cochrane, 2006). Thematic analysis is a qualitative methodology that can be utilized to organize qualitative data into patterns with the goal of eventually developing theories or models to account for phenomena or to explain change (e.g., Taylor & Bogdan, 1984). In the present study, all interviews were transcribed by the principal investigator and the initial screening for general categories and sub-themes was undertaken throughout this process. Two additional independent raters were then asked to read the transcripts and identify categories and themes. All three raters then met, discussed the findings, and agreed on three general global themes, one of which was further broken down into three sub-themes.

RESULTS

Participant Characteristics

Fifty-two individuals completed the quantitative measures, 20 lesbian and 6 gay couples. Due to time zone differences, work schedules and parenting responsibilities, only 15 couples were available to participate in the interview and be included in the qualitative analyses. The mean age of all couples was 48.8 years (range = 23–72 years). The average number of years together was 10.8 years (range = 1–35 years). Five couples had children with one to three children per couple. Twenty-two of the participants reported having had a previous heterosexual relationship. A majority of participants had a postsecondary education (33.4% post graduate, 26.7% undergraduate degree, 11.7% community college diploma) with 6.7%: A majority of participants had a post-secondary education (33.4% post graduate, 26.7% undergraduate degree, 11.7% community college diploma) with 6.7% having a high school diploma and 3.3% having less than a high school diploma. Most had incomes over $75,000 per year with 63.3% above $75,000, 30% at $25–75,000 and 3.3% less than $25,000.

Relationship Satisfaction

Results of the Dyadic Adjustment Scale measurement indicated that the 26 same-sex couples had a mean relationship satisfaction score of 126.71 with a standard deviation of 8.94. The population mean on this scale for married heterosexual couples is 114 (Spanier, 1976). Cronbach's alpha for these responses was .926. Thus, the same-sex marriage group in the present study had significantly higher levels of relationship satisfaction than did the sample of married, heterosexual couples reported on by Spanier, t (26) = 7.25, p, < .001.

Attachment Security

The population mean chosen for comparison on the Experiences in Close Relationships-Revised measure was the Married Population Norm as this is the most rigorous norm for this measure. Other available norms were for clinical populations experiencing psychological and relational distress. Results of the ECR-R suggest that these married heterosexual couples were reporting levels of Attachment Anxiety with an average of 1.79 out of a possible 3.00 t (26) = −13.59, p < .001 and Attachment Avoidance with an average of 1.60 out of a possible 3.00 t (26) = −13.832, p < .001 (Brennan, Clark, & Shaver, 1998). Cronbach's alpha for these responses was .611. The same-sex marriage group reported significantly less attachment-related anxiety and avoidance than married norms, t (26 anx) = −13.59, p < .001 and t (26 avoid) = −13.832, p < .001 respectively. In addition, all of the couples in the present study fell within the "secure" range of attachment compared to 70% for the normative heterosexual married couples.

Qualitative Interview Findings

In total, 15 couple interviews were carried out either by telephone or in person. Analysis of differences in interview length, general responsiveness of participants, and content did not reveal any qualitative differences based on method of interview. The three global themes that emerged from every interview were characterized as Social elements, Relational elements, and Political elements. Each theme is described below with representative quotes reflecting representative ideas and thoughts from participants that led to the thematic characterizations.

Social Elements

All of the participants described social elements related to the impact of being legally married on them personally and/or on their relationships. The three sub-themes that fell under the Social category were: (1) the Language of Marriage, (2) Being Out, and (3) Rights and Responsibilities.

Sub-theme 1: The Language of Marriage

Ninety-two percent of participants discussed the impact of the language of marriage as an element of their experience of becoming legally married. Almost all indicated that words such as spouse, marriage, wife, husband, and daughter-in-law, were understood by everyone and that through this language they felt understood and known by their friends and families in a different way that created a new and deeper acceptance of their partnerships. For most, this language had a very positive influence.

> The language of marriage helped us feel more a part of this world. Everyone knows what it means. It helps others start to realize that a relationship is a relationship and we are dealing with the same issues that everyone else deals with. It helped me realize, the word marriage, what was important to me; getting married, having a wedding. The language was really intentional; showing others that that's what we mean. (*Tessa*, 37)

Only two couples discussed the negative impact of language. In both cases, their families had previously been only minimally tolerant of their relationship and marriage broke the limits of tolerance and caused a breach in their relationships with these family members.

A majority of female participants described their experiences with the word "wife." They discussed how this has been a patriarchal word throughout history and illustrated their struggle with deciding whether to use this word or not. A number of women joked that they would like to have a wife but would not like to be one. A lot of humour and thought was put into these decisions and the majority of participants had chosen to continue using the word spouse or partner. A smaller number of participants chose to reclaim the word wife in a more positive frame or to make up their own word.

> … for me it's like reclaiming the word queer or dyke, taking something that's been used as a negative and defining itself. (*Grace*, 56)

Participants indicated that there was no more mystery about their relationships as everyone knows that a marriage is about a lifelong emotional and sexual relationship that is primary and equal to the relationships that heterosexual couples have with their partners.

> The word has taken us from being legal partners to being wives with the status that the word conveys, it puts this relationship into a context that everyone, homophobic or not can understand. (*Chris*, 50)

Sub-theme 2: Being Out

Three quarters of participants commented on the fact that legalized marriage had an impact on their level of being out. In particular they felt more comfortable and entitled to be out but also a sense of responsibility about the need.to be out. They talked about an increased personal level of social awareness and felt that this had come about as a result of their being more out and in particular, as a result of their public declaration of marriage.

> It's a problem cause if you're going to have a gay wedding you need to tell people you're gay! It's not that people didn't know, it's that I wasn't silent anymore. (*Sue*, 36)

Participants discussed the impact that legal marriage had on their own levels of internalized homophobia and the external homophobia of others. In fact, a number of participants observed that they had not even been aware that they had any internalized homophobia until it came time to announce their marriage. They talked about coming out again in a new way with a new found sense of pride and a decreased level of internalized homophobia.

> We would have thought that we were really even on the scale of internalized homophobia. I've been out for 25 years and we're out to friends, family, at work in community but this resurfaced issues and dynamics with the decision to wed publicly. I moved from a place of being grateful to feeling entitled … from "Am I really allowed to tell people to come to my wedding" to celebrating, revelling in, and claiming the legitimacy. I used to simply feel grateful for being accepted but now I feel entitled and legitimate. It was another layer of coming out. (*Pat*, 48)

Seventy-two percent of participants discussed how the language of marriage and the increased "outness" of being married had the combined impact of creating normalization for their relationships and for same-sex couples in general and that these things led to social change. They felt that being out, proud and having affirmed their relationships publicly through marriage showed the world more about their relationships. Further, they noted that simply living their married lives publicly and openly demonstrated that their relationships were no different than those of their heterosexual peers.

> Marriage opens the door for people to know that we're not really any different from any other couple who decides to make a commitment to each other … and that we get up, go to work, pay our bills, buy gas for our cars, help our kids, and just live ordinary, everyday lives … I would invite anyone to come into our home to see just how very ordinary we really are! (*Helen*, 50)

In effect, these participants felt that living their lives and loving publicly has led to greater levels of acceptance and support from their communities.

> People have said that having experienced our wedding, they are more willing to challenge other people when the subject comes up which is very affirming. (*Will*, 40)

Sub-theme 3: Rights and Responsibilities

Three quarters of the participants indicated that the rights and responsibilities of marriage were important to them and that this had an impact on them since getting married. They felt that they and their relationships were full participants in society in the sense that the ability to file taxes together as spouses and to have the immediate practical benefits of marriage, such as receiving immediate spousal health insurance benefits, had given them a newfound sense of empowerment and inclusion in a system that they had been restricted from in the past. These couples embraced the opportunity to be responsible for their partner in all of the legal and social ways that come with marriage and articulated a deep sense of belongingness and feelings of entitlement that had historically been denied to them and their relationships.

Relational Elements

All of the participants described experiencing an impact on their relationship through the act of legally marrying their partner. In particular this impact was felt in the areas of family and safety or security. While all couples talked about the impact that legal marriage had on their sense of commitment, the majority reported that it had not changed their level of commitment.

The legal ceremony did not change our level of commitment at all ... our first commitment ceremony three years ago had a tremendous impact ... the unlegal deepened our
commitment and the courts simply caught up to us. (*Bryn*, 37)

Ninety-two percent of participants discussed the impact that legal marriage had on their
sense of family and almost all of them described feeling more open to or ready for the idea of
having children. They also felt more entitled to apply to adopt and many were, in fact, either in
the process of beginning adoption applications or assisted fertilization and some were already
pregnant. Among the couples contemplating having children, a number had previously decided
not to have children and indicated that being legally married had changed something for them
that allowed them for the first time to imagine that they could become parents.

Adoption and parentage was a big part of getting married. We felt it would legitimize
us as co-parents and make the child feel more secure. (*Leslie*, 42)

Most participants talked about family from the perspective of creating family and bringing family
together. Some talked with animation and emotion about their experiences of being welcomed
into the family of their partner and a number recounted how previously anxious or unaccepting
parents had introduced their child's partner to others as their daughter-in-law or son-in-law. Most
described this kind of experience as one of the impacts of legal marriage that was tremendously
enriching. For example, a woman whose partner's rural father had been very uncomfortable
and even negative when his daughter came out to the family describes how over time he had
changed his attitude and openly embraced the marriage of his daughter and included her as a
full member of the family.

It's the reason that everyone gets married, to feel a part of each other's family ... we really
are ... we stopped to get a coffee and I thought he'd want to stay in the truck so I offered
to go in and get it but he said he wanted to go in to show ofifhis new daughter-in-law.
I call her father "Dad" now and he gets a kick out of it ... he calls us his girls. (*Abbie*, 38)

In contrast, two couples experienced further distancing from already strained family relationships
because their families saw in legal marriage the kind of public profession of love from which
they had to withdraw. The couples told these stories with sadness but also with a sense of having
made a decision to move forward in deepening their relationship with a full understanding of
the potential consequences.

Eighty-six percent of participants also discussed the impact that legal marriage had on their
level of safety and security in the relationship with most describing this as a newfound sense of
peacefulness and feeling relaxed and at ease in the relationship in ways that they had not before. Among the many who talked about an increased feeling of closeness, a majority indicated
that they had been overwhelmed and tremendously surprised that it was even possible to feel
closer to the partner they had been with for many years. This is an interesting observation in
relation to the couples that did not necessarily feel any greater level of commitment; possibly
something did increase in terms of emotional closeness and security. Some couples expressed
both awe and anger at the amazement of actually being able to feel closer to someone that they
had loved for so long and then at realizing that they had been denied this feeling throughout
their relationship.

> The minute we got married all of the conversation about security and houses and money stopped ... the bottom line was that when you get married you are taking on a responsibility for that person and if something happens to her it is my problem ... I finally felt safer, more secure and knew that she was not going to walk out the door. (*Sue*, 36)

> I had no idea that I could feel any closer to him than I already did after 35 years together. It is unbelievable and I can't believe that we have been denied this experience all of these years. (*Len*, 68)

Political Elements

All of the couples talked about the political climate around same-sex marriage and the impact that this element of the issue has had on them. All couples described the importance of being granted legal rights of marriage and full equality in society. In terms of legal rights, all of the participants described their feeling of finally being protected by society. They described a profound sense of safety and security in knowing that they would be able to have the right to make decisions for an ill partner, care for children together and have the benefits related to inheritance and insurance. Almost all talked about the importance of being married for access to parental rights and their desire to be given equal rights under the law in cases of adoption and automatic parental rights to a child born into the marriage. As mentioned above, many of the participants were in the process of starting families at the time of the interviews and these issues were foremost on their minds.

> We did insemination a couple of days ago. We were going to do this anyway but I wanted to be legally married before the baby was born. From a legal perspective I want to be legally protected and secure. (*Donna*, 39)

Most participants also talked about their feeling that legal marriage had the impact of legitimizing their relationships. They reported feeling like they finally existed and were accepted by society and not just by their immediate social circle.

> I think that changing the law has set a moral standard by which people's attitudes are changing; it does legitimize it ... like corporal punishment. In Sweden they changed the laws and it changed from 90% of people believing that it was okay to hit their kids to only 10% in less than twenty years ... it is insisting that cultural change be instigated by government. (*Sandra*, 43)

> It really changed the status that I am allowed to claim in the world. (*Dale*, 39)

In discussing the political issues related to same-sex marriage, 92% of participants indicated that offering same-sex couples civil unions instead of marriage was not acceptable to them and certainly not equal. These couples expressed deep concern about the possibility of a political watering down of the judgment that denying marriage to same-sex couples is unconstitutional.

If civil unions were what was there for everyone then fine but if same-sex couples can only have civil unions where heterosexual couples can have marriage, it isn't fair. It is the same as having to sit at the back of the bus. (*Lynn*, 39)

DISCUSSION

Participants in the present study were among the first same-sex couples to get legally married in Canada. Our findings indicate that they experienced primarily positive consequences subsequent to marriage and it is therefore not surprising that this sample showed significantly higher levels of relationship satisfaction and attachment security compared to heterosexual married population norms. While others have reported comparatively high levels of relationship satisfaction and happiness in cohabiting same-sex couples (e.g., Balsam et al., 2008; Kurdek, 2008b), another explanation for this finding may be that couples in this sample have been in committed relationships for extended periods of time and have undoubtedly weathered the inevitable struggles of long-term relationships in a social environment that may not have always been supportive. High scores on attachment and relationship satisfaction. may therefore reflect the fact that these are highly successful couples who simply renewed their commitment by getting married legally.

Our qualitative analyses documented the overall positive experience of marriage for these couples as reflected in the three overarching thematic elements that emerged from their observations: (a) Social elements, (b) Relational elements, and (c) Political elements.

Socially, participants indicated that the language of marriage had an important impact in helping the people in their lives to better understand and validate their relationship. Marriage also increased their level of being out, decreased their own internalized homophobia, and apparently decreased externalized homophobia in the people around them. In many cases, participants were not even aware that they had residual internalized homophobia after having been out for many years. They welcomed taking on the rights and responsibilities of legal marriage and felt that this allowed them to finally be full participants in society.

Relationally, most participants indicated that legal marriage had not deepened their level of commitment to their partners but it did have the effect of helping them feel more fully a part of each others' families. Participants noted that legal marriage had deepened their feelings of closeness to their partners and peacefulness in their relationships and were struck by this unexpected outcome. They said they could not have imagined feeling any closer to their partners after many years of committed deep relationship.

Politically, participants found in the legal right to marry the feeling of being protected by society in terms of inheritance, power of attorney, parenting rights, and other areas where marriage protects partners. In this sense, marriage had a profound impact on their sense of security and entitlement. They were clear that a civil union was not the same as or equal to a legal marriage that provided couples with a measure of equality and legitimization.

In areas where comparisons are possible, the foregoing observations are generally comparable to those in the few other studies of the impact of legal marriage on same sex couples (Alderson, 2004; Lannutti, 2008; Ramos, et al., 2009). One difference is that Alderson (2004) and Ramos et al. (2009) found that their participants felt more committed to their partners whereas that feeling was less apparent in the present study although our couples did comment on an increased sense of closeness to their partner and a greater feeling of peace and relaxation about their relationship status.

Perceived Implications of Same Sex Marriage

Although our participants decided to marry for personal reasons, as did the couples studied by Alderson (2004) and Ramos et al. (2009), they also recognized that the positive effects on their relationships also had the potential to impact on society through increased exposure and normalization. People who had witnessed their marriages and who continued to support them had become more willing to speak out against homophobia and to support governmental initiatives that legalized and now protect same-sex relationships. However, participants also expressed concern that same-sex marriage could have a negative impact on queer culture in that the inclusion of gay and lesbian couples in the traditions of heterosexual society might cause divisions within the GLBTQ community. Would advocates for same-sex marriage and those who reject marriage as sublimation into the dominant patriarchal society become split off from each other? Another concern was that some members of the GLBTQ community who might not be prepared for marriage would decide too quickly, without having contemplated the consequences, and marry simply because they have the opportunity.

Limitations and Summary Observations

Our comparison of relationship satisfaction and attachment-related anxiety, avoidance and security in heterosexual married couples and same-sex married couples may have been limited by the age of the measure (Spanier, 1976) and by the fact that the scale used was designed for heterosexual respondents. Researchers should now consider psychometric validation of measures on couple function and satisfaction for gay and lesbian married couples. Another limitation was that our participants were highly self-selected couples who were committed and secure enough to make the decision about getting married once the opportunity was available to them. Future investigations may benefit from a comparison group of heterosexual married couples and a sample of same-sex couples chosen to be demographically representative of married couples in general.

While it is important to understand the impact of legalized marriage on this first cohort, over time it will also be necessary to examine the impact of access to marriage on the next generation of LGBT youth. For example, it will be interesting to follow the relational lives of youth who are coming of age in this period of change and increased rights. Future research might also study matched heterosexual and gay and lesbian couples who met their partners after the legalization of same-sex marriage to determine the impact of marriage on couples who had always had marriage as a legal option

Overall, our assessment of the impact of legal marriage on Canadian same-sex couples demonstrated positive impact across the personal, interpersonal, and political realities of the couples. The fact that participants reported feeling legitimized, understood, supported and protected by both society and their communities suggests a compelling impact that extends beyond the individuals to encompass the larger society.

REFERENCES

Alderson, K. (2004). A phenomenological investigation of same-sex marriage. *The Canadian Journal of Human Sexuality, 13*, 107–122.

Angus Reid Strategies. (2009). *Canada more open to same-sex marriage than U.S., UK*. Retrieved from http://www.angus-reid.com/polls/view/canada_more_ open_to_same_sex_marriage_than_us_uk/

Balsam, K.F., Beauchaine, T.P., Rothblum, E.D., & Solomon, S.E. (2008). Three-year follow-up of same-sex couples who had civil unions in Vermont, same-sex couples not in civil unions, and heterosexual married couples. *Developmental Psychology, 44*, 102–116. doi: 10.1037/0012-1649.44.1.102

Brennan, K.A., Clark, C.L., & Shaver, P.R. (1998). Self-report measurement of adult attachment: An integrative overview. In J.A. Simpson & W.S. Rholes (Eds.), *Attachment theory and close relationships* (46–76). New York, NY: Guilford Press.

Cabaj, R., & Purcel, D. (1998). *On the road to same-sex marriage: A supportive guide to psychological, political and legal issues*. San Fransisco, CA: Jossey-Bass.

Fereday, J., & Muir-Cochrane, E. (2006). Demonstrating rigor using thematic analysis: A hybrid approach of inductive and deductive coding and theme development. *International Journal of Qualitative Methods, 5*, 1–11.

Gottman, J.M., Levenson, R.W., Gross, J., Frederickson, B., McCoy, K., Rosenthal, L., Ruef, A., & Yoshimoto, D. (2003). Correlates of gay and lesbian couples' relationship satisfaction and relationship dissolution. *Journal of Homosexuality, 45*, 23–43. doi: 10.1300/J082v45n0l_02

Johnson, S.M., & O'Connor, E. (2001). *For lesbian parents: Your guide to helping your family grow up happy, healthy, and proud*. New York, NY: Guilford Press.

Jordan, K.M. (2000). Substance abuse among gay, lesbian, bisexual, transgender, and questioning adolescents. *School Psychology* Review, *29*, 201–207.

Kurdek, L. (2003). Differences between gay and lesbian cohabiting couples. *Journal of Social and Personal Relationships, 20*, 411–436. doi: 10.1177/02654075030204001

Kurdek, L.A. (2004). Are gay and lesbian cohabitating couples *really* different from heterosexual married couples? *Journal of Marriage and Family, 66*, 880–900. doi: 10.1111/j.0022-2445,2004.00060.x

Kurdek, L.A. (2005). What do we know about gay and lesbian couples? *Current Directions in Psychological Science, 14*, 251–254. doi: I 0.1111/j.0963–7214.2005.00375.x

Kurdek, L.A. (2006). Differences between partners from heterosexual, gay, and lesbian cohabiting couples. *Journal of Marriage and Family, 68*, 509–528. doi:10.1111/j.1741-3737.2006.00268.x

Kurdek, L.A. (2007). The allocation of household labor by partners in gay and lesbian couples. *Journal of Family Issues, 28*,132–148. doi:10.1177/0192513X06292019

Kurdek, L.A. (2008a). A general model of relationship commitment: Evidence from same-sex partners. *Personal Relationships, 15*, 391–405. doi:10.1111/j.1475-6811.2008.00205.x

Kurdek, L.A. (2008b). Change in relationship quality for partners from lesbian, gay male, and heterosexual couples. *Journal of Family Psychology, 22*, 701–711.doi:10.1037/0893-3200.22.5.701

Lannutti, P.J. (2008). "This is not a lesbian wedding": Examining same-sex marriage and bisexual-lesbian couples. *Journal of Bisexuality, 7*, 237–260. doi:10.1080/15299710802171316

Moore, K.A., McCabe, M., & Brink, R. (2001). Are married couples happier in their relationships than cohabiting couples? Intimacy and relationship factors. *Sexual and Relationship Therapy, 16*,35–46. doi:10.1080/14681990020021548

Ramos, C., Goldberg, N.G, Badgett, M.V.L. (2009). *The effects of marriage equality in Massachusetts: A survey of the experiences and impact of marriage on same-sex couples*. Los Angeles, CA: The Williams Institute, UCLA.

Rosario, M., Hunter, J., Maguen, S., Gwadz, M., & Smith, R. (2001). The coming-out process and its adaptational and health-related associations among gay, lesbian, and bisexual youths: Stipulation and exploration of a model. *American Journal of Community* Psychology, *29*, 113–160.

Saphira, M., & Glover, M. (2001). The effects of coming . out on relationships and health. *Journal of Lesbian Studies, 5*, 183–194.

Skinner, K.B., Bahr, S.J., Crane, R.D., & Call, V.R. (2002). Cohabitation, marriage, and remarriage: A comparison of relationship quality over time. *Journal of Family Issues, 23,* 74–90. doi:10.1177/0192513X02023001004

Solomon, S.E., Rothblum, E.D., & Balsam, K.F. (2004). Pioneers in partnerships: Lesbian and gay male couples in civil unions compared with those not in civil unions, and married heterosexual siblings. *Journal of Family Psychology, 18,* 275–286. doi:10.1037/08933200.18.2.275

Solomon, S.E., Rothblum, E.D., & Balsam, K.F. (2005). Money, housework, sex, and conflict: Same-sex couples in civil unions, those not in civil unions, and heterosexual married siblings. *Sex Roles, 52,* 561–575. doi:10.1007/sl 1199-005-3725-7

Spanier, G.B. (1976). Measuring dyadic adjustment: New scales for assessing the quality of marriage and similar dyads. *Journal of Marriage and the Family, 38,* 15–28.

Taylor, S.J., & Bogdan, R. (1984) *Introduction to qualitative research methods: The search for meanings.* New York, NY: John Wiley & Sons.

The Strategic Counsel. (2002). *Canadian attitudes on the family: Focus on the family Canadian national survey.* Toronto, ON: Author.

Wienke, C., & Hill, G.J. (2009). Does the "marriage benefit" extend to partners in gay and lesbian relationships?: Evidence from a random sample of sexual active adults. *Journal of Family Issues, 30,* 259–289. doi:10.1177/0192513X08324382

Zicklin, G. (1995). Deconstructing legal rationality: The care of lesbian and gay family relationships *Marriage and Family Review, 21,* 55–76.

(UN) COVERING NORMALIZED GENDER AND RACE SUBJECTIVITIES IN LGBT "SAFE SPACES"

By Catherine O. Fox in collaboration with Tracy E. Ore

> We need to look seriously at what limitations we have placed in this "new world" on who we feel "close to," who we feel "comfortable with," who we feel "safe" with.
>
> —Minnie Bruce Pratt

Writing about her experiences as an activist, Minnie Bruce Pratt interrogates her assumptions about the function of safe spaces in feminist coalition building. After coming out as a lesbian and losing her children to a homophobic ex-husband, she describes her desire for "a place where [she] could live without the painful and deadly violence, without the domination: a place where [she] could live free, *liberated*, with other women." However, even as Pratt begins to envision a different place, or community, from which to create nonoppressive ways of interacting with other women, she reveals how her desire for what she calls a "safe place" is dangerously rooted in her history and identity as a privileged woman and in a noninnocent understanding of what constitutes safety. She writes, "I had not admitted that the safety of much of my childhood was because Laura Cates, Black and a servant, was responsible for me; that I had the walks with my father because the woods were 'ours' by systematic economic exploitation, instigated, at that time, by his White Citizens' Council." She explains that "my experience of a safe space ... was based on places secured by omission, exclusion or violence, and on my submitting to the limits of that place"—limits such as being a good mother and obedient wife.[1] To carry over those notions of safety into feminist coalitions would necessitate bringing the very values that she actively attempts to deconstruct in challenging her privileges and prejudices. She goes on to reflect upon how her notion of safety had been based upon finding a comfortable and secure place where she could simply be herself, how her notion of safety was conflated with feeling "protected" and with a history of racism, sexism, and heterosexism through the "chivalric" behavior of white men. Pratt's purpose is not to undermine the dream of a new world, a world free of psychic and physical violence, but to examine how the vision of safety that operated in the early women's movement was limited by white, heterosexist notions

Catherine O. Fox with Tracy E. Ore, "(Un)Covering Normalized Gender and Race Subjectivities in LGBT 'Safe Spaces,'" Feminist Studies, vol. 36, issue 3, pp. 629-649. Copyright © 2010 by Feminist Studies Inc. Reprinted with permission. Provided by ProQuest LLC. All rights reserved.

that sought safety and security for a few women at the expense of many women. Ultimately, she insists that new places must be forged in coalitions through a process of struggle, examining our own assumptions and privileges, challenging not only others' ignorance, but our own ignorance, and seeking new ways of interacting with those who are differently positioned from ourselves.

Safety continues to be an important element for communities committed to creating the conditions in which oppressions are addressed and marginalized peoples can live and thrive. In particular, university communities have attempted to foster "safe zones" for lesbian/gay/bisexual/transgender (LGBT) people since the 1990s. The need for LGBT safe spaces is clear, as high rates of violence, disproportionate rates of suicide and substance abuse, high dropout rates, and overall alienation continue to affect the lives of LGBT people on our campuses.[2] Safe space initiatives aim to raise visibility and create educational programs for LGBT students that increase awareness of LGBT issues and address the presence of heterosexism and homophobia in campus culture. However, too often, our commitments in LGBT campus communities have been organized around uncomplicated notions of heterosexism and homophobia; and, as Kevin Kumashiro notes, "in our commitment to change oppression and embrace differences, we often fail to account for the intersection of racism and heterosexism, and of racial and sexual identities. Ironically, our efforts to challenge one form of oppression often unintentionally contribute to other forms of oppression, and our efforts to embrace one form of difference exclude and silence others."[3]

Turning more specifically to the discourse of LGBT safe space, we must recognize that one of its effects is the reinstitution of regulatory forces that support a white, heteronormative order. Insofar as the central organizing feature for queer people is the eradication of homophobia and heterosexism, safe space discourse continues to operate within a normalizing gaze of a white, masculinist, middle-class subject, rendering queer subjectivity in a most simplistic and reductive manner and producing an illusionary "safety." Such normalization within the discourse of LGBT safe spaces elides how we are all multiply positioned in relation to power and privilege and the ways "identities" come into being relationally, or in other words, "how a variety of forms of oppression intertwine systemically with each other; and especially how the person who is disabled through one set of oppressions may *by the same positioning* be enabled through others."[4] We lose sight of the relationality of our subjectivities and the necessity of building ally relationships outside of a hetero/homo binary that constructs a gay white male as the proper "subject" of those safe spaces.

In this article we want to advance how we think and write about safe spaces, troubling the discourse of "safety" for LGBT people on college campuses such that we are not re-creating normalized gender and race relations. In the analysis that follows we first explore the logic of safe spaces that have often been organized around two normalizing devices that serve to construct a white male subject at the center of LGBT safe spaces. We then move to discuss the organizing of a large, student-run queer conference at our university around an intersectional theme and the fallout that occurred in the midst of planning the conference in order to illustrate how the discourse of LGBT safe spaces can occlude coalition work across and between differences when safety is conflated with feelings of comfort and security in such a manner that perpetuates ignorance. Finally, we propose how we might counter this normalizing discourse by reconceptualizing queer student spaces as safe(r) spaces so that we can bring intersectional analyses of oppressions to the foreground of conversations with LGBT students such that they can engage in the kind of questioning of "safety" that Pratt describes is necessary for coalition work.

Normalizing Devices and the Conflation of Safety with Comfort The concept of "safe spaces" has been central to changing the campus climate for LGBT people wherein the focus in the spaces has been trained on eradication of homophobia and heterosexism.[5] Herein lies part of the problem with the discourse of safe space: it has been decided that the social problem for LGBT people is relatively easy to identify—homophobia and heterosexism. Embedded in this discourse are two devices that reproduce normalized gendered and raced subjects: dichotomizing and universalizing. That is, a focus on homophobia and heterosexism is built upon a binary logic that constructs "gayness" as a primary identity and other identities as peripheral or marginal. And this discourse further suggests that all gay people experience homophobia and heterosexism in similar ways.

Often framed around providing support as students come out, campus safe spaces support a strategy that mandates homogeneity by demanding primacy for a core sexual identity. On the surface, these spaces create a welcoming space for all of us who are considered outcasts, and yet upon closer examination they actually obscure differences between us. It is a common mantra in academia that sex, gender, race, and sexuality are not mutually exclusive categories existing in unrelated ways; however, as John D'Emilio has noted, queer spaces historically have not been very good at recognizing or incorporating this diversity.[6] The discourse of safe space fails to account for this intersectionality because it relies on a binary logic that focuses on the elimination of homophobia/heterosexism, thereby creating a singular, marginalized identity around which the spaces are organized. In the construction of this singular identity, other oppressions and privileges often are unaccounted for in the discourse of safe space; or if they are accounted for, they are represented in an additive manner (e.g., being Asian and gay is to experience "double oppression").

For example, the Gay, Lesbian, and Straight Education Network's (GLSEN) detailed How-To Guide for Starting an Allies Program describes safe spaces for LGBT people as those spaces that are free from homophobia, transphobia, and heterosexism and enforce the idea that "there is a need for programs that specifically address Anti-LGBT bias," as if anti-LGBT bias is experienced similarly by all LGBT people. And although the writers recognize that "none of us is just one thing—we all have sexual, gender, religious, ethnic, racial, class, and other identities that mingle together in complex ways," the suggestion that anti-LGBT bias can be constructed over and against antiwomen bias or anti-Black bias or anti-Asian bias deploys the kind of binary logic that serves to construct a singular marginalized identity that is addressed in safe spaces. The How-To Guide suggests that "a Safe Space program that protects LGBT people should therefore be designed to incorporate other 'isms' through coalitions and partnerships with other groups both on and off campus."[7] Such an approach suggests that "other" identities are experienced in additive ways (e.g., experiencing "Asianness" and "gayness" as two separate experiences rather than a complex and dynamic relationship to sexuality and ethnicity). The assumption that other "isms" are the work of "other groups" produces a particular kind of subject—one whose gender or race or ethnicity are not central to her/his experience of oppression and violence in society—and renders other subjects as marginalized in the discourse of safe space. There is a tacit message here: examinations of intersections of oppressions and privileges, the intersections of sex, gender, race, ethnicity, and class, are not the work of LGBT safe spaces and thus not an issue for LGBT communities.

Like GLSEN's How-To Guide, much of the literature on working with LGBT youth references racism and sexism as if they are parallel to heterosexism and homophobia rather than inter-related. Jonathan Rutherford describes the additive approach in this way: "Individuals simply piled up any number of categories of oppression—Black, gay, working-class, disabled, rather like layers in a cake. There [is] no sense that complex interaction between these experiences existed." For example, as Evelynn Hammonds notes, "Blackness" often is added to "lesbianness," which renders the experiences of Black lesbians as intelligible only through the lens of white lesbians' experiences. This approach fails to account for the complex interaction of norms around race, gender, sexuality, such that we fail to acknowledge how Black lesbians often are cast as "race traitors" in relation to normalized Black female sexuality.[8] An additive model centers gay white male experiences as the foundation upon which all other experiences are to be built.

Through the implication that all gay people similarly encounter heterosexism and homophobia, we enact the second device, universalizing, in normalizing gendered and raced subjects in safer spaces. This illusory unity enforces a premature solidarity that does not consider the strategic significance of the meanings attached to sex, gender, and race. Thus, although safe zones may be "nurturing spaces" for a little while, they ultimately provide an illusion of community based on the "freezing of difference."[9] Further, the impact of such false universals is the erasure of the realities of members of the queer community, ignoring their very different experiences.[10] Indeed, there is no universal "gay" experience. The discourse of LGBT safe spaces fails to acknowledge how our experiences in relation to our sexuality are profoundly connected with our gendered and raced experiences. And although many white people attempt to group all LGBT people of color together, it follows that there is no universal experience for LGBT people of color—no "gay African American" experience, no "Chicana lesbian" experience. There is a kind of false intimacy created by discourses built upon the logic of binaries and universals. Emma Pérez argues that "the mistake made within any arena, whether academic or political, is that a common enemy bonds 'us' and makes 'us' all the same, while 'they,' the common enemy, are also all the same."[11]

Recent scholarship about queer youth of color points to the kind of "false intimacy" many queer youth of color experience in LGBT student organizations comprised predominantly of white people. Lance McCready illustrates how some Black queer students choose to deemphasize their sexuality in order to not risk ostracism or ridicule from Black straight students. Such students often choose not to associate with LGBT groups because they are not "safe"; that is, the spaces don't provide the kind of support in which the intersection of homophobia, racism, and (hetero) sexism is addressed or look at how different racial and ethnic communities express homophobia and heterosexism. Michael Dumas adds that many queer youth of color perceive a white discourse around issues of coming out, such that coming out often tends to be represented as an individualistic action with queer white people; but for many queers of color, coming out is about a larger social uplifting and social change and thus involves a greater consciousness about challenging social practices that constitute normative and nonnormative subjects in society.[12]

It is the binary and universal logic embedded in discourses of LGBT safe spaces that ultimately produce marginalization, or "that complex and disputatious process by means of which certain people and ideas are privileged over others at any given time,"[13] and fails to address the multifarious nature of all LGBT people. Again, it is not just that heterosexism and homophobia are constructed in contradistinction to other oppressions; it is also the assumption of a universal experience in relation to homophobia and heterosexism for all LGBT people. Such a logic within the discourse enable spaces of safety for gay white males—and often white heterosexual females—but not for others in the LGBT community. We must address the workings of this logic so that we can broaden our notions of safety by creating contexts and conversations in which we can better understand the interactions and influences of multiple aspects of our identities.

As an example of how the logic embedded in discourses of safe space inhibits coalition building and intersectional analyses of queer identities, we turn to our work with queer undergraduate students on our campus. In the spring of 2004 students wanted to revitalize the campus queer community. Two LGBT student organizations submitted a proposal to host the student-run, student-centered Midwest Bisexual, Lesbian, Gay, Transgender, and Ally College Conference (MBLGTACC). The conference had been hosted by students at our university in 2000 and had included a diversity of speakers whose messages focused on activism and intersectional analyses of race, class, gender, and sexuality. Students wanted to bring these conversations back to campus and use the conference as a way to inspire activism and coalition building. Their proposal, submitted to the previous year's conference organizers, states the following goals:

- Provide a safe and supportive forum for discourse about diverse issues of interest to LGBT youth.
- Educate participants about HIV/AIDS prevention, building activism, sexuality, and gender.
- Examine the relationship between sexism, racism, classism, ageism, ableism, and homophobia.
- Foster localized, grassroots networking among LGBT youth and their allies.
- Promote visibility of LGBT individuals and organizations throughout the Midwest.

After their proposal was accepted, students delved into the complicated process of planning a conference. They titled the conference "Building the Bridges to Bring It All Together" to emphasize their vision of "creating common ground instead of falling into the us vs. them attitude" and created a steering committee that divided the labor of organizing the conference (this included everything from creating the conference call and inviting keynote speakers to the logistics of securing blocks of hotel rooms and conference rooms on campus). Students did not want faculty involved in decision making because it was a student-run conference, and they didn't want faculty "taking over." They did, however, want to ensure that "bridges were built" with faculty and invited us to support their process by attending meetings, negotiating bureaucratic process, such as setting up accounts, and speaking on such subjects as white privilege and corporate sponsorship. As might be expected with such a large undertaking, students faced problems around communication issues, particularly how to create egalitarian communication channels, leadership styles, and how to deal with conflicts when they arose in planning meetings. It was at these junctures that faculty members were called upon to provide students with tools for working through and with these differences. Although there were about five faculty members involved through the nine-month planning process, students were adamant about faculty staying on the periphery of the planning process; and, for the most part, faculty members were supportive of this because there is much more for students to gain from a conference that is owned and planned without heavy-handed involvement from faculty.

As the planning for the conference progressed, divisions increased among the students, and patterned behaviors started to become more visible—patterns that belied the intent of the conference to build bridges. White students routinely talked over students of color in conference-planning meetings, or simply ignored them; students of color were expected to do the "cultural work" for the conference, that is, to build bridges with various student-of-color organizations. Conversations and behaviors played out gendered norms—the word "bitch" frequently circulated in arguments, overtly sexualized gestures and behaviors pervaded conference-planning banter, and some lesbians were named "man-hating bitches" when disagreements arose. These tensions culminated when three students (a straight woman of color, a gay man of color, and a white lesbian) discontinued their involvement in office activities and organizations because they no longer felt "safe." In a dramatic performance, they came to a steering committee meeting, read an open letter to their peers announcing their resignation, called upon the conference organizers to confront the racism and sexism embedded within the conference planning if they genuinely hoped to enact the thematic focus, and then exited the meeting.

After the initial shock, students took their peers' resignation as a "reality check moment" and focused their next meeting on how to create safe spaces. Students conducted an informal survey to determine what safe space meant to LGBT students and used this feedback to initiate a conversation. Believing that race, class, and gender are not LGBT issues, a handful of students felt that safe space was a space where they could be comfortable to say and do whatever they wanted—to "just be gay," and they felt their "safe space" was being infringed upon by students who brought discussion of race and gender to the table. Other students believed safety had to be a place where gender and race could be discussed because these were not separate identities for them. Perhaps not surprisingly, a handful of vocal, white students, who believed that LGBT safe spaces are places to "just be me," instructed female participants to go to the Women's Center if they wanted to deal with sexism and told students of color to go the Multicultural Student Center if they wanted to deal with racism. White gay male students who were adamant about making visible the interconnections between race, gender, and sexuality were ostracized by this vocal minority and named "traitors" and "sell outs to the femi-nazis." Conflicts around what exactly constituted a safe space as well as conflicts about who would get to decide what made it a safe space ultimately led to a very (un)safe space for all participants. Overwhelmingly, all the students equated safety with feeling comfortable to "be who I am" and the "freedom to say and do what I want."

At the heart of the conflicts that arose in the conference planning lies the unexamined logic embedded in discourses of safe space, a logic built upon binaries and universals that serves to re-center a normatively gendered and raced subject through the *conflation of safety with comfort*. In fact, much of the literature about safe spaces for LGBT people on college campuses tends to conflate feeling *safe* with feeling *affirmed* and *addressed* and comfortable.[14] Part of the reason for this conflation is the multidimensional level of violence against queers in the forms of physical and psychic violence. Psychic violence manifests itself in the form of verbal harassment, negative perceptions and stereotypes of LGBT people, and general invisibility in curriculum and campus activities. Such psychic violence has affected LGBT peoples' sense of self-esteem and success in institutions of higher education and has led to higher rates of depression, substance abuse, social isolation, and failure in school or work.[15] However, experiences of psychic violence are often conflated with threats of physical violence in discourses of safe space so that pride, or feeling comfortable and affirmed and addressed, become the organizing factors in establishing such spaces. Organizing queer spaces around notions of pride often centers white male privilege.

Judith Halberstam's critique of gay pride and uses of gay shame at the "Gay Shame" conference at the University of Michigan is useful in understanding the workings of white male privilege in LGBT safe spaces. Positioning shame as the experience of being exposed and failing to be "powerful, legitimate, proper," she argues that

> the subject who emerges as the subject of gay shame is often a white and male self whose shame in part emerges from the experience of being denied access to privilege ... .

[S]hame for women and shame for people of color plays out in different ways and creates different modes of abjection, marginalizations and self-abnegation; it also leads to very different political strategies ... . While female shame can be countered by feminism and racialized shame can be countered by what Rod Ferguson calls "queer of color critique," it is white gay male shame that has proposed "pride" as the appropriate remedy and that focuses its libidinal and other energies on simply rebuilding the self that shame dismantled rather than taking apart the social processes that project shame onto queer subjects in the first place.[16]

Through an analysis of interactions and presentations at the "Gay Shame" conference, Halberstam illustrates how shame is projected systematically onto females and people of color such that it allows white gay males to create an "illusion of mastery," as if they have acquired a complete understanding and overcome their shame. LGBT safe spaces created as sites to *feel comfortable, affirmed,* and *addressed* are similarly inflected by the impulse to reconstruct a self with accesses to privilege rather than addressing the systemic and interconnecting violence and inequities that bring about the kind of illegitimacy and impropriety many different kinds of queer people experience.

The unexamined assumption that safety should be equated with feeling affirmed and addressed fails to address the normalization of gender and race in these social spaces and, in fact, operates to re-center and privilege gendered and racialized norms. In excluding race and gender from communities and movements organized around sexuality, Riki A. Wilchins argues that

left untouched is any problem which is about "sexual orientation AND." So, we're not going to deal with queers of color, because that's sexual orientation AND race. We're not going to deal with issues of working-class queers or queers on welfare, because that's about gay AND class. And we're not going to deal with the concerns of lesbians, because that's about gay AND gender. Pretty soon, the only people we represent are those fortunate enough to possess the luxury of a simple and uncomplicated oppression.[17]

The normative subject of LGBT safe spaces is often secured through identification of "other" oppressions as "deviant" or extraneous. Indeed, it is an expression and luxury of race and gender privilege to assert one's right to feel *comfortable* and *affirmed* at the cost of others feeling alienated by both individual acts and systemic practices of racism and sexism.

At work in the reproduction of these gender and racial norms is the maintenance of social safety for centered subjects in which they can exist in a place of ignorance. Kumashiro insists the problem is not simple inclusion of queers of color in the conversation: the problem is the kind of willful ignorance involved in resistance to "troubling" what we already know. He questions, "Is this because White queers resist disrupting their own privileges? Is this because White queers resist acknowledging the racist stereotypes that color the ways they see and interact with the of-colors among them ... . Is there comfort, in other words, in seeing queerness and racial difference as separate and distinct?" Here again, we can see how social safety and comfort are conflated when we choose to fall into discourses that dichotomize and categorize race, sexuality, and gender along different trajectories rather than examining their intersections. The problem, then, is not lack of diversity in LGBT safe spaces but resistance to knowing differently in these spaces, a resistance that is circulated through an epistemology of ignorance. Eve Kosofsky Sedgwick has articulated the ways in which ignorance can operate in powerful ways: "Knowledge, after all, is not itself power, although it is the magnetic field of power. Ignorance and opacity collude or compete with knowledge in mobilizing the flows of energy, desire, goods, meanings, and persons." Marilyn Frye has also written extensively about how willful or "determined ignorance" operates within white consciousness, "creating the conditions which ensure its continuance." Frye discusses the impact of white ignorance on the ignored, explaining that there is nothing that people of color can do to be seen and heard in the face of such determined ignorance, with the consequence of being ignored "nearly to death."[18] Sedgwick and Frye illustrate that ignorance is not innocent. When coupled with constructions of safe spaces as sites in which to feel pride, comfort, affirmed, and addressed, ignorance often operates as resistance to acknowledging privilege in LGBT safe spaces such that, in Sedgwick's words, it "mobilizes the flow of meanings and persons" within those spaces and re-centers a normative gendered and racial subject.

It is the power of ignorance that a core of students (white and of color, female and male) set out to challenge at the outset of choosing to host the MBLGTACC. Through course work and conversations with queer faculty, they had learned about the history of Stonewall, civil rights, Black Power, women's liberation, and gay liberation; and they were cognizant of the need to recognize how their own ability to speak out as "gay subjects" is built upon a history of struggle by many movements for social change. They wanted to *not* repeat history, to *not* leave anyone behind, to *not* separate their activism from other activist projects and movements. Despite their active desire to engage in coalition work and intersectional analyses of oppression, when done within the operative logic of LGBT safe spaces, the kind of revolutionary and invigorating work students wanted to effect through the conference was not achieved. The effect of the discourse of safe space in the meeting where tensions came to a head was further justification for the marginalization of conversations about sexism and racism and, ultimately, the marginalization of students who resigned from the conference planning. On the surface, students were left behind as the exigency to plan the conference became more pressing, or perhaps more "doable," than the need to face the internal divisions that became visible midway through the planning process. However, one student in particular continued to dialogue with students and faculty about what had occurred. In hindsight he describes feeling foolish at the time for not seeing the rampant sexism and racism occurring in meetings before the three students publicly resigned. He worked behind the scenes to continue building bridges with students of color through conversation, interacted one-on-one with faculty to continue to educate himself, and was active in conference planning to make sure that the opinions and voices of students of color and female students were not ignored. There is something to be learned from this student's continued engagement that moved him well beyond a place of "comfort" or "safety," something to be learned by both faculty and students who wish to engage in ally relationships and coalition work.

The conference was ultimately well attended, and participants indicated in their evaluations that it was successful; however, by the time the conference occurred, the "bridges" were seemingly all but gone and the queer "community," both student and faculty, dissolved. In hindsight we see that had we as faculty members been more cognizant of how the logic of safe space was operating in the conference planning we might have presented students with a different set of tools for examining what occurred. We facilitated conversations about white privilege and male privilege, and we asked everyone to consider three questions: What was my role in the process of students resigning? What did I learn? Is there anything that I could have done differently? Ultimately these conversations did not get to the heart of the conflicts, which were rooted in the discourses of LGBT safe spaces that subtly framed all of the interactions around the conference. Indeed, our conference experience as faculty members made us rethink the questions we might pose to students if we are to engage in coalition politics. We are not suggesting that more central involvement of faculty would have avoided the complications and alienation that occurred for both students and faculty members. Indeed, less would have been learned had faculty been heavy handed in our involvement because it would no longer have been a student-owned conference. We might, however, have acted as better guides and facilitators to help students learn from the past. For example, we might have reflected on the kind of coalition work Minnie Bruce Pratt details in "Identity: Skin Blood Heart," for it is in the confrontations and discussions of oppression and marginalization that we are unmoored from comfort zones and must call into question the equation of safety with comfort, must call into question the systemic forces that have secured our own privilege to be ignorant. We know from activists such as Bernice Johnson Reagon, Audre Lorde, Dorothy Allison,[19] and others that coalition work involves pain and discomfort; and unfortunately, when the conference planning began to implode, faculty members' own sense of safety (read: comfort) became threatened, and several faculty slowly began checking out—some disengaged because they were uncomfortable with conflict, some because they were targeted as creating discomfort for others and were under fire, and others because it was simply emotionally exhausting. Most significant is the way in which discourses of LGBT safe space—a discourse that is integral to the way faculty and students *literally* frame our offices, dorms, hallways through safe space posters—occluded the vision of the students because of the unexamined assumptions embedded within the discourse.

RECONCEPTUALIZING SAFE(R) SPACES

To discursively construct LGBT safe spaces as those spaces that are free from antigay bias is to speak one's privileged status into being. It is to speak out of a place of singularity that denies the interconnections between race, class, gender, and sexuality—it is to assume that only people of color have a racial identity, and only women have a gendered identity, and only those of the working class have a class identity. As we imagine these spaces we must attend to how we can create the conditions in which we are interrupting and challenging "hegemonic social structures by which certain subjects are rendered 'normal' and 'natural' through the production of 'perverse' and 'pathological' others."[20] This takes a degree of reflexivity about our own subject positions and how we are all multiply positioned in relation to power, privilege, and oppression. Such spaces cannot be created until we begin to create bridges that focus on solidarity rather than unity and until we begin to understand how we are all subjects-in-process.

One way to begin this work is reconceptualizing our notion of safety. Barclay Barrios suggests that we might use the metaphor of the briar patch to imagine our work in helping students queerly navigate the world. Barrios explains:

> The briar patch, like the world, is a dangerous place—it is, after all, filled with brambles and that's just what keeps Brer Fox out. What makes it a refuge for Brer Rabbit is not something inherent in its nature but the fact that it's where he was raised. And having been raised there means that he knows how to move through the briar, how to use the thorns to his advantage, how to find his way through the thickets, how to, in short, negotiate its dangers successfully.[21]

Barrios's metaphor moves us beyond the binary between safe and dangerous spaces and calls us to imagine strategies and tactics for negotiating a necessarily unsafe world. Thus, we can direct our attention from creating "safe" spaces to creating "safe(r)" spaces. Such a shift moves us away from the belief that safe spaces can be secured in a manner that they are free of struggle or discomfort. Placing the "r" in parentheses calls attention to the tensions inherent in any discussion and action aimed to counteract multiple forms of terror and violence. It calls us to "unfix" our understanding and interpretation of safety and, instead, engage safety as a process through which we establish dialogues that create and re-create spaces where queer people are more free from the physical and psychic violence of those normalizing processes in which we all move and operate through our quotidian experiences. It calls us to consider the ways that safety has too often been equated with comfort around normative gender and race identities that reproduce a white male gay subject at the center of these spaces.

Certainly, queer theorists have produced rich scholarship in the last two decades, attuning us to the fluid nature of subjectivity and the ways race, nation, sexuality, and gender are bound within a heteronormative order. William J. Spurlin argues that queer theory

> has also enabled further exposure of the white, masculinist, middle-class, and Western bias historically encoded in gay studies and helped to mobilize, over the course of the 1990s, a new corpus of academic theorizing that considered sexuality in relation to the persistent pressures of other normalizing regimes pertaining to race, class, gender, geopolitical spatializations, citizenship, nationalism, and the effects of economic globalization and transnational exchange.[22]

However, in a recent introduction to a special issue of *Social Text*, "What's Queer about Queer Studies Now?" David Eng, Judith Halberstam, and José Esteban Muñoz insist we need to be "ever vigilant to the fact that *sexuality is intersectional*, not extraneous to other modes of difference" (emphasis ours). Calling attention to Hiram Perez's and Judith Halberstam's critiques of the "'transparent white subject' [that remains] at the heart of queer studies," they go on to argue that "the political and intellectual promises of queer studies [is] yet unfulfilled to the extent that queer too quickly collapses back into 'gay and lesbian' and, more often than not a 'possessive individualism' that simply connotes 'gay,' 'white,' and 'male.'"[23] We still have much to do, and part of that doing, we believe, is an obligation to bring these kinds of analyses and conversations to student activists.

In thinking through our work four years ago with queer students during the "Building the Bridges to Bring It All Together" conference, we return to Gloria Anzaldúa's work on, ironically, bridges and liminal spaces. We have found her metaphors tremendously useful in recent dialogues with queer students about the importance of questioning who we are as a community, what our goals should be, and what we mean when we invoke the need for safe spaces. Anzaldúa describes bridges as necessarily (un)safe spaces because they bridge worlds. She explains, "Transformations occur in this in-between space, an unstable, unpredictable, precarious, always-in-transition space lacking clear boundaries. *Nepantla es tierra desconocida*, and living in this liminal zone means being in a constant state of displacement—an uncomfortable, even alarming feeling." Bridges are never permanent; they must be built again and again through dialogue and coalition work. Anzaldúa insists that we recognize the pain and discomfort of these in-between, "borderland" spaces, but she also recognizes them as necessary in order to create a different world. She argues that there are no safe spaces, even the space of "home":

Home can be unsafe and dangerous because it bears the likelihood of intimacy and thus thinner boundaries. Staying "home" and not venturing out from our own group comes from woundedness, and stagnates our growth. To bridge means loosening our borders not closing off to others. Bridging is the work of opening the gate to the stranger, within and without. To step across the threshold is to be stripped of the illusion of safety because it moves us into unfamiliar territory and does not grant safe passage.[24]

Much like her earlier work suggesting a shift from identity politics to "affinities,"[25] Anzaldua gives us and our students a language to hold on to, a language in which to think differently about safety, a language to begin questioning our assumptions about who is served by the discourse of LGBT safe spaces, who is served when we equate safety with comfort. She gives us a way to enter into dialogues about the discomfort that is involved when we work through the ambiguities, tensions, and pains that constitute a community as variegated as the one denoted by L-G-B-T.

With the murders at Northern Illinois University and the murder of Lawrence King,[26] our physical vulnerability in educational institutions comes to the foreground again. Instead of simply using these recent atrocities to shore up the need for safe spaces in education we might instead use them in dialogues with students to interrogate institutional responses, dialogues framed with the language and metaphors that Anzaldúa has so adeptly offered us. Brandon McInerney, the fifteen-year-old boy who shot Lawrence King, will be tried as an adult. Some may applaud this as an appropriate institutional response that creates greater safety for other queer students. However, this response suggests that McInerney came up with the homophobia and genderism on his own, thereby freeing society from an analysis of the larger problem—which is precisely where he got those ideas. McInerney becomes a scapegoat, and the state and society are freed from dealing with the issue. This move to place absolute guilt on the individual is the same logic used in the sexual torture and humiliation of the prisoners in Abu Ghraib, sexual torture and humiliation that occurred at the intersections of racism, homophobia, and imperialism and fed by discourses of national safety and security. As we discuss and think through the very real issue of physical safety with our queer students we must move our conversations with them to distinguish the difference between physical safety and psychic safety and further interrogate discourses of safety so that we can engage in the kinds of intersectional analyses that might enable a more complex understanding of varied subjectivities and needs that we aim to account for under the umbrella of LGBT safe spaces.

Our intent in this article is not to dismantle programs and spaces that provide refuge from the psychic and physical violence that LGBT people experience. However, it is imperative to acknowledge the potential limits of such projects: "Recognizing that challenging oppression always begins with a construction of margins and that full inclusion is impossible does not mean that change is not possible. Rather, it means that our approaches cannot be treated as panaceas."[27] Safe spaces are not panaceas, particularly if we wish to engage students in coalitional processes. If we find it easy to shore up the boundaries of LGBT safe spaces, we fall into the trappings of assuming our identities are easily defined by singular notions of homophobia and heterosexism, which fails to account for the complex interplay of our sexed, gendered, and raced identities with our sexualities within specific spaces. Spaces for queer folks have the radical potential to be countersites for the establishment of solidarity that can allow marginalized people to flourish in the context of the larger university; however, we must begin by questioning and complicating the very concept of safety around which queer activism on campuses is often organized.

NOTES

We are grateful for extensive conversations with three students (who wish to remain anonymous) and the insights they provided. Although faculty members were involved throughout the conference planning and execution, we would not have had an understanding of student motivations for the conference nor sense of their impressions of its successes and failures without these dialogues. We are also thankful for the critical commentary these students provided on earlier drafts of this article.

1. Minnie Bruce Pratt, "Identity: Skin Blood Heart," in *Yours in Struggle: Three Feminist Perspectives on Anti-Semitism and Racism*, ed. Minnie Bruce Pratt, Barbara Smith, and Elly Bulkin (Ithaca, NY: Firebrand Books, 1984), 25–26.

2. Physical violence has been initiated and supported by societal institutions as evidenced by a history of experimentation with lobotomies within the medical establishment to "cure" homosexuals in the 1940s and 1950s, and sixty years of police raids on gay bars and bath houses prior to Stonewall. Additionally, there are numerous examples of murder and other forms of violence perpetrated against queer folk: the murder of Rebecca Wight and the near killing of her partner, Claudia Brenner, in 1989; the killing of Brandon Teena in 1993; the murder of Roxanne Ellis and Michelle Abdill in 1995; the killing of Julianne Marie Williams and Laura "Lollie" Winans in 1996; the brutal beating of Matthew Shepard in 1998; the slaying of Billy Jack Gather in 1999; the murder of Sakia Gunn in 2003; the countless number of undocumented rapes and beatings of queer youth; as well as the over 1,000 FBI-reported hate crimes in 2005. See Federal Bureau of Investigation, *Uniform Hate Crime Statistics 2005*, www. fbi.gov/ucr/hc2005/. Also see Robert D. Brown and Carl A. Happold, *Campus Climate and Needs Assessment Study for Gay, Lesbian, Bisexual, and Transgender (GLBT) Students at the University of Nebraska-Lincoln: Moving beyond Tolerance toward Empowerment* (Lincoln: University of Nebraska, 2002), www.unl.edu/cglbtc/climate.shtml; Susan Rankin, *Iowa State University Campus Climate Assessment Project* (Ames: Iowa State University, 2004), www.hrs.iastate.edu/diversity/doc/finalreport.pdf.

3. Kevin Kumashiro, ed., *Troubling Intersections of Race and Sexuality: Queer Students of Color and Anti-Oppressive Education* (Lanham, MD: Rowman and Littlefield, 2001), 1.

4. Eve Kosofsky Sedgwick, *Epistemology of the Closet* (Berkeley: University of California Press, 1990), 32.

5. Anthony R. D'Augelli and Charlotte J. Patterson, *Lesbian, Gay, and Bisexual Identities and Youth: Psychological Perspectives* (New York: Oxford University Press, 2001). See also Ronni L. Sanlo, *Working with Lesbian, Gay, Bisexual, and Transgender College Students: A Handbook for Faculty and Administrators* (Westport, CT: Greenwood Press, 1998), *Unheard Voices: The Effects of Silence on Lesbian and Gay Educators* (Westport, CT: Bergin & Garvey, 1999), and *Gender Identity and Sexual Orientation: Research, Policy, and Personal Perspectives: New Directions for Student Services* (San Francisco: Jossey-Bass, 2005); Roger L. Worthington, Sarah Inez McCrary, and Kimberly Howard, "Becoming an LGBT Affirmative Career Advisor: Guidelines for Faculty, Staff, and Administrators," in *Working with Lesbian, Gay*, 135–43; Gay, Lesbian, and Straight Education Network (hereafter GLSEN), *GLSEN Safe Space: A How-To Guide for Starting an Allies Program* (New York: GLSEN, 2003), www.glsen.org/binary-data/GLSEN_ATTACHMENTS/file/294-2.PDF.

6. John D'Emilio, *Making Trouble: Essays on Gay History, Politics, and the University* (New York: Routledge, 1992), 123. See also Amber Ault, "The Dilemma of Identity: Bi Women's Negotiations," in *Queer Theory/Sociology*, ed. Steven Seidman (Cambridge, MA: Blackwell, 1996); and Scott Bravmann, *Queer Fictions of the Past: History, Culture, and Difference* (New York: Cambridge University Press, 1997).

7. GLSEN, *GLSEN Safe Space*, 4. We acknowledge that GLSEN is an organization primarily committed to serving the needs of K-12 educators and students; however, their Safe Zone Training and Ally Program is the preeminent model adopted by most college campuses in the United States.

8. Jonathan Rutherford, quoted in Linda Scholl, "Narratives of Hybridity and the Challenge to Multicultural Education," in *Troubling Intersections*, 142–43; Evelynn Hammonds, "Black (W)holes and the Geometry of Black Female Sexuality," *Differences: A Journal of Feminist Cultural Studies* 6 (Summer/Fall 1992): 140.

9. Bernice Johnson Reagon, "Coalition Politics: Turning the Century," in *Home Girls: A Black Feminist Anthology*, ed. Barbara Smith (New York: Kitchen Table/Women of Color Press, 1983).

10. Darren Rosenblum, *Queer Intersectiomlity and the Failure of Recent Lesbian and Gay "Victories"* (New York: Pace University Law School, 1994), http://digitalcommons.pace.edu/lawfaculty/210.

11. Emma Pérez, "Irigaray's Female Symbolic in the Making of Chicana Lesbian Sitios y Lenguas (Sites and Discourses)," in *Living Chicana Theory*, ed. Carla Trujillo (Berkeley, CA: Third Woman Press, 1994), 95.

12. Lance T. McCready, "Understanding the Marginalization of Gay and Gender Non-Conforming Black Male Students," *Theory into Practice* 43 (Spring 2004): 136–43; Michael J. Dumas, "Coming Out/Coming Home: Black Gay Men on Campus," in *Working with Lesbian, Gay*, 79–85; Mollie V. Blackburn, "Agency in Borderland Discourses: Examining Language Use in a Community Center with Black Queer Youth," *Teachers College Record* 107 (January 2005): 89–113.

13. Russell Ferguson, "Introduction: Invisible Center," in *Out There: Marginalization and Contemporary Culture*, ed. Russell Ferguson et al. (New York: New Museum of Contemporary Art, 1990), 7.

14. See, for example, Katya Salkerver and Roger L. Worthington, "Creating Safe Space in College Athletics," in *Working with Lesbian*, Gay, 193–202; GLSEN, *GLSEN Safe Space*; Kathleen Hothem (KC) Burns, and Christopher D. Keene, "Creating a Safe Zone Project at a Small Private College: How Hate Galvanized a Community" (363–69) and Charles Outcalt, "The Life Cycle of Campus LGBT Organizations: Finding Ways to Sustain Involvement and Effectiveness" (329–37), both *in Working with Lesbian*, Gay; and Nancy J. Evans and Vernon A. Wall, *Beyond Tolerance: Gays and Lesbians and Bisexuals on Campus* (Alexandria, VA: American College Personnel Association, 1991).

15. Brown and Happold, *Campus Climate*; Rankin, *Iowa State University*.

16. Judith Halberstam, "Shame and White Gay Masculinity," Social Text 84–85 (Fall/Winter: 223–24.

17. Riki A. Wilchins, *Read My Lips: Sexual Subversion and the End of Gender* (Ithaca, NY: Firebrand Books, 1997).

18. Kumashiro, *Troubling Intersections*, 12; Sedgwick, *Epistemology of the Closet*, 4; Marilyn Frye, "On Being White: Thinking Toward a Feminist Understanding of Race and Race Supremacy," in her *The Politics of Reality: Essays in Feminist Theory* (Freedom, CA: Crossing Press, 1983), 119.

19. See Reagon, "Coalition Politics"; Audre Lorde, *Sister Outsider*: *Essays and Speeches* (Trumansburg, NY: Crossing Press, 1984); Dorothy Allison, *Talking about Sex, Class, and Literature* (Ithaca, NY: Firebrand Books: 1994).

20. David Eng, Judith Halberstam, and José Esteban Muñoz, "What's Queer about Queer Studies Now?" *Social Text* nos. 84–85 (Fall/Winter 2005): 3.

21. Barclay Barrios, "Of Flags: Online Queer Identities, Writing Classrooms, and Action Horizons," *Computers and Composition* 21 (September 2004): 344.

22. William J. Spurlin, "Theorizing Queer Pedagogy in English Studies after the 1990s," *College English* 65 (September 2002): 9–10.

23. Eng, Halberstam, and Muñoz, "What's Queer," 1, 12.

24. In an earlier version of this article, a reviewer for another journal suggested that Anzaldúa's work is passé and relies too much on "identity politics." We see this as a dismissal of the work and theorizing of a feminist of color that serves to reify the privileged status of "high" "white" theory. In fact, Anzaldúa is an author and theorist who is able to make accessible to many undergraduate students theories of fluidity and mobility that would otherwise not be available to them. See Gloria Anzaldúa, *This Bridge We Call Home: Radical Visions for Transformation* (New York: Routledge, 2002), 3.

25. Gloria Anzaldúa, "La Prieta," in *This Bridge Called My Back: Writings by Radical Women of Color*, ed. Cherríe Moraga and Gloria Anzaldúa (New York: Kitchen Table/Women of Color Press, 1981), 209.

26. On February 14, 2008, Steven Kazmierczak opened fire from a stage in a lecture hall at Northern Illinois University, killing five people before he turned the gun on himself. On February 12, 2008, Lawrence ("Larry") King was shot in the head and murdered by a fifteen-year-old student, Brandon McInerney, at E.O. Green Junior High School in Oxnard, California. McInerney had bullied King because of his perceived sexuality and gender-noncomforming behavior. Interestingly, the NIU shooting has received much more media attention than the Lawrence King murder.

27. Kumashiro, *Troubling Intersections*, 17.

DUDE, YOU'RE A FAG: MASCULINITY AND SEXUALITY IN HIGH SCHOOL

By C.J. Pascoe

MASCULINITY AND DOMINANCE

The weight room, a freestanding module by the football field, stank with a familiar musty smell of old sweat, metal, and rubber. Colorful diagrams of deltoids, biceps, quads, and other muscle groups adorned the walls. Each day Coach Ramirez, a gentle, soft-spoken man, called roll and told the (mostly male) students to run a lap or two as he entered the module to place his folders in his office and turn on the stereo. After running their laps, the sweaty boys filed in as loud hip-hop music blared from the stereo. Dressed in regulation black gym shorts and T-shirts, boys milled about, picking up weights, completing a few sets, and then moving on to other machines. Some of the African American boys danced to the music, while, inevitably, Josh and his white friends asked for country music.

One fall morning, as some of the boys grew tired of lifting, they gathered around a set of benches in the front of the weight room. Reggie, a white rugby-playing junior, asked the gathering group, "Did you hear about the three 'B's?'" Before anyone had a chance to respond, Reggie announced triumphantly, "Blow job, back massage, and breakfast in bed!" Rich asked skeptically, "Shouldn't the back massage come first?" The conversation soon turned to the upcoming Winter Ball and their prospects for *sex* with their dates. Jerome complained that he was not "gonna get laid at Winter Ball." Josh admonished, "That's why you gotta go for the younger ones, fool! Like twelve years old!" Reggie, Rich, and Pedro laughed at Josh's advice. Pedro, never quiet for long, told the rest, "If you can put their legs behind their head and eat them out they'll have the fattest orgasm." The conversation quickly evolved into a game of sexual one-upmanship as Reggie, Rich, Jerome, and Josh began talking over each other, each with a more fantastic story. Josh claimed he was "so good" that he couldn't "control the girl from thrashing around on the bed and hurting herself on the headboard." In response Jerome advised, "That's why you gotta start out at the headboard!" Reggie shouted, "My girlfriend's bed broke!" Rich jumped in with "One time my girlfriend's dad came home while we were doing it and I had to hide in the closet." Josh, not to be outdone, replied, "Hey man, try getting a b.j. [blow job] while you are driving home!" This challenge was answered by a chorus of groans and "I've done that!"

This sort of locker-room talk is what one expects to find when researching teenage boys and masculinity. Indeed, the public face of male adolescence is filled with representations of masculinity in which boys brag about sexual exploits by showing off a girl's underwear (as in the 1980s film *Pretty in Pink),* spend the end of their senior year talking about how they plan to lose their virginity *(American Pie),* or make cruel bets about who can bed the ugliest girl in the school *(She's All That).* In many ways, the boys at River High seemed much like their celluloid representatives. As this scene in the weight room indicates, heterosexual, innuendoes, sexual bravado, and sexual one-upmanship permeated these primarily male spaces. This chapter looks at these gender practices and, instead of taking them at face value as testosterone-fueled verbal jockeying, pays attention to the meanings of masculinity embedded in them. In these sorts of interactions and gendered spaces, masculinity, in spite of boys' talk about the gay boys' ability to be masculine as discussed in the previous chapter, is assumed to be synonymous with hetero-sexuality. But, as they do when invoking the fag discourse, boys talking about heterosexuality are and are not talking about sex. Their talk about heterosexuality reveals less about sexual orieiitation and desire than it does about the centrality of the ability to exercise mastery and dominance literally or figuratively over girls' bodies (Wood 1984). These heterosexually based gender practices serve to defend boys against emasculating insults like those in the fag discourse (Hird and Jackson 2001). Engaging in very public practices of heterosexuality, boys affirm much more than just masculinity; they affirm subjecthood and personhood through sexualized in-teractions in which they indicate to themselves and others that they have the ability to work their will upon the world around them. Imposing one's will and demonstrating dominance in this way aligns boys with personhood and subjectivity, historically coded as masculine (Jaggar 1983; Mackinnon 1982). Demonstrating dominance in a variety of ways is a central part of contemporary American masculinity (Peirce 1995).

Compulsive heterosexuality[1] is the name I give to this constellation of sexualized practices, discourses, and interactions. This term builds on Adrienne Rich's (1986) influential concept of "compulsory heterosexuality."[2] Rich argues that heterosexuality not only describes sexual desires, practices and orientations but is a "political institution" (23). The "enforcement of het-erosexuality for women as a means of assuring male right of physical, economic and emotional access" (50) is a central component of gender inequality. The microprocesses of heterosexuality as an institution are so embedded in daily life that, while heterosexuality may be personally meaningful, it can simultaneously function as an oppressive social institution. While compulsory heterosexuality may regulate both men and women, "their experiences of it and the power and privilege that accompany it are different" (V. Robinson 1996, 120).

Practices of "compulsive heterosexuality" exemplify what Butler (1995) calls "gender performativity," in which gender "is produced as a ritualized repetition of conventions, and ... this ritual is socially compelled in part by the force of a compulsory heterosexuality" (31). Compulsive heterosexuality is not about desire for sexual pleasure per se, or just about desire to be "one of the guys"; rather, it is "an excitement felt as sexuality in a male supremacist culture which eroticizes male dominance and female submission" (Jeffreys 1998,75). Indeed, ensuring positions of power entails boys' constant "recreation of masculinity and femininity" through rituals of eroticized dominance (Jeffreys 1998, 77). Looking at boys' ritualistic sex talk, patterns of touch, and games of "getting girls" indicates how this gender inequality is reinforced through everyday interactions. Taken together, these ritualized interactions continually affirm masculinity as mastery and dominance. By symbolically or physically mastering girls' bodies and sexuality, boys at River High claim masculine identities.

[...]

GETTING GIRLS

Chad sneered at boys who, unlike him, couldn't "get girls." Getting girls, like the "girl watching" documented by Beth Quinn (2002), "functions as a game men play to build shared masculine identities and social relations" (387). Boys who couldn't engage in this game of "getting girls" lost masculine capital. School rituals such as the homecoming assembly mirrored Chad's derision of boys who failed to play at "getting girls." At the Homecoming Assembly two boys, Lamar and Tonio, stood in front of the cheering student body, lip-synching a comedy routine between Chris Rock and Michael Jackson.[3] Leering and pointing at two attractive girls clad in hip-high leather boots, black miniskirts, and white tank tops walking across the stage, the two boys pulled each other aside. Lamar, as Chris Rock, dared Tonio, as Jackson, to "get a girl." They paced back and forth in front of the girls, "Chris Rock" saying, "That girl! Oh man!" "Michael Jackson" responded in a high-pitched voice, "Goodness gracious! She is too fine!" "Rock" agreed, "She sho' is fine!" "Rock" turned to "Jackson," challenging him, "You can't get that girl!" "Jackson" responded defensively, in a high voice, "I *can* get her!" Again "Rock" challenged him, "I *bet* you can't get that girl! Michael, you are going to Neverland again!" The students roared in laughter as the two boys strutted back to "get" the girls.

The ritual of "getting girls" played out in this homecoming skit illustrates one of the ways compulsive heterosexuality becomes a part of boys' friendships and interactional styles. "Rock" and "Jackson," like boys at River High, jokingly challenged each other to dominate—or, in their words, to "get"—a girl. In these rituals girls' bodies functioned as a symbol of male heterosexuality and tangible evidence of repudiation of same sex-desire (Butler 1999). That is, if boys desired girls, then they couldn't possibly desire each other.

Both of the Mr. Cougar sketches I have outlined thus far involved stories of getting girls. In each one the victorious pair of boys was rewarded with girls as confirmation of their dominance. When Brent and Greg defeated the "gangstas," they were rewarded with "their girls," and when Freddy and Randy, as River High wrestlers, defeated their wrestling foes, the "dancing girls" ripped off their shirts to reveal a color pattern that symbolically linked them to Freddy and Randy. Rituals of getting girls allowed boys to find common ground in affirming each other's masculinity and positioned them as subjects who had a right to control what girls did with their bodies. A close examination indicates that rituals of "getting girls" relied on a threat of sexualized violence that reaffirmed a sexualized inequality central to the gender order at River High.

On Halloween, Heath arrived at school dressed as an elf carrying a sprig of mistletoe and engaged in a fairly typical ritual of getting girls. He told anyone who would listen that an elf costume was a brilliant idea for Halloween because "it's the wrong holiday!" We stood by his friends at the "water polo" table who tried to sell greeting cards as a fundraiser for the team. Heath attempted to "help" by yelling at girls who passed by, "Ten dollars for a card and a kiss from the elf! Girls only!" Girls made faces and rolled their eyes as they walked past. Graham walked up and Heath yelled to him, arms outstretched, "Come here, baby!" Graham walked toward him with his hips thrust forward and his arms open, saying, "I'm coming!" and quickly both of them backed away laughing. Graham challenged Heath's kissing strategy, saying that the mistletoe sticking out of his green shorts wouldn't work because it wasn't Christmas. Heath, to prove his point that mistletoe worked at any time of the year, lifted the mistletoe above his head and, moving from behind the table, walked up to a group of girls. They looked at him with a bit of trepidation and tried to ignore his presence. Finally one acquiesced, giving him a peck on the cheek. Her friend followed suit. Heath strutted back to the table and victoriously shook hands with all the boys.

Heath, in this instance, became successfully masculine both through renouncing the fag—he emphasized he was kissing "girls only," he imitated a fag by coming on to Graham—and through "getting girls" to kiss him.[4] Graham then congratulated Heath on his ability to overcome the girls' resistance to his overtures. This sort of coercion, even when seemingly harmless, embeds a sense of masculinity predicated upon an overcoming of girls' resistance to boys' desire (Hird and Jackson 2001). Indeed, if one of the important parts of being masculine, as stated by the boys earlier, was not just to desire girls, which Heath indicated through his "girls only" admonition, but also to be desired by girls, Heath demonstrated this in a quite public way, thus ensuring a claim, at least for a moment, on heterosexuality.

While the boys laughed and celebrated Heath's triumph of will, the girls may not have had the same reaction to his forced kisses. In a study of teenagers and sexual harassment, Jean Hand and Laura Sanchez (2000) found, not surprisingly, that in high school girls experienced higher levels of sexual harassment than boys did and were affected more seriously by it. The girls in their study described a hierarchy of sexually harassing behaviors in which some behaviors were described as more problematic than others. The girls overwhelmingly indicated that being kissed against their will was the worst form of sexual harassment, rated more seriously than hearing boys' comments about their bodies or receiving other types of unwanted sexual attention.

Of course, it is unlikely that boys, or girls, would recognize these sorts of daily rituals as sexual harassment; they are more likely seen as normal, if perhaps a bit aggressive, instances of heterosexual flirtation and as part of a normal adolescence (N. Stein 2005).[5] In fact, I never saw a teacher at River recognize these seemingly flirtatious interchanges as harassment. In auto shop, Tammy, the only girl, often faced this sort of harassment, often at the hands of Jay, a stringy-haired white junior with a pimpled face. One afternoon he walked up to Tammy and stood behind her deeply inhaling, his nose not even an inch away from her hair. Clearly uncomfortable with this, she moved to the side. He asked her if she was planning to attend WyoTech (Wyoming Technical College, a mechanic school), and she responded, "Yes." He said, "I'm going too! You and me. We're gonna be in a room together." He closed his eyes and started thrusting his hips back and forth and softly moaning as if to indicate that he was having sex. Tammy said, "Shut up" and walked away. Used to this sort of harassment, she had developed a way of dealing with such behavior. But no matter how many times she dismissed him, Jay continued to pepper her with sexual innuendoes and suggestive practices.

Both Jay's and Heath's behaviors show how heterosexuality is normalized as a sort of "predatory" social relation in which boys try and try and try to "get" a girl until one finally gives in. Boys, like Jay, who can't "get" a girl often respond with anger or frustration because of their presumed right to girls' bodies. Marc reacted this way when a girl didn't acknowledge his advances. As usual, he sat in the rear of the drama classroom with his pal Jason. A tall, attractive blonde girl walked into the room to speak to Mr. McNally, the drama teacher. As she turned to leave the class, Marc, leaning back with his legs up on the chair in front of him and his arm draped casually over the seat next to him, yelled across the room, "See you later, hot mama!"

Jason, quickly echoed him, yelling "See you later, sweet thing." She didn't acknowledge them and looked straight ahead at the door as she left. Marc, frustrated at her lack of response, loudly stated, "She didn't hear me. Whore." Instead of acknowledging that not getting her reflected something about his gender status, he deflected the blame onto her. In fact, he transformed her into the female version of the fag: the whore.[6]

Getting, or not getting, girls also reflects and reinforces racialized meanings of sexuality and masculinity. Darnell, the African American and white football player who, in chapter 3, talked about how boys were told from a young age to avoid becoming a fag, made it clear that this sort of rejection was embedded with racialized meanings: pacing up and down the stairs that line the drama classroom, he yelled across the room to me.

"There's just one thing I hate! Just one thing I hate!" Shawna, an energetic, bisexual African American sophomore, and I simultaneously asked, "What's that?" Darnell responded, frustrated, "When mixed girls date white guys! Mixed girls are for me!" Shawna attempted to interrupt his rant, saying, "What if the girl doesn't want to date you? Girls have a say too." Darnell responded, not in as much jest as one might hope, "No they don't. White boys can date white girls. There's plenty of 'em. They can even date black girls. But mixed girls are for me." Darnell's frustration reflects a way in which racialized, gendered, and sexual identities intersect. While he felt that he had a claim on "getting girls," as a "mixed" guy he saw his options as somewhat limited. Girls and girls' bodies were constructed as a limited resource for which he had to compete with other (white) guys.

[...]

TRADING ON HETEROSEXUALITY

College Women's Gender Strategies and Homophobia

By Laura Hamilton

Scholars note that homophobia plays a central role in the construction of masculinities (Connell 1987; Corbett 2001; Kimmel 2001; Pascoe 2005). Indeed, as Corbett (2001) notes, the term *faggot* stands in for more than sexual insult: It connotes a failure to be fully masculine. "Real" men repudiate the feminine or that which they perceive to be weak, powerless, and inconsequential (Kimmel 2001). The hegemonic form of masculinity thus supports men's dominance over women and other men in subordinated positions because of race, class, or sexuality (Connell 1995). The literature on masculinities suggests that homophobia occurs when men try to perform hegemonic masculinity. By verbally or physically attacking men whom they perceive as not masculine, men may reassert their own manhood (Corbett 2001; Kimmel 2001; Pascoe 2005). When relying solely on this conceptualization, homophobia takes on gendered characteristics, underscoring a particular masculine manifestation of antihomosexual behaviors as quintessentially homophobic.

Past research seems to support the association of homophobia with men: For instance, studies often find that women have more positive attitudes toward homosexuality (Loftus 2001). Giddens (1992, 28) has even predicted that women will be the vanguard in creating a space for "the flourishing of homosexuality." Yet, it is possible that women's homophobia remains obscured when conceptualizing homophobia as a singular phenomenon. As Stein (2005) suggests, homophobia can take many forms and operate through multiple mechanisms. Homophobia may also be central to the development of certain feminine selves but not in the same way as for masculine selves. Because women and men are in different positions with regard to power, women's homophobia may support gendered identities that are most successful in garnering men's approval

AUTHOR'S NOTE: This article is part of a larger project about collegiate life that the author conducted in collaboration with Elizabeth A. Armstrong, director of the study. The author wishes to thank her for her insights and support. Thanks is also given to Sibyl Bedford, Katie Bradley, Teresa Cummings, Aimee Lipkis, Evelyn Perry, Brian Sweeney, and Amanda Tanner for research assistance. The author also appreciates Elizabeth A. Armstrong, Nancy Davis, Donna Eder, Timothy Hallett, and Brian Powell for comments on the article and is grateful to Dana Britton, Christine Williams, and anonymous reviewers for their helpful suggestions.

(Rich 1980). Some women may distance themselves from others who do not perform the erotic selves that they perceive as valued by men. These women may exhibit homophobia to maintain the believability of their traditionally feminine identities.

In this article, I draw on ethnographic and interview data from a women's floor of a residence hall on a public university campus to suggest that heterosexual women may display homophobia against lesbians as they negotiate status in a gender-inegalitarian erotic market. First, I describe the Greek party scene on this campus, the erotic hierarchy linked to it, and lesbians' low ranking within this hierarchy. I then explain that women who were active partiers excluded lesbians from social interactions and spaces while critical partiers and nonpartiers were more inclusive. Finally, I describe how heterosexual women conceptualized the same-sex eroticism that they used to garner men's attention and the consequences that this had for lesbians. I conclude by discussing how gender inequality and heteronormitivity combine to create homophobia among women.

GENDER STRATEGIES: "TRADING ON" HETEROSEXUALITY

Scholars have used Swidler's (1986) concept of "strategies of action" to show how women create "gender strategies" that help them navigate inegalitarian gender conditions. A gender strategy is a course of action that attempts to solve a problem using the cultural conceptions of gender available to the individual (Handler 1995; Hochschild 1989). Gender strategies are thus both cognitive and behavioral. They are not, however, always reflexive. In interaction, decisions and actions often occur quickly and nonreflexively. Women may fall into well-established patterns of behavior that pull from available cultural definitions of femininity and masculinity. Consequently, they can engage in gender strategies without awareness of the gendered aspects of their actions (P. Y. Martin 2003).

Gender strategies involve the use of particular gender presentations over others. These presentations do not reflect preexisting internal qualities but become engrained in people's bodies through the constant repetition of particular movements, acts, and thoughts (Butler 1990; K. A. Martin 1998). Premised on gender difference, heterosexuality is one of the key mechanisms through which women and men learn to embody gender. Given women's subordinate position, much of what makes a woman traditionally feminine is her ability and desire to attract a man (Bartky 1990). Women learn to produce feminine bodies and to have desires for men that conform to heterosexual imperatives. Many of the roles from which they gain their identities—such as girlfriend, wife, and mother—further emphasize the centrality of heterosexuality to gender identity (Jackson 1996).

Depending on the rules governing a particular social field, some gender presentations will garner more rewards than others will (McCall 1992). As Connell (1995) notes, while political, cultural, and economic practices benefit hegemonic masculinity, they but subordinate masculinities that eschew heteronormativity. Many of these same practices similarly disadvantage women. However, femininities that conform to heteronormative ideals of feminine charm and beauty can operate as a form of embodied cultural capital (McCall 1992).[1] One strategy that women may use to deal with gender inequalities is to "trade on" their embodied capital (Chen 1999). That is, they may rely on their ability to signal heterosexuality to acquire better treatment and more status than other women (Butler 1990; McCall 1992; Rich 1980; Schwalbe et al. 2000). Homophobia can result when women who have embodied capital disassociate themselves from those who do not. Any benefits that women may accrue through homophobia come at a cost: They ultimately reinforce the gendered inequalities that made such a gender strategy necessary (Schwalbe et al. 2000).

Gendered-embodied capital is not equally available to all individuals: Instead, material resources, the physicality of bodies, and prior gender performances all restrict the femininities/masculinities that individuals can enact. Audiences hold people accountable for the types of gender performances that they expect from particular bodies in particular social positions (Bettie 2005). Gender identities thus reference locations within social hierarchies. Hegemonic masculinity, for example, relies not only on heterosexuality but also on race and class statuses (Chen 1999). Similarly, women's embodied capital privileges whiteness and requires classed knowledge and resources (Bettie 2005; Collins 1990). Therefore, heterosexual women in socially dominant race and class positions may have greater access to the dividends of hegemonic masculinity as they are most likely to embody cultural notions of an "ideal" femininity.

Erotic Markets and Heterosexual Privilege

A ubiquitous element of youth cultures, erotic markets are expanding to include larger segments of the population for longer periods of their lives. Erotic markets are public sexualized scenes in which individuals present erotic selves that are subject to the judgments and reactions of others (Collins 2004). These markets require a mass of individuals who share similar assumptions about the kinds of sexual activity that are open for negotiation and how to interpret the sexual activity that does occur.

Many erotic markets operate using heteronormative cultural logics. This does not mean that all people within these scenes are heterosexual or that all erotic behaviors in this scene occur between women and men; rather, the available cultural understandings in heterosexual erotic markets reflect heteronormative ideas about sexuality, what "sex" is, and for whom it is performed. Because heterosexuality presumes gender difference, these meanings also code "real" sex as that which is penetrative or initiated by men and position women as desired objects rather than desiring subjects (Armstrong 1995; Jackson 1996). As a result, same-sex eroticism between conventionally feminine women becomes a performance for men, one that inevitably ends in heterosexual sex (Jenefsky and Miller 1998).

[...]

Same-Sex Eroticism among "Straight Girls"

Only active partiers, those in the two outer rings of social distance from lesbians, participated in same-sex eroticism (4 out of 6 women in the "never okay" group; 17 out of 24 women in the "okay for others but not in my space" group). Same-sex eroticism included kissing (on the mouth, often involving tongues) and fondling (of breasts and buttocks), particularly while dancing; no heterosexual women reported oral or digital stimulation of the genitals. These women openly discussed such behaviors with researchers, talked about them with their friends, and posted pictures of themselves kissing women in their rooms and on the Internet.[6] Heterosexual women who were more open about homosexuality did not either engage in the same behavior or advertise it in the same way.

As Jenefsky and Miller (1998) note, the performance of lesbianism for men may signal heterocentric eroticism. Women on the floor who engaged in this behavior claimed that they intended their same-sex kissing for an audience of heterosexual men. Several noted that they liked to get reactions from men. One described, "You get guys that you just like to see their expressions. It's just so funny to see them be like, 'Oh my god, I can't believe you just did that, that was awesome.'" Another woman explained, "Guys said, 'Do it, do it!' just screwing around.... [They] were like, 'These girls are going to kiss!' So you think you're cooler and guys think you're cooler." The value in the same-sex kiss, therefore, was in the attention that it could garner from men. Like a sexy outfit or new stilettos, heterosexual women could deploy same-sex eroticism as a statement of style to get attention amid a sea of scantily dressed young women. One resident even noted that unlike doing drugs, this way of getting attention did not cause bodily harm.

Heterosexual women were careful to claim that their kisses had little meaning behind them, noting that they were not involved and not "serious." They often contextualized their behaviors so that others (and perhaps themselves) would interpret them as heterosexual. As two roommates told me when I asked if they had ever seen two girls kissing,

> R1: Well, sometimes we're drunk. (Both laughing)
> R2: Like trashed.
> R1: We have a wall of shame of pictures.
> R2: Sometimes we get a little out of control and trashed, but it's not like we're going crazy on each other. Like, it's just to be funny. It's random kisses. It's not serious.
> R1: Right (laughs). It's not like I want you or anything. Eww.

Women often attributed these kisses to alcohol. Among this crowd, however, intoxication was rarely an embarrassing state. Drunken pictures were most likely to make it into public view as they provided proof that one could party hard. Same-sex sexuality was just another way to mark oneself as edgy and spontaneous—"stepping outside of your box," as one woman called it.

Floor residents who employed woman-to-woman eroticism were careful to distinguish their behaviors from those whom they considered to be "real lesbians." As many felt that lesbians were identifiable through their unfeminine appearance, they seemed sure that those in their social networks were heterosexual even if sexual orientation was never a topic of conversation. As one respondent noted,

> R: It's totally different if you're into it. Like lesbians or something. It's just your friend.
> I: How can you tell like if somebody is really into it or not?
> R: I don't know. I always just assumed everyone wasn't. Just 'cause it's people I knew. I've never seen real lesbians kiss.

All of these women agreed that you only kissed close friends whom you trusted to be heterosexual. One even described it as a "bonding" activity between her and another woman on the floor. When they saw other women kissing at parties, they usually applied the same assumptions.

These women felt that encountering lesbians making out in the heterosexual space of the party scene was unlikely. They understood that women achieved status and even basic inclusion in the party scene through their ability to attract men. In their eyes, most lesbians were incapable of doing so; lesbians were "boyish" and "weird" and therefore unlikely to be "hot" or "blonde." They assumed that lesbians simply could not succeed in passing as heterosexual women. This assumption allowed them to construct seeming boundaries between their same-sex erotic practices and those of who they deemed to be "real" or "actual" lesbians. The maintenance of these boundaries played a central role in their ability to maintain heterosexual identities and define their behaviors as hetero-, rather than homo-, erotic.

Reducing Lesbian Spaces

Heterosexual women's enactment of same-sex eroticism worked to further marginalize lesbians. Displays of eroticism between women perceived as undesirable to heterosexual men invited ridicule or worse. Because the heterosexual party scene encompassed all Greek houses, many off-campus houses, and all but a few bars in town, lesbians were effectively excluded (both by choice and by design) from most public erotic spaces in town. A lesbian in a focus group suggested that heterosexual women even encroached on the few lesbian- and gay-friendly party spots. Della's, the bar to which she referred, is a widely known gay bar.

> One night I was at Della's and waiting for my friends to meet me there. I'm sitting alone at this table, and a group of approximately 50 girls in matching T-shirts with sorority lettering across the front, came in, took over the dance floor, and were makin' out and givin' lap dances to each other.... I called [my friend] and I was talkin' to her about how just disgusted I was by it because it's making a mockery of us. These two girls overheard me 'cause I was being loud (laughter).... And I tried to explain to them that if I went to the straight bar with my girlfriend and stood next to her, let alone kissed her, that would not be okay. But that these little girls kissing and giggling is A-okay because it's implied that there's no pleasure there or that it's to please men rather than to please themselves.

This woman experienced the sorority women's presence in her space as invasive and their behavior as insulting. Acting as heterosexual "tourists," these sorority women consumed the experience of the "exotic other" but could safely leave it behind (Casey 2004). As most erotic spaces privileged their sexuality, they felt entitled enough to invade one of the few lesbian-identified spaces in pursuit of a thrill.

None of the women in the focus group felt that heterosexual women's use of same-sex eroticism would lead to claiming a lesbian identity. One explained, "There doesn't seem to be any ... authentic lesbian in between there." However, heterosexual women's enactment of same-sex eroticism in a gay bar suggests that their appropriation may not be only about garnering men's attention. It is possible that claiming a heterosexual identity allows them to enjoy experimentation with other women. On the floor, two roommates told me and another woman about a night when they danced together naked. They did this alone and were not recounting the story to get men's attention. Yet neither described this experience as a "lesbian" encounter, instead jokingly dismissing it as something to do when they were bored. They may have privately experienced this as a moment of questioning their sexuality; however, their ability to tell others without facing challenges to their heterosexual identity was dependent on the existence of out lesbians from whom they could differentiate themselves.

As Casey (2004) notes, heterosexual women's intrusion into gay and lesbian identified spaces can reduce lesbians' comfort, safety, and sense of inclusion. Women who claimed heterosexual identities may have experienced freedom from men's gaze and possibly played with same-sex desire while in the bar; however, as a result of their intrusion, lesbians lost the right to define the meaning of same-sex eroticism in their own space. By claiming same-sex eroticism as a heterosexual practice, heterosexual women made lesbian desire invisible and reconfigured it as a performance for men. Ironically, in the lesbian bar take-over, heterosexual women took up space with their bodies and their sexuality—something that scholars find to be particularly difficult for women (K. A. Martin 1998; Tolman 2002). Yet they did so only at the cost of women who were more disenfranchised on campus than they were.

DISCUSSION

The literature on masculinities suggests that men's dominance over women encourages adherence to heteronormative ideals of manhood that support aggression against gays (Connell 1987; Corbett 2001; Pascoe 2005). These analyses present the flipside of that story; women's efforts to navigate inegalitarian gender contexts may fortify their efforts to meet heteronormative standards of femininity. Although disadvantaged relative to men, heterosexual women may raise their status among other women by distancing themselves from those who do not perform traditionally feminine identities. Lesbians, who often avoid signaling availability to men through behavior or appearance, thus encounter systematic social exclusion.

Past scholarship may have minimized homophobia among women because it does not look the same as among men. Men's homophobia often takes the form of physical or verbal violence against gay men. My analyses suggest that homophobia among women instead renders lesbians socially invisible. For example, when someone covertly dismantled the Rainbow Week bulletin board in the hall, no one, save the resident assistant, said anything. The unceremonious removal of the board and its subsequent replacement with healthy eating suggestions fittingly represented the situation of the lesbians on the floor. Most of the floor was so busy avoiding them, they were almost socially nonexistent.

BECOMING A BLACK MAN

By Daisy Hernandez

Louis Mitchell expected a lot of change when he began taking injections of hormones eight years ago to transition from a female body to a male one. He anticipated that he'd grow a beard, which he eventually did and enjoys now. He knew his voice would deepen and that his relationship with his partner, family and friends would change in subtle and, he hoped, good ways, all of which happened.

What he had not counted on was changing the way he drove. Within months of starting male hormones, "I got pulled over 300 percent more than I had in the previous 23 years of driving, almost immediately. It was astounding," says Mitchell, who is Black and transitioned while living in the San Francisco area and now resides in Springfield, Massachusetts.

Targeted for "driving while Black" was not new to Mitchell, who is 46 years old. For example, a few years before transitioning, he had been questioned by a cop for simply sitting in his own car late at night. But "he didn't really sweat me too much once he came up to the car and divined that I was female," Mitchell recalls.

Now in a Black male body, however, Mitchell has been pulled aside for small infractions. When he and his wife moved from California to the East Coast, Mitchell refused to let her drive on the cross-country trip. "She drives too fast," he says, chuckling and adding, "I didn't want to get pulled over. It took me a little bit longer [to drive cross country] 'cause I had to drive like a Black man. I can't be going 90 miles an hour down the highway. If I'm going 56, I need to be concerned." As more people of color transition, Mitchell's experience is becoming an increasingly common one.

The transgender community has experienced a boom in visibility in the last decade. Some of this has come about through popular culture, including the acclaimed 1999 film *Boys Don't Cry* and more recently with Mike Penner, the *Los Angeles Times* sports columnist who came out as transgender and is now known as Christine. In recent years, there's also been a growing number of memoirs, including *The Testosterone Files* by the Chicano and American-Indian poet Max Valerio, as well as more academic books on the subject, like *The Transgender Studies Reader*.

Just as key has been the work of transgender people themselves, who have transitioned due to the more widespread availability of hormones and surgeries. Rather than passing as heterosexual, an increasing number of them in the last decade have identified as "trans" and begun support, advocacy and legal-rights groups. The widespread use of the Internet and the new online social networks are also helping to break the isolation that trans people often feel in their own communities.

In Asia, Latin America and Africa, the place of transgender people is likewise changing. While trans women in many cultures have been marginally accepted, they have been largely confined to traditionally feminine roles as caretakers—a situation that is changing now in places like Ixhuatan, Mexico, where Amaranta Gomex, a muxe, or trans woman, ran for political office in 2003. In some countries, trans activists are going to court and winning key changes in public policies. In Brazil, a court ruled in August 2007 that sexual-reassignment surgery is covered by the constitution as a medical right.

While it's extremely difficult to say how many people identify as transgender, the National Center for Transgender Equality has estimated that about three million people are transgender today in the United States. It's hard to say how many of those are people of color, but one online group for Black trans people called Transsistahs-Transbrothas has about 300 members, and another group specifically for Latino trans men has 98 members.

In the last four years, there's also been an increase in the number of people seeking top surgeries, or removal of their breasts, according to Michael Brownstein, a well-known doctor specializing in gender surgeries in San Francisco. He does about four to six top surgeries a week, and he notes that while 30 years ago, trans people would come to his office alone, they are now arriving with partners, siblings and friends for moral support.

These social and political changes have ushered in a time when it is increasingly acceptable for men and women to alter their physical bodies to match their gender identity. Left largely unexamined, however, has been the issue of racism and how trans men and women experience it. Trans people of color are finding that they have an extremely different relationship to gender transition than white people. London Dexter Ward, an LAPD cop who transitioned in 2004, sums it up this way: a white person who transitions to a male body "just became a man." By contrast, he says, "I became a Black man. I became the enemy."

In short, people of color know that racism works differently for men and women, and transgender people like Mitchell and Ward are getting to experience this from both sides of the gender equation.

Louis Mitchell is the type of man who immediately puts people at ease as he advises them about how cheap the housing is in Massachusetts. He calls himself "a big Black man" (he's 5 feet 9 inches tall and 250 pounds). In 2006, after much soul searching, he began attending divinity school. Talking to Mitchell, it's easy to imagine him in a pulpit. He is simultaneously warmhearted and sure of himself. He could sell a two-bedroom condo as easily as convincing a congregation to be honest with God.

Growing up in West Covina in Southern California, Mitchell attended church with his mother and devoured history books. At the age of 3 or 4, he knew that he was a boy, regardless of having been born into a girl's body. He also believed that God created miracles. So he prayed that he would grow into a boy's body when he reached puberty. That didn't happen, much to his surprise.

Near the end of 1970, when Mitchell was 18 years old, he hitchhiked with a friend to Corpus Christi, Texas, where the legal drinking age was lower than in California. There, he met drag queens, and he felt hopeful for the first time. If the queens could be women, his thinking went, then there might be options for him to live as a man.

At the time, a Black transsexual woman had already been the first person to undergo sex reassignment surgery at John Hopkins University, according to Joanne Meyerowitz's classic book *How Sex Changed: A History of Transsexuality in the United States*. Avon Wilson's transition in 1966 at John Hopkins marked a turning point for the transsexual community. It was the first time a medical clinic in the United States performed the surgery, and so while it remained rare to be approved for surgery, it was at least a possibility. However, Mitchell went on to identify as a butch, even though he felt that he was masquerading as a lesbian.

Then, 15 years ago, a friend of his began the process of transitioning to a male body. "That lit a fire that I couldn't put out," he says now. He met a few Black trans men at a conference but took many years to think about his own transition. He considered the consequences of transitioning, including the impact on his mother, who he's very attached to, and the loss for him of his lesbian community. He didn't think too much about racism. Mitchell already had a goatee without taking hormones and was used to being followed in stores. He had grown accustomed to women clutching their purses at the sight of him. So he was somewhat surprised about the changes that came after he began taking injections of the hormone testosterone—the degree to which he became a target and also the emotional changes he felt as a Black man.

Before transitioning, Mitchell recalls being "cavalier and reckless" about what he did in public and about his interactions with police officers. "I didn't think about it so much," he says about cops. "At some point they would find out I was female" and that would diffuse the situation. Now, Mitchell finds that he doesn't engage in small transgressions like jaywalking or spitting on the sidewalk. "I never know if they're just waiting for something to happen to roll up, and I do not want find myself in custody. That would be just precarious and dangerous in so many ways."

When living in San Francisco, he moved out of the historical gay neighborhood of the Castro because he got tired of being followed in stores. During the cross-country trip with his wife Krysia, he refrained from being affectionate with her in public. He didn't want to run the risk of drawing attention to himself as a Black man and her as a mixed-race Latina who at times is perceived as white. "More than a trans man, I'm a Black man," Mitchell says. "I'd be in intensive care by the time they realized I was a trans man."

Prado Gomez, a 33-year-old Chicano who transitioned in 2001, describes the situation with racism and violence as a "trade off." "I'll be able to walk down the street and not be raped, unless they know my status [as a trans man]", he says. "But there's a different kind of threat from men." Before transitioning, Gomez was used to being pulled over in the car with his brothers by cops in San Francisco. "Cops called me an asshole until they saw the F on my license," he recalls, and small verbal fights on the street back then did not escalate. Gomez says that a guy would call him a "bitch" and leave it at that. Now, Gomez knows he has to be more careful. A small exchange of words could lead to more violence.

London Dexter Ward has also seen his life change because of the ways that racism is gendered. "I do a lot of shopping online now," says Ward, who got tired of being followed in book and clothing stores.

A 44-year-old police officer, Ward began hormone treatments in 2004 and transitioned while working for the LAPD, where he's now an instructor at the police academy. The transition on the job was no small feat, since it meant moving to the men's locker room and showers. But Ward's coworkers and supervisors, like his family, accepted him.

In typical men's locker-room humor, his sergeant created a penalty jar where the cops had to deposit a quarter if they referred to Ward by a female pronoun. Ward, like Mitchell and Gomez, felt that he had planned for just about every change that would come with transitioning. "What I did not prepare for was being a Black man," he says.

He finds that people now look at him with fear in bars and restaurants where he once used to go for a good time. "When people are afraid of you, you stop wanting to hang out in those places," Ward says. Experiencing racism as a Black man, though, doesn't necessarily give Mitchell and Ward a bond with their peers, who grew up in Black male bodies, experiencing racism as Black boys and then men. "It's a matter of living for them, at this point," Mitchell says. "It's no longer some strange thing that they notice. It just is. It's like gravity. I am a Black man, and therefore if something is stolen while I am in the neighborhood, then I am a suspect."

The racism that Black trans men experience is only part of the story, of course. Mitchell says his manhood is not about the racism he encounters. "It is more about integrity and a sense of being the truest person I can be," he says, adding that his gender transition has been about "having my insides and my outsides match finally." Rather than see himself as joining a group of men who are perpetual targets, he feels he's joined a community of men that are strong but not ashamed of their tenderness. Mitchell also finds that he's in a unique position now to mentor young Black men. As someone who came of age in the lesbian community and has feminist politics, Mitchell jokes with Black boys who talk about "fags" and refer to women as "bitches." He pulls the teenagers aside and uses a bit of reverse psychology, telling them that it's okay if they're gay. When the teens protest that they're not, Mitchell says, "You have no respect for women, and you're fixated on gay men. What am I supposed to think?"

Johnnie Pratt, a Black trans man who lives in the San Francisco area, also jokes that he now enjoys certain perks. Finally, he is taken seriously by the guys at Home Depot. Before transitioning, he says, "They'd be looking at me like, 'Shut up girl.' Now they want to talk to me." Trans men of color are finding that some things stay the same on both sides of the gender equation. Cultural expectations, for example, are hard to shake. As is common for Latinas, Gomez has raised his brother's two children with his partner, Mariah, and is now taking care of his mom, who suffers from Alzheimer's disease. Gomez sees no contradiction in the fact that as a man, he bathes his 60-year-old mother. "I am the only one my mother trusts," he says. "She sees here is this man, but she knows this man is her daughter."

The experience with racism is flipped in some ways for Black trans women. Monica Roberts, who is 45 years old, transitioned in 1994. As a Black woman, she is happy to no longer be considered, as she says, "a suspect." Since transitioning, she has not been pulled over for "driving while Black," although she quickly adds that it has happened to a friend who is also a Black trans woman. Roberts and her Black trans-women friends have experienced something else since transitioning: "We've noticed a power shift," she says. "Black culture is matriarchal-based … most of the leadership in the Black community is made up of very powerful women. There's a lot of that in my hometown." And so as Roberts transitioned, she has stepped into that role. Roberts grew up in Houston, Texas, and in the Black church. Her mother is a teacher, and she was surrounded by women who were historians and leaders in the community. She understood the influence of Black women. "You might have a minister up here pontificating on the pulpit on Sunday," she says, "but the real power behind the throne is the women's auxiliary that's meeting on Tuesday."

Her father, a local radio commentator, tried to groom Roberts for leadership as his eldest child. Yet, it was only after transitioning that Roberts felt able to take on such a leadership role. Perhaps it was due to the toll that living in the "tr*nny closet" had taken on her self-esteem. But Roberts also noticed a difference in the responses she received from other people to her leadership as a Black woman. She got positive reactions, she says, "because I was basically doing the traditional work of Black women in the community in terms of uplifting the race." In 2005, Roberts and other transsexual and transgender activists started the first conference for Black trans people. It took place in Louisville, Kentucky, where she now lives. She also writes these days for a local LGBT outlet and blogs at transgriot.blogspot.com. In 2006, she became the third Black person to receive the Trinity Award, which recognizes people for their contributions to the transgender community.

Pauline Park also found that transitioning to become a woman of color altered her place in the world. A Korean adoptee who was raised in the Midwest, Park transitioned in 1997 but chose to not physically alter her body. Park is now 46 years old and a founding member of the New York Association for Gender Right Advocacy, which got legislation passed in New York City to protect transgender people from discrimination in housing and employment. In transitioning from living as an Asian man to an Asian woman, Park found that she was finally able to have "the joy of actualizing something I've always wanted to be." But she also finds that she has gone from invisibility to a visibility that is at times unwelcomed. Being an effeminate Asian male, Park says, "tends to—if anything—put you in either invisibility or derision, ridicule [and] harassment. But if you're perceived to be an Asian woman, what happens is the exact opposite, which is sexual interest and even harassment."

Now Park finds herself at times the target on the subways in New York City, where she lives. Recently, when she got off the No. 7 train in Queens, she realized that she was being followed by a man. She didn't know if it was because he saw her as an Asian woman or a transgender Asian woman. She ran home and slammed the door shut. "I always wear shoes I can run in," Park says. She concedes she knew that Asian women were exoticized, but "it's one thing reading about something in a book and another to be running down the street."

Listening to Monica Roberts, it's hard to imagine a time when she wasn't a leader. She's adamant that Black trans people need their own spaces. For example, she says, there's a lot of hostility in the white transgender community toward Christianity, and some of that is justified. But when it comes to Black trans folks, she says, it's impossible to just walk away from the church. "You can't leave out Christians if you want people of color" at a conference, she says. "We were all raised in a church." Roberts also highlights another small but important detail of trans life for people of color: There's a level of animosity between trans women and men in the white community that doesn't exist to the same degree in the Black community. Some of that is due to the fact that white trans women are often dealing with a loss of power in public life, while white trans men are coming to positions of power and all its ensuing emotions and consequences. It's different for Black transsexuals, Roberts says.

"There's a lot of information sharing … They [Black trans men] can talk to us about being women, and we can talk to them about DWB." At the end of the day, Roberts also says, "People don't see me as a trans woman. They see me as Black … and that's the thing that people notice. The bottom line is, we're Black first."

Mitchell concurs. "More than I'm a trans man, I'm a Black man," he says. "Many of the things that I see in the world and many of the things that I respond to in the world have more to do with how I am treated as a Black man rather than how I am treated as a trans man.

70 PERCENT OF ANTI-LGBT MURDER VICTIMS ARE PEOPLE OF COLOR

By Michael Lavers

It's an all too common, if shocking story: A transgender Latina woman with HIV is attacked on a street close to her home in a low-income neighborhood in the Bay Area. Making a bad situation worse, police officers literally drag her from her bed at 6 a.m. because they think she committed the crime herself.

"They kept telling her she wasn't who she was, and that she was a man," explained María Carolina Morales of the San Francisco-based Communities United Against Violence as she recounted the incident to Colorlines. "She was arrested. She was taken to the station. She wasn't listened to. She spent the weekend in jail."

The woman went to court a month after her arrest, but disappeared shortly after her court date.

"She was somebody who was unemployed, who didn't have a safety net," noted Morales. "We don't know if she ran away, if she ended up in jail or [was] transferred to another place, another city. Her phone was disconnected the day after court. We just don't know—don't know what happened."

The National Coalition of Anti-Violence Programs released its annual report on hate violence motivated by sexual orientation, gender identity and expression and HIV status last week. The report documents 27 anti-LGBT murders in 2010, which is the second highest annual total recorded since 1996. A whopping 70 percent of these 27 victims were people of color; 44 percent of them were transgender women.

The study also found that transgender people and people of color are each twice as likely to experience violence or discrimination as non-transgender white people. Transgender people of color are also almost 2.5 times as likely to experience discrimination as their white peers.

"It wasn't a shock," said Morales, whose organization is among the 17 anti-violence programs from across the country that contributed data to the NCAVP report. "For the last four years we've seen that trend—of transgender women and people of color in our communities experiencing higher levels of violence. Sadly that continues."

Recent headlines certainly bear witness to this disturbing trend.

A Milwaukee judge sentenced Andrew Olaciregui to an 11-year prison sentence in December after he pleaded guilty to shooting Chanel Larkin three times in the head on a street corner in May 2010. Prosecutors maintain Olaciregui shot Larkin after he offered to pay her $20 to perform a sex act and found out she was transgender. Larkin was 26 at the time of her death.

In another high-profile case, Hakim Scott and Keith Phoenix both received decades-long prison sentences last summer for their role in the death of Ecuadorian immigrant José Sucuzhañay on a Brooklyn street in December 2008. Prosecutors contend Scott and Phoenix shouted anti-gay and anti-Latino slurs at Sucuzhañay as they attacked him with a baseball bat and bottles.

Juan José Matos Martínez received a 99-year prison sentence in May 2010 after he pleaded guilty to stabbing gay Puerto Rican teenager Jorge Steven López Mercado to death before decapitating, dismembering and partially burning his body and dumping it along a remote roadside in November 2009.

So what causes disproportionate rates of violence against transgender people and queer people of color?

"What the 2010 report allows us to do is document something we've seen and experienced for a long time," said Ejeris Dixon of the New York City Anti-Violence Project, which wrote the bulk of the NCAVP report. "It's really about an intersection of oppression."

Dixon, who was a long-time staffer at Brooklyn-based Audre Lorde Project until she joined AVP earlier this year, said a lack of employment, housing and health care for transgender people all contribute to disproportionate rates of violence. Morales said that ongoing police harassment against these communities is an additional factor, making those most at-risk for hate violence also least likely to seek help.

"All of those things sanction violence," said Dixon.

The NCAVP report found that half of those who experienced hate violence did not contact the police after their attack. The report further found that 25.4 percent of transgender women did not file a report. So what can be done to reduce these rates of violence against LGBT people and communities of color?

The Audre Lorde Project is among the groups that organize LGBT people in communities of color that are increasingly looking beyond law enforcement and the criminal justice system for a solution. The Safe OUTside the System Collective works with bodegas, businesses and organizations within Brooklyn's Bedford-Stuyvesant neighborhood and surrounding areas to create safe spaces for LGBT people of color to curb violence.

"What's true and important is our communities have been and continue to organize around issues of harassment—whether it's neighborhood or community harassment or [harassment] by the police," said Kris Hayashi, executive director of the Audre Lorde Project.

Morales stressed that empowering transgender people and people of color to participate in decision making processes around employment, health care, improved access to food and affordable housing is another key component to addressing the problem. "For that, our organizations and institutions need to prioritize opening spaces for people to develop their leadership, to be able to engage, to learn and make decisions and so that they can see themselves not only reflected, but see themselves in the process."

Another potential solution is for anti-violence programs to tackle some of the underlying disparities that contribute to increased violence against LGBT people and people of color.

"That can mean a lot of things: We can talk about low-cost programs, intersections with immigration rights groups," said Dixon. "It's about crafting programming that focuses on these populations and also developing leadership of LGBT people of color and trans people."

While Morales conceded these most recent statistics are grim, she said she remains hopeful that they will allow her organization and others around the country to develop more effective strategies to tackle hate violence. She stressed, however, this hasn't happened as much as she would like to see.

"It hasn't been significantly stepped up enough," said Morales, referring to strategies to further engage community members in the solution. "However, I have seen a lot more conversations and dialogue opening up around the community—the prison population continues to significantly increase every year, and violence continues to increase. I don't believe its working. COAV doesn't believe its working. I am hopeful [the report] will open up more opportunities to question the strategy to violence response."

THE DRAG QUEEN AND THE MUMMY

The late star of *Paris Is Burning* and the mystery man in her closet

By Edward Conlon

The apartment on West 140th Street in Harlem was filled with bolts of fabric, feathers, sequins and beads, headdresses, tailpieces, and elaborate gowns which were thrifty facsimiles of exorbitant foreign fashions. A prior tenant was a drag performer who also had a business as a dress and costume designer, and she—polite usage requires the feminine pronoun—required clothing for theatrical, millinery, and everyday use. The apartment was not large and, in addition to her considerable personal effects, contained the belongings of her boyfriend and his brother. But whatever the clutter and overcrowding, the remark by a sergeant from the local precinct that "You could lose a small child in there," was both a truism and an understatement, because the body of a grown man had been concealed there for years.

The drag performer was named Dorian Corey, and she thus inspired three headlines in 1993, in even, two-month intervals—a coup for any entertainer, but something of a triumph when the first story was her obituary. Corey was a principal subject of *Paris Is Burning,* a successful and acclaimed documentary about the drag balls of Harlem, and when she died last August, at the age of fifty-six, the *New York Times* ran a picture of her in drag, the first and only time it has ever done so. In October, two men went to her apartment in hope of finding a costume for Halloween. Their search, led by a friend of the deceased's, took them to a large closet space, the size of a small bedroom. Finding nothing to their immediate satisfaction among the dresses and costumes, they were intrigued by the sight of a large, musty garment bag. They asked permission to open it and received casual approval to do so. Inside, they discovered the mummified body of a man, bound up and wrapped in plastic, folded into the fetal position with a bullet hole in his head. He was identified as a onetime Bronx resident who was last seen by his brother around 1968. The incident was the sort of gory but routine oddity that rates a tabloid paragraph, buried far from the first page. For some reason, it was not until December that Dorian Corey was connected with the story, when it made the gossip column of the *New York Post* before being picked up by the wire services. Chi Chi Valenti, a hostess and producer at various downtown nightclubs, was quoted saying "This makes her more legendary in death than she was in life."

The word "legend" is one of the thematic compasses of *Paris Is Burning,* and it is invoked in the dual sense of great stature and dubious reality. It takes its title from a drag ball of the same name, which was held in an Elk's Club on 129th Street in Harlem, and it too is a hub of doubled and tripled meanings: the capitol of black America as the City of Light, its burning suggestive of a sudden fashionable demand as well as a progressive annihilation. The legends are the eminences, gray and otherwise, of the drag scene, who arrive and endure in status by force of personality and performance. At the balls, they "walk" in various categories, and the original "grandes dames" who modelled themselves on figures from Lubitsch films or Las Vegas floor shows became, over time, only a small part of an eclectic pageant of talents and tastes. The old divas whose costumes forbade much movement beyond the statuesque entrance were joined by break dancers and voguers, who fluidly moved through the histrionic, almost hieroglyphic poses of fashion photography. As the expansion continued to an egalitarian extreme, ostensibly mundane categories such as Executive, College, and even Homeboy "Realness" are lent pathos and bite by the sense that they represent lives that are as out of reach to the walkers as those in the rarefied realm of celebrity. For some, the exclusion is final, beyond mediation. Others perfect the pose in order to reject it, so that which for others is the labor of a lifetime becomes a light-operatic amusement, done and dispensed with in a moment. The ironies are double-edged, and cut deep.

The film was attacked by the African-American scholar bell hooks as exploitative, and the immediate prospect of poor black men who wanted to be wealthy and famous white women suggests, at least, a subculture of acute maladjustment. But many of the devotees of the more aggressively theatrical categories are secure in their understanding that the walk, and the life, is a performance, an artform, suffused with a sense of fun and play, however serious in purpose and expert in craft. The breach between life, on and off-stage, lends a tension that is vibrantly explored: an off-duty drag queen, unshaven, in a t-shirt and jeans, might not look so different from an off-duty fireman. Others seek to put as much distance as possible between them and their original condition, through hormone treatments and breast implants, a medical transformation toward femaleness whose radical conclusion is referred to as "the change."

The ambitions of the ball-goers veer between bold dream and pure delirium. Some have a talent; others, merely a wish. The rather severe divide between those who fail and those who do not seems to lie in whether one wants to do something, or simply be something. Willie Ninja sought celebrity as a dancer and choreographer, and in large measure he has attained it in the fashion and music industries. A slim, knobby blonde named Venus Xtravaganza, on the other hand, wanted to be a "rich white girl," and a famous actress or model; she also wanted to be "loved, taken care of, spoiled," and married in a church, wearing white. But Venus was equidistant from the worlds of Norman Rockwell and *Paris Match,* and as unlikely to attain conventional fame as she was to make a conventional home. A teenage runaway, she admitted that she once hustled but demurely insisted the dangers of that life persuaded her to put it behind her. She might see a "very handsome young gentleman" on occasion, who might give her some money "to buy a dress, or some shoes, to make myself more beautiful." Most of the time—"99 percent, or ah, 95"—there was no sex exchanged for the money, and in any case, she insisted, it was no different from what a housewife does for a new washer-dryer. While she may have been making a joke at the expense of the camera, it would be wrong to believe that she was in anything but deadly earnest; in a culture steeped in the double entendre, it is the rare statement whose meaning is unmixed. A friend tells of her unambiguous ending: Venus was strangled in a motel room, and days passed before her body was found.

In spite of its tough-mindedness, its countless lessons in hard luck, the ball world sees the larger world, at least in potential, as a place of delicacy and exquisite promise. Throughout the tessel—lated pattern of the film, its fragments of lives broken or never whole, the motif of indignant optimism is almost perversely repeated. "Life hasn't been fair to me," said one queen, relaxing in a negligée, "Not yet."

Paris Is Burning treads the minefields of race, class, and sex with a light and stylish step, provoking without crude polemic and letting the subjects tell of their predicament with aching poignancy and a sometimes refulgent wit. Its most compelling presence is Dorian Corey. Almost fifty at the time of the filming, she was a generation older than most of the subjects; given the velocity of the life-cycle in that milieu, perhaps more than two generations older. Tall and plump, light-skinned, with a smooth and rueful, smoke-burnished voice, she speaks, for the most part, as she looks at the mirror, daubing on eye shadow and rouge. Amid the vanities and mockeries, hers is a singularly generous perspective, self-possessed and self-assured but never dismissive or jealous of her competitors. Corey sketches an astute overview of the culture and customs of the balls, providing a lucid view into its festivity and bitter feuds. While the younger crowd is frankly mercenary, Corey is refreshingly retrograde, an oldtime Broadway trouper with a rugged workethic, a shrewd sense of history and a knack for pleasing the crowd. The generational points of reference are as different, in era and dimension, as Cindy Crawford and Sarah Vaughn.

"With the current children, the children that are young, they've gone to television, you know," she muses. "I've been to several balls and they actually had categories—'Dynasty!' You know, they want you to try to look like Alexis, or Crystal. I guess that's just a statement of the times. When I grew up, you wanted to look like Marlene Dietrich, Betty Grable. Unfortunately, I didn't know that I really wanted to look like Lena Horne. When I grew up, of course, you know, black stars were stigmatized. Nobody wanted to look like Lena Horne. Everybody wanted to look like Marilyn Monroe."

The criticism, or connoisseurship, of the gay life uptown is never made from an arrogant remove, as the stakes and risks are ones she has undertaken herself: "When you're undetectable, when they can walk out of that ballroom into the sunlight, and onto the subway, and get home, and still have all their clothes and no blood running off their bodies—those are the femme realness queens." And the frivolity, while undeniable, is also hardwon: "Daytimes, if they go out they're only going out to try to hustle up a quarter or two, to get their things for the ball, or go to little jobs. A lot of them have little jobs, they work—don't think they're lazy. In New York City, you work or you starve. You work, some kind of work, legal or otherwise, but you have to work to sustain yourself."

But Corey also has an acuity of insight that makes many of her observations resonate beyond the world of the balls. She translates in a way that the street corner carollers of "All I want for Christmas is my two, front tits" do not. "If you have on a label, it means that you've got wealth, when it doesn't really. Because any shoplifter can get a label," she said, noting a trend that was hardly confined to her own subculture." (There was a time when you could spend a great deal of time making outfits, and preparing for something. Now they come very quickly. And the moods change, very quickly. But I come from the old school of big costumes—feathers and beads. And they don't have that anymore. Now it's all about designers. And it's not about what you create, it's about what you can acquire."

Jennie Livingston, who produced and directed *Paris Is Burning,* recalls meeting Dorian Corey in 1985 or 1986, just after moving to New York after graduating from Yale. She noticed the dancers in Washington Square Park and, intrigued, began to go to the balls. She began filming in 1987, in part at Dorian's apartment at 150th Street and St. Nicholas Avenue, which Livingston recalls as "quite a neighborhood": "The first shoot we did, there was a gun battle right outside. And there were crew members in the van, and they had to go down to the floor of the van so they wouldn't get caught in the crossfire." Corey moved to another apartment, ten blocks down, around 1988, and Livingston was relieved to continue her visits in less hazardous territory. "We got to be friends, and I'd go up to her place to play scrabble, which was something she liked quite a bit. She always had a TV set or two going on. She was always one of the more entertaining people I've met, she was great to hang out with."

Dorian Corey studied at the Parsons School of Design, and had a successful business as a dressmaker and costumer, selling to both the ball world and the local community. Lois Taylor, another friend, said that she was an exceptional graphic artist. In her vivid phrase, "Dorian could paint her ass off." But Corey considered herself an entertainer first, and for several years she travelled all over the country with a drag show called the Pearl Box Revue. She danced with a boa constrictor, and later regaled friends with anecdotes of the sudden moods and inconvenient deaths of the snakes. Jessie Torres, another friend, managed to communicate the impression it must have made: "It would bite her, affectionately. She was bleeding, but it was part of the act."

Dorian performed most often at Sally's II, a Times Square drag club, where she lip-synched and sometimes served as *mistress* of ceremonies. Between songs, said Livingston, she did "a great, slightly insulting sort of patter, a kind of African-American verbal eloquence with a gay camp sensibility, one-upping someone before they got you." The lush, dark satires of the forties and fifties, such as *Sunset Boulevard* and *All About Eve,* could be quoted at length, and a heckler, or someone who merely caught her eye, might be asked, "Didn't we meet last night at Rikers Island?"

Sally's is on West 43rd Street, across from the *New York Times* and next to the Hotel Carter, which advertises its $49 nightly rate as "cheaper than most cab rides." On the stairs which lead up to the bar, there is theatrical memorabilia and a program for the next week's entertainment, which features Go-Go Boys, Mother Herself Sally, and Dorian Corey's Drag Doll Revue. Around the dark, circular bar, red-lit from above, the patrons were roughly, evenly divided between drag queens and their admirers. Some queens succeeded admirably in their "realness," elegant or funky but impeccably feminine; others were aging endomorphs in helmets of platinum blonde, with gothic mascara and powder caking about the dewlaps. The sartorial males were just as diverse, a "gorgeous mosaic" sent up from central casting: a young tough in a white t-shirt and leather jacket, a classic Brooklyn cornerboy with—"Heya doin'!"—accent to match; two athletic young black men, in sweatpants and windbreakers, who looked like high school football coaches; a suited executive and a goateed bohemian; a middle-aged man with a long beard and thick glasses, in a white shirt and black gabardine suit, with an anomalous blue baseball cap: an Orthodox Jew disguised as a Mets fan, or a Mets fan disguised as an Orthodox Jew. The music was a deafening alternation between bump-and-grind disco and sentimental ballads. Whitney Houston was a favorite, as was "A Whole New World," the theme song from *Aladdin,* and perhaps Sally's as well. Below the bar is the stage, with gold tinsel on the curtain and gold glitter-dusted records suspended from the ceiling. White plastic picnic chairs line the peeling walls and surround a dozen-odd fiberboard tables. The atmosphere is both seedy and earnest, its almost comically overripe decadence undercut with an insistent, stage-struck idealism.

Raphaela, husky-voiced and Latin, with long, straight black hair and a black miniskirt, was pointed out as an old friend of Dorian's. Raphaela strutted with deceptive speed, and had finished a lap and a half around the bar before I caught up with her. A tap on the shoulder brought a sensuous, polysyllabic "Hello!" in a voice that dropped half an octave when press credentials were rapidly presented: "Oh. Sure." She knew Dorian for over ten years, and recalls her as "Fabulous!" When asked what Dorian's favorite song was, she belted out, "I ... can't stop *thinkin'* about you, baby!" The conversation ended somewhat abruptly, as Raphaela grew somewhat teary-eyed, and also attempted to frisk the interviewer, "to make sure you're not a cop."

Jessie Torres, who lived with the eponymous Sally for over ten years, now manages the club. She was a close friend of Corey, "not family, but one of *the* girls." She remembers her as prodigiously talented, kind-hearted, and engaging: "You would be somewhere serious and she would crack you up. She had the gift of the gab. She was a headliner, even before *Paris Is Burning.* She was what people came to see." Her costumes combined expert skill and extravagant fantasy, and Jessie recalls "dresses like chandeliers," centaurs, wolf-women, and Marie Antoinette, complete with guillotine. "When people come to a drag show, they don't want to see a dress that could be bought on 34th Street." Offstage, as well, Dorian could not be taken lightly: "She lived in a hardcore neighborhood, and had to take care of herself."

"There was definitely an edge, a hard edge," agreed Livingston. "The life she led was not easy although she made a great go of it, and had everything pretty well worked out, particularly compared to other people in that world. She'd survived and gone on and found a way of living the way she wanted to live. Dorian had a lot of talent and an ability to parlay her—I don't know if it's a need or a propensity, however you want to say it—she certainly wasn't transgender in a way that Venus was transgender, but to parlay her camp sensibility and her love for drag into survival. Not an easy thing to do. She was a hard person, because she'd been through some hard things, and she said a lot of nasty things behind peoples' backs—you wondered what she said about you when you left the room. That I think goes along with the wit, the picking the world apart, as a way of remaining dignified. And clear about who you are."

Who she was, originally, was Fred erick Legg, a boy raised in relative comfort on a farm outside of Buffalo. Asked if there was any contact with the Legg family, Livingston said, "Not much, not much. I think the cord had been cut. She talked about 'the farm,' and the wood stove, and the memories, because she was not originally an urban person. But she didn't talk to me about particular people, it was something she definitely put behind her. There are people who can walk on back home and say 'Hi, what do you think of my tits and my spangled gown?' And there are people who can't. Most people can't."

For the last eleven years, she lived with a man named Leon, a thirty-five year old employee of the trophy shop, which supplies awards for the balls. They met at a bar near Times Square, and moved in together not long after. In the words of one friend, they were "an unlikely couple. An odd match. But they were together, and there was a home there, and some comfort there." There was a slight tremble in Leon's voice when he spoke of Dorian, and most of his answers did not extend beyond one or two words. He recalled that her favorite singer was Eartha Kitt, but could not remember a particular song, or any jokes she told on stage. "I moved in with Dorian before my parents moved out of the city," he said. "She always helped me out when I was down and out, you know, when I needed carfare to get to work and all. I loved Dorian very much."

Dorian Corey was diagnosed with AIDS not long before the release of *Paris Is Burning,* and though she went on one last tour in the wake of publicity for the film, she was hospitalized intermittently during the three years before her death. Livingston was disturbed by the lack of visitors when she was sick, but Lois Taylor, who said she was the reigning Mother of the House of Corey, said that she wanted still less, preferring to be left alone. They agreed that her treatment at the hospital was "appalling," with the strain of terminal illness exacerbated by what they considered callous treatment by her physicians. Nor was Dorian a tractable patient. Taylor said she often had to "outslick" her just to get her to speak with her doctor. She continued to drink, and Livingston was torn between the desire to make her kick a bad habit and the wish to see her as comfortable as possible in her last days. When she asked for a prescription for tranquilizers, in the hope that Corey would switch to a less toxic balm for her nerves, she was told, "You know, that's habit-forming." A promised move to a specialized AIDS unit never materialized.

In August of 1993 she slipped into a coma and died several days later. After her cremation, a memorial service was hosted by Sally and Jessie Torres at the club. "Dorian was just there for a lot of people," said Torres. "We played a couple of songs in her honor—Patti Labelle, 'You Are My Friend,' Regina Belle, 'If I Could.' People from all over came, from all walks. She was very well-liked, and had a wit about her, a humor. She was very theatrical, she could do anything. She was a very special person, very special. Dorian was Dorian, just legendary."

Two months later, after two men expressed an interest in having a look around Dorian's apartment for Halloween costumes, Lois Taylor agreed to show them around. Taylor said that they were straight men, looking for a black cape for a vampire costume. In the closet, they came across "one of those old-time cloth bags that you put suits in and fold it over. It was dark blue with checks on it, one of those old-time bags." Taylor tried to pick it up, but was unable to: "And I couldn't, you know, because I'm only 135 pounds! And I went to lift the bag, and I couldn't! You know, because I knew Dorian had some heavy, heavy stuff up there in that closet. And I just said, 'Honey, well just go on and cut the bag.' You know what I'm saying? And he cut the bag, and he says, 'This is a lot of plastic here.' So I say, 'Maybe its one of her beaded gowns,' 'cause, I mean, she's got some tremendous beaded gowns. I didn't know what the hell was in there. So then he stuck it, and then he cut the thing, and then he says, 'There's a scent!' He says, 'I don't know. Is there a dead dog, or what?' And I said 'Dead dog!' and I ran like hell. And then, honey, he says, 'Well, I don't know what it is.' And then he identified himself as a policeman. And I says, "Ohhhh!" So he says, 'Well, I'm going to call the precinct.' And I say, 'Sure, go ahead, do it.' That's when they discovered it. I probably should have gone back there to look at it, because I would have saw something that I never would have got nowhere in my life.

"After that, they forgot about the costumes."

The news that Dorian Corey may have been in possession of a corpse for almost half her life was greeted with uniform shock. Rumors then began to spread in manner befitting a society skilled in extravagance: there was talk of a diary that explained the event, and a deathbed note. At Sally's, the doorman said, "You know they were lovers, right? He was a shady guy, used to beat her up." He then remarked that the body had been dead two or three years. When it was asserted that ten times that amount of time may have passed since the death, it did not seem to unsettle his account. Chi Chi Valenti told a tale that cast Dorian as a blend of Douglas Fairbanks and Gracie Allen, dashing but flighty, handily foiling a burglary but too busy dressing for a show to bother with the clean-up. Among her friends, an initial amazement was often followed by an avowal that whatever happened, Dorian must have been richly provoked. "God only knows what he did. Dorian never mentioned a word to me. If she did do it, he had to push her," said Lois Taylor. "The whole thing is," said Jessie, "Dorian was not a violent person but, excuse my expression, she was not going to be fucked with, either."

"I guess anyone I know could possibly be a murderer, could possibly be framed for murder," said Livingston. "I guess anyone in this city, in self-defense, could do just about anything. It struck me always as more likely that she would be framed than she would commit this murder and then carry this thing around. She always struck me as such a normal, balanced person who was in control of her life. I certainly don't remember Dorian as a perfect person, but this is beyond my picture of who she is or could have been."

"I don't know if she had a gun," she continued. "I wouldn't be surprised. I think actually that when the gun battle erupted, when we were filming in 1987, that she might have said something about having a gun. I would have had a gun if I lived in that building."

Jessie confirmed that Dorian did own a handgun. "One time she was going on stage, and she told me to hold this little evening bag," she said. "When she gave it to me, my hand went *down,* and I said, 'What the fuck do you got in here?' It was a little .22. She would have these jokes, 'Someone's gonna mess with me, I'm gonna shoot 'em up with lead.' We had a standing joke then, that the thing was rusty, and it would never work."

When a detective said that he had been told, in the course of his investigation, that Corey "had a temper when she hit the bottle," the prospects of her unblemished innocence seemed still more doubtful. One can watch *Paris Is Burning* over and over without the slightest, subtlest hint of violence in Dorian Corey, or duplicity, or fear. But she was, after all, an actress. The closest she came to what might be considered commentary on the situation is the last scene of the film, as she sits in front of the mirror, applying colors to her face: "I always had hopes of being a big star. Then I look—as you get older, you aim a little lower and you say, 'Well, you still might make an impression.' Everybody wants to leave something behind them, some impression, a mark upon the world. Then you think, you've left a mark upon the world just by getting through it. And if a few people remember your name, you've left a mark. You don't have to bend the whole world. It's better to just enjoy it. Pay your dues and enjoy it. If you shoot an arrow and it goes real high, hooray for you."

• • •

If Dorian Corey killed a man fifteen years ago, there would have been over 25,000 homicides in New York City between that time and the present. If the death was in 1968, which appears to be the better estimate, there would have been more than 40,000. In that context, the event might seem a historical curiosity, like the vanished settlers of Roanoke, an event in need of explanation, not a verdict. There is no statute of limitations for murder, however, and the police were obliged to proceed as if the crime had been committed yesterday.

They began with the elementary information: Dorian Corey moved from 150th Street to 140th Street in the late eighties, and a dead man was found in the apartment on 140th Street. These two facts bred a sizable family of possibilities, and while some were more or less likely than others, the entire episode had long departed from the realm of the probable. There was not one mystery but several, and the first—the identity of the dead man—was not the least difficult.

The photographic record of Dorian Corey is extensive, flattering, and fond, a wealth of old snapshots and glossies, and hours of documentary footage. The only known picture of the man found in her apartment is a polaroid, which has the grisly universality of a *memento mori* and the clinical circumscription of unique misfortune. The body is set against a black background, posed in half-profile, from the chest up, hunched over as if to listen closely. The complexion is purple and yellow, the nose and ears are nibs of cartilage, and a slight overbite is exaggerated by the loss of flesh. Pertinent facts are noted on an information sheet below: the body is of a black male, 5'10", 140 pounds, wearing blue and white boxer shorts. The case is one of many in a red ledger in the office of Raoul Figueroa, a licensed mortician and a detective in the Missing Persons Squad of the New York City Police Department.

[...]

"So I had to come up with something to try to be able to deal with the fingers, because of the skin, it was—we all have microorganisms, that either were near the body when he was enclosed, or on the body itself. They will eat through the skin, leaving these micro-little holes, that you can't really see but where you can't inject anything because its gonna leak out. Very slowly, but it leaks out. So there's not much you can do. If you try to put ink on that it will not adhere to the skin. It was a problem, and I ended up—I can't give away secrets because, well, it's beneficial to us to keep it more or less secret. But I worked out something, and I was able to close those holes. Then drying, which is a common-known thing with acetone and a variety of other things, drying the skin, then using a little bit of heat. You might have to soften it, put it in special liquids to soften it. And I was able to secure the print."

To do so, Figueroa put the skin on his own fingers, like a glove, over the latex gloves he wears, inked them and rolled them for the print. His success was better than he expected, and he was able to get prints from all ten fingers. A match was made with one Robert Wells, who was born in December, 1938, and arrested in the Bronx in 1963. A sister was located in Fairmont, North Carolina, who informed him that his real name was Robert Worley. Another brother, who lived in Harlem, told Figueroa that he had not seen his brother since 1968.

"He seemed like a very nice individual, very courteous, very decent," said Figueroa. "He was surprised that we found [his brother's body]. He used to live in the Bronx, he lived with him, and he disappeared. The weird thing, he was living not too far from where the body was found. He spoke with the rest of the family and he gave us permission to bury him. He says, 'We know where he's at, we know what happened to him.'"

Were it not for his arrest, there would be no useful social record of Robert Worley. Family and friends would be deprived of the consolation of at least knowing when to mourn, and why. A law-abiding citizen in a like circumstance would simply be assigned a number and put in the ground. The occasion which enabled the state to inform the Worley family of their brother's demise occurred on March 27, 1963, when he was arrested for rape.

For anyone familiar with the criminal justice system in New York City, to hear the number 347/63, and know that it refers to an April indictment in the Bronx, is to be sent into a rapture of nostalgia. 347 indictments by April suggests a rate of just over one thousand per year. In 1993, there were over 9000, and the record, set in 1990, was 10,892. In 1963, New York City was safer than it is today in most meaningful and measurable ways, with the compelling exception of sexual offenses. The abuse of children and crimes occurring within the home were rarely exposed to public view. Rape, in particular, has undergone a dramatic legal and social transformation. The entire category of acquaintance rape was virtually exempt from prosecution, and wholesale classes of victims, from prostitutes to divorcees, might not have been considered presentable to a jury. At the same time, those rapes which were prosecuted might be pursued with great vigor, especially when a woman's "virtue" as well as her body had been subject to violence and violation. In several states, generally southern ones, rape was a capital crime.

Linda Fairstein, Chief of the Sex Crimes Unit of the Manhattan District Attorney's Office, said that the most salient reform of the rape statute was the abolition, in 1972, of the corroboration requirement. Three elements of the crime had to be established independently of the claims of the victim: the identification of the assailant; the sexual nature of the offense, usually through medical evidence; and the use of force, either through visible injury or the recovery of a weapon. "If all three of those elements were not independently proved, then the case could not go forward. For example, as the *New York Times* printed in 1970, more than a 1000 men were arrested in New York City for sexual assault, and only eighteen were convicted of the crime. The overwhelming number of cases, before 1972, never got past the arrest phase."

According to court documents, Worley forced a woman into the vacant store below his apartment and raped her. It might be supposed that they were acquainted before the incident: the woman lived right around the corner from him, and the arrest occurred within hours after the crime. Worley was charged with kidnapping, assault, and having intercourse with "a female, not his wife, against her will and without her consent." The woman was employed as a nurse's aide, and she had a common English name, which makes it likely that she, too, was African-American. Worley gave his "true name" as "Robert Wells," and stated that his parents were dead, which was also false. His occupation is listed as "finisher," his race as "C" for "colored." In an affidavit, Detective Robert Rose wrote that "the defendant stated that he did perpetrate acts of sexual intercourse with the deponent at the above location. He also stated that he had been drinking wine and didn't know what happened to him." There was no record of any prior arrests. His bail was originally set at $3500 and then reduced to $1500. Three weeks after his arrest, he pleaded guilty to assault, and was sentenced to two to four years in state prison, of which, his brother recalls, he served almost the full term.

Worley was represented by the Legal Aid Society, and there are three different attorneys of record at arraignment, plea, and sentencing. None are listed in the most prominent directory of attorneys, and neither is the prosecutor and the judge. They may have retired, or they might not practice law, or they might practice, but not at a law firm. They also might be dead. According to police records, there have been two detectives named Robert Rose. One was eight years old in 1963, and the other died in 1991.

While the information in the court file is too sparse to permit all but the most speculative interpretation, Ms. Fairstein was able to offer the following observations: "A confession doesn't automatically satisfy all the requirements. It sounds like he's admitting that he's the guy, but he's not admitting force. My guess would be that it's a better case than many if it was indicted and got into the system, but it must have been lacking something for there to be that kind of plea bargain. For the time, the bail is probably high. The whole thing really depends on an evaluation of the victim and her story. Whether or not they knew each other would be an issue. Is she somebody who was drinking with him at that location? That case is more likely to be pleaded down than if they'd never seen each other before and he just pulled her off the street in his drunken state. There are too many variables missing for me to say much, but I would say that there was certainly some merit to the case and it sounds, with an assault charge, that he certainly smacked her around at some point. It might well have started—I'm guessing this because of proximity of location—as an evening drinking together, and that's why it was pled down. That's simply an educated, experienced guess."

[...]

Robert Worley is still an open case. As such, a full and frank discussion was not possible for legal reasons, as well as frequent practical ones ("Not today, I got a fresh double murder"). Roe conceded that Worley's death probably occurred not long after his disappearance, and he said that he was convinced that Dorian Corey knew of the body. To me, this knowledge strongly suggests responsibility. The theories that depend on proxies and oversights—that the body was there when she moved in, that she was "protecting" someone, and so on—began to seem desperately wishful and elaborate, although the ultimate conjecture—that Corey killed Worley, and brought the body with her when she moved—is hardly a prosaic deflation of the event. My initial guess was that it was a street pick-up that turned into a robbery attempt. Eventually, someone told me that something like that did occur, and though I found it persuasive, the information was of a piece with the rest of what I heard—speculative, sketchy, and never better than second-hand.

Jessie Torres said that in her last days, Dorian began to tell Sally about her secret, on the phone, over two or three calls. Although Sally's health was fair at the time, she would die three months after Dorian. During one such call, Sally asked Jessie to listen in on the extension. "God forgive me," said Jessie, "And may she rest in peace, I said, 'Sally, that AZT is eating that queen's mind up.' She was in a delirious situation. I said it was impossible—she lived in two different places—why would she? Girls do have a tendency to exaggerate."

Until October, all practical and reasonable belief dictated against the story, and Jessie assumed it to be a melancholy delusion. After the discovery of the body, the lesser details of the account converged in support of its implausible premise. "In Harlem there are guys that we would call take-off artists," she explained. "They would come around and just want to take from the queens the little bit you have. From what I'm told, this is the situation. He had robbed her before, from what I'd heard. He was known in the neighborhood as a junkie. If he knew you had a little bit of money, he would come around here, come around there with the attitude, 'Fuck you, you all are faggots.' Fuck you bitch! He'd take women off too. Seeing that society frowns on junkies, they feel, you know, they could frown on us. I could imagine. I have been in situations like that—guys who say, 'Go ahead, call the police, you faggot!' He had taken things from her a couple of times. One time, she was fed up. And she was not having it."

While there is no reason to dispute the sincerity of the confession, Dorian was suffering from a neurological impairment and recalling an event of perhaps twentyfive years before, an event which itself may have occurred in a chaotic instant, amid a welter of terror, fury, and dismay. The account that Jessie overheard may differ substantially from what in fact transpired. Then again, it may not. If Dorian was entirely justified in her actions, she remained a black drag queen in possession of a cadaver, and did not expect more sympathetic treatment from the police than she would from society at large. At the same time, it is unknown what force, still less lethal force, might have been called for; it is likely that her gun was unlicensed, and she may have been reluctant to call the authorities because of some additional culpability. Robert Worley's version of the incident will never be known.

The greater wonder, and one which will abide, is why she never disposed of the body. Those who understand her position are unlikely to make public their own. As a movie buff, Dorian knew that it is the rare mystery where some clue, some trick of the plot does not betray the identity of the killer. In a way, she read the situation correctly, leaving well enough alone until she was unavailable for comment. The Corey–Worley mystery ended with a twist that she could not predict, though one she would have appreciated, as shoppers in her closet wanted a vampire costume and got a mummy instead. The ironies, at least, were to her taste.

• • •

Over half a century ago, in places in the countryside to the north and the south of the city, two women held children whom they cannot have expected would ever meet. Nor could they have imagined the way each life would take shape, and were they to see photographs of their sons, one shrunken and stiff on a morgue slab, the other with breasts and a blonde wig, gyrating beneath a live boa constrictor, it would be difficult to guess which woman would be more shocked. Corey and Worley were black men without much money, close in age, who moved to New York City from rural areas. As victims of AIDS and homicide, they embody two of the main statistical bases for abbreviated life expectancy in Harlem. Worley was buried in Potter's Field, on Hart Island in the western Long Island Sound, in a common grave. Corey was cremated, and her ashes were scattered off City Island in the Bronx. The two islands are separated by half a mile of water.

There seems to be an instructive likeness between them but their moral and material resemblance is tangential, shifting. There are travels, changes of name. One was sent to prison for a crime against a woman, and the other made a living as a female impersonator. When Corey left, Worley came back. The relation is arrhythmic, oblique, like the pattern of droplets that fall from a tap. The intersection of their lives was brief, and none were aware of it until both were gone. They left behind unanswerable questions, pained and fond memories, loved ones in mourning. One left a legend; the other a child. And for worse and for better, together and apart, each made a mark upon the world.

HOW TO CLOSE THE LGBT HEALTH DISPARITIES GAP

By Jeff Krehely

SUMMARY AND INTRODUCTION

In the past decade lesbian, gay, bisexual, and transgender, or LGBT, people have made rapid progress in winning and securing equal rights. Fifteen states and Washington, D.C. now give same-sex couples at least some of the same rights afforded to heterosexual married couples. Even more states offer nondiscrimination protections based on sexual orientation, gender identity, or both. Polling data show that the general public has increasingly positive views of LGBT people and are becoming more supportive of their civil and political rights.[1] In short, heterosexual Americans are finally recognizing LGBT people as a legitimate social minority that should have equal access to our society's basic rights, opportunities, and responsibilities.

Despite this progress, however, members of the LGBT population continue to experience worse health outcomes than their heterosexual counterparts. Due to factors like low rates of health insurance coverage, high rates of stress due to systematic harassment and discrimination, and a lack of cultural competency in the health care system, LGBT people are at a higher risk for cancer, mental illnesses, and other diseases, and are more likely to smoke, drink alcohol, use drugs, and engage in other risky behaviors.

People who are both LGBT and members of a racial or ethnic minority will often face the highest level of health disparities. For example, as the National Coalition for LGBT Health notes, a black gay man faces disparities common to the African-American community as well as those suffered by the LGBT community, and a transgender Spanish-speaking woman, regardless of her sexual orientation, must navigate multiple instances of discrimination based on language, ethnicity, and gender.[2] A companion CAP brief, "How to Close the LGBT Health Disparities Gap: Disparities by Race and Ethnicity," explores these in more detail.

Health surveys cannot continue to treat populations in isolation: Members of the LGBT community who are members of other populations that are recognized as suffering from health disparities must be allowed to identify themselves fully on surveys, including their sexual orientation and gender identity.

We can only estimate the full extent of LGBT disparities due to a consistent lack of data collection on sexual orientation and gender identity. No federal health survey includes a question on sexual orientation or gender identity, and only a few states ask respondents their sexual orientation or gender identity, severely limiting researchers' ability to fully understand the LGBT population's needs and hindering the development of public policies and programs that seek to improve the LGBT population's health and well-being.

To overcome this lack of data and make it easier for researchers and advocates to get a full and accurate accounting of LGBT health outcomes and needs—and ultimately to close the gap between the health and well-being of LGBT people and the heterosexual population—the U.S. Department of Health and Human Services should establish a dedicated Office of LGBT Health. This office would take the lead in coordinating a consistent and scientifically driven response across HHS to LGBT health issues. A top priority of this office should be to ensure that any federally funded health study that collects demographic information—be it age, sex, race, ethnicity, primary language, or socioeconomic status—must also include questions about sexual orientation and gender identity.

This memo will outline the health disparities LGBT populations face, look at why these disparities occur, and examine why we need better data on these populations and what we can do to solve this problem.

Access to health care and health insurance

■ Heterosexual ■ LGB ■ Transgender

Health Disparity #1: Heterosexual adults are more likely to have health insurance coverage.[5]

% of adults with health insurance

- 82%
- 77%
- 57%

Health Disparity #2: LGB adults are more likely to delay or not seek medical care.[6]

% of adults delaying or not seeking health care

- 17%
- 29%

Health Disparity #3: LGB adults are more likely to delay or not get needed prescription medicine.[7]

% of adults delaying or not getting prescriptions

- 13%
- 22%

Health Disparity #4: LGB adults are more likely to receive health care services in emergency rooms.[8]

% of adults receiving ER care

- 18%
- 24%

Impact of societal biases on physical health and well-being

■ Heterosexual ■ LGB ■ Transgender

Health Disparity #5: Heterosexual adults are more likely to report having excellent or very good overall health.[9]

% of adults reporting excellent or very good health

- 83%
- 77%
- 67%

Health Disparity #6: Lesbian and bisexual women are less likely to receive mammograms.[10]

% of women receiving a mammogram in past 2 years

- 62%
- 57%

Health Disparity #7: LGB adults are more likely to have cancer.[11]

% of adults ever diagnosed with cancer

- 6%
- 9%

LGBT Health Disparities[3]

The right-hand columns of Pages 2, 3, and 4 show 18 data points on key LGBT health disparities. They are organized into four categories: access to health care and health insurance, impact of societal biases on physical health and well-being, impact of societal biases on mental health and well-being, and how societal biases lead to engagement in risky behavior.

The indicators show significant disparities in the mental and physical well-being of the LGBT population when compared to the heterosexual population. Members of the LGBT population are less likely to have health insurance coverage and more likely to have to resort to visiting emergency rooms for care. They also have higher rates of some diseases, lower rates of testing and screening for certain illnesses like heart disease, and higher engagement in risky behaviors that can compromise overall health or well-being, such as alcohol and tobacco use.

Many of the statistics presented are based on data collected through the California Health Interview Study, or CHIS. CHIS is one of the very few comprehensive, ongoing state-level health surveys that regularly collects information on sexual orientation. Although statistics on California's lesbian, gay, and bisexual residents cannot be generalized to the national LGB population, it is useful to analyze California since it has the largest LGB population in the United States. The Williams Institute, a think tank at the UCLA School of Law dedicated to sexual orientation law and public policy, estimates that 1.3 million LGB adults live in California, representing about 15 percent of the estimated 8.8 million LGB adults in the United States.[4]

No national government surveys include questions related to gender identity or expression. To date, Massachusetts is the only state that we found to include a question on gender identity in a government health survey. Several researchers and advocates have done surveys of local transgender populations, and we include data from their work in our review below. Many of these data points can be found in the Movement Advancement Project's "Advancing Transgender Equality" report from January 2009, which included a meta-analysis of studies on the transgender population.

CHIS collects demographic data on race and ethnicity as well as sexual orientation. This data is presented in a companion brief to this report.

Health Disparity #8: LGB youth are more likely to be threatened or injured with a weapon in school.[12]

% of youth threatened or injured with a weapon

5%
19%

Health Disparity #9: LGB youth are more likely to be in physical fights that require medical treatment.[13]

% of youth in a physical fight requiring medical treatment

4%
13%

Health Disparity #10: LGB youth are more likely to be overweight.[14]

% of youth who are overweight

6%
12%

Impact of societal biases on mental health and well-being

■ Heterosexual ■ LGB ▨ Transgender

Health Disparity #11: LGB adults are more likely to experience psychological distress.[15]

% of adults experiencing psychological distress in past year

9%
20%

Health Disparity #12: LGB adults are more likely to need medication for emotional health issues.[16]

% of adults needing medication for mental health

10%
22%

Health Disparity #13: Transgender adults are much more likely to have suicide ideation.[17]

% of adults reporting suicide ideation

2%
5%
50%

Health Disparity #14: LGB youth are much more likely to attempt suicide.[18]

% of youth reporting suicide attempts

10%
35%

Sources of LGBT Health Disparities

Negative health outcomes for LGBT people are due to the cumulative and intersecting impact of many different factors, particularly their reduced access to employer-provided health insurance, the social stigma that exists against LGBT people, and a lack of cultural competence in the health care system.

Lack of Health Insurance

LGBT people lack health insurance for several reasons. First, persistent workplace discrimination and harassment means that LGBT people are more likely to lose or quit their jobs or to not get hired in the first place.[23] A study by the National Gay and Lesbian Task Force and the National Center for Transgender Equality shows that 97 percent of transgender people report being mistreated at work because of their gender identity or expression. For example, transgender people consistently report being verbally or physically harassed, removed from direct contact with clients, or fired without cause. Because most people get their health insurance through their employers, these employment gaps also create insurance coverage gaps.

Second, many workplaces do not provide health insurance benefits for the same-sex domestic partners of their employees. Given the high cost of purchasing private individual health insurance and administrative barriers to accessing coverage, many LGBT people must go without insurance. Research shows that if all employers offered domestic partner benefits, the uninsured rates for same-sex and different-sex unmarried couples would decrease by as much as 43 percent.[24]

Third, most insurance plans do not cover the specific care that LGBT people need. Transgender individuals are often unable to access even basic preventative and primary care due to insurance exclusions. Similarly, because discriminatory health care practices lead LGBT people to either not seek preventative treatment or to receive low-quality treatment, they are more likely than others to have HIV/AIDS or certain cancers. Insurance companies almost always classify these diseases as pre-existing conditions, which means the people who have them are either ineligible for coverage or are charged exorbitant rates when they seek coverage in the non-group market.

Without insurance, people are less likely to be able to afford regular health screenings and treatment for specific health problems. Such barriers to care often delay treatment until a condition is extremely difficult or even impossible to manage or cure.

LGBT Stigma

Another reason LGBT people tend to have worse health status than heterosexuals is the social stigma around being lesbian, gay, bisexual, or transgender. Because of this stigma, LGBT people face frequent harassment and discrimination from young ages, leading to negative mental health outcomes and high rates of risk-taking that increase the likelihood of physical harm.

Impact of societal biases on engaging in risky behavior

■ Heterosexual　■ LGB　■ Transgender

Health Disparity #15: LGB adults are more likely to have problems with alcoholism.[19]

% of adults reporting alcohol abuse
- 33%
- 44%
- 24%

Health Disparity #16: LGB adults are more likely to smoke cigarettes.[20]

% of adults who smoke
- 16%
- 27%
- 15%

Health Disparity #17: LGB youth are more likely to smoke cigarettes.[21]

% of youth who smoke
- 14%
- 38%

Health Disparity #18: LGB youth are more likely to take risks in automobiles.[22]

% of youth who rarely or never wear seatbelts
- 5%
- 14%

% of youth who have ridden with a driver who had been drinking
- 24%
- 37%

% of youth who drove after drinking
- 11%
- 26%

For example, the Family Acceptance Project's research shows that "adverse, punitive, and traumatic reactions from parents and caregivers in response to their children's LGB identity" is closely correlated with LGB youth having poor mental health and an increase in substance abuse.[25] To cope with stress and discrimination, some LGBT people turn to "self-medication," resulting in higher rates of tobacco, drug, and alcohol use compared to the heterosexual population. Moreover, given that LGBT people often do not want to disclose their sexual orientation or gender identity in health care settings for fear of discrimination and provider bias, they are less likely to seek timely treatment.

Lack of Competent Care

Given the social stigma that leads members of the LGBT population to not disclose their minority status to health care providers, doctors and others are often unaware of their LGBT patients' specific needs. This ignorance results in conditions going undiagnosed as well as doctors being unable to educate their patients about risky behaviors or other physical or mental health concerns. Furthermore, many LGBT people face outright hostility from their health care providers. One of the few existing studies of the transgender community shows that up to 39 percent of all transgender people face some type of harassment or discrimination when seeking routine health care.[26]

Similarly, a general lack of data on LGBT people makes it difficult for doctors and other health care providers to learn about the LGBT population's needs. This lack of information and data is reflected by the fact that most medical schools do not offer any coursework or instruction on the health needs of LGBT people. For example, researchers have found that over half of medical school curricula include no information about gay and lesbian people.[27] Programs in public health schools are also unlikely to include such information beyond work related to HIV/AIDS.[28]

This exclusion from curricula and trainings matters: Students with exposure to lesbian, gay, bisexual, or transgender patients are more likely to perform more comprehensive patient histories, hold more positive attitudes toward LGBT patients, and possess greater knowledge of LGBT health care concerns.[29] All of these factors strongly contribute to better care and improved health outcomes for LGBT people.

This connection between training and actual practice—and the fact that many medical and health care students receive little exposure to LGBT issues—means that many doctors, nurses, therapists, and other health professionals are unable to meet the needs of LGBT patients. It is also highly unlikely that these caregivers create an atmosphere that makes LGBT people feel comfortable disclosing their sexual orientations or gender identities. Without a clear signal from a doctor or other health care professional that he or she is comfortable treating an LGBT person, for example by having "partner's name" instead of "spouse's name" on intake forms, many members of the community will not feel safe "outing" themselves, leaving health care providers with inadequate information and preventing LGBT individuals from getting the treatment that they need.

We Need More Comprehensive Data on LGBT Health

Many of the data points shown earlier are from convenience samples of LGBT people in specific states or cities. Overall, current data and information on LGBT health can best be described as a loosely knit patchwork that often raises more questions than it answers. Fundamentally, despite the recent inclusion of sexual orientation and gender identity on a handful of state health surveys, significant gaps still exist in our knowledge of LGBT people's health status and health care needs.

HOW TO CLOSE THE LGBT HEALTH DISPARITIES GAP: DISPARITIES BY RACE AND ETHNICITY

By Jeff Krehely

INTRODUCTION AND SUMMARY

The original "How to Close the LGBT Health Disparities Gap" demonstrated that significant health disparities exist between lesbian, gay, bisexual, and transgender, or LGBT, and heterosexual populations. This brief will examine how health disparities for LGB people vary among different racial and ethnic groups. (The data analyzed do not include gender identity variables, so the "T" is excluded from most instances of the "LGBT" acronym in this report.) It finds that a person's race or ethnicity and their sexual orientation are important factors for health policy researchers and advocates to consider when conducting their work.

Unfortunately, very few representative health-related surveys ask questions about a person's sexual orientation in addition to race or ethnicity. No surveys ask similar questions about gender identity. This lack of data severely hampers efforts to design and implement programs that would best and most effectively serve all LGBT populations.

The Center for American Progress therefore calls on the U.S. Department of Health and Human Services, or HHS, to establish an Office of LGBT Health and to collect data on sexual orientation and gender identity in any federally funded health research. HHS already collects data based on race and ethnicity—adding sexual orientation and gender identity to the demographic data collected would improve our nation's ability to serve LGBT people of all races and ethnicities.

This memo will outline LGB health disparities by race and ethnicity before discussing why these disparities occur, why we need better data on these populations, and why creating an Office of LGBT Health in the Department of Health and Human Services would be an effective way to address the problem.

LGB Health Disparities by Race and Ethnicity[1]

The right-hand columns of Pages 2 and 3 present eight data points on health disparities for LGB people across different races and ethnicities.[2] The statistics are based on data collected through the California Health Interview Study, or CHIS. CHIS is one of the few comprehensive, ongoing state-level health survey that regularly collects information on sexual orientation. Although statistics on California's LGB residents cannot be generalized to the national LGB population, it is useful to analyze California since it has the largest LGB population in the United States. The Williams Institute—a think tank at the UCLA School of Law dedicated to sexual orientation law and public policy—estimates that 1.3 million LGB adults live in California, representing about 15 percent of the estimated 8.8 million LGB adults in the United States.[3] Unfortunately, CHIS does not currently collect data on gender identity.

Source of Health Disparities

The companion piece to this brief shows that the cumulative and intersecting impact of three main factors contributes to significant negative health outcomes for LGBT people: their reduced access to employer-provided health insurance, the social stigma that exists against LGBT people, and a lack of cultural competency in the health care system. For people of color, a lack of affordable health care and insurance and culturally competent service providers—along with persistent racism in society—are some of the largest causes of health disparities.[13] An LGBT person of color faces the combined impact of these barriers, increasing the likelihood of negative health outcomes.[14]

- ■ African-American heterosexual
- ■ Asian or Pacific Islander heterosexual
- ■ Latino heterosexual
- ■ White heterosexual
- ■ African-American LGB
- ■ Asian or Pacific Islander LGB
- ■ Latino LGB
- ■ White LGB

Health Disparity #1: LGB Latino adults are least likely to have health insurance.[4]

% of adults with health insurance

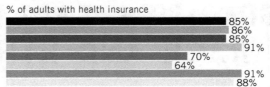

85%
86%
85%
91%
70%
64%
91%
88%

Health Disparity #2: White, African-American, and Latino LGB adults are most likely to delay or not seek health care.[5]

% of adults delaying or not seeking health care

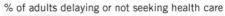

21%
29%
12%
22%
13%
28%
21%
31%

Health Disparity #3: LGB African-American adults are most likely to delay or not get needed prescription medicine.[6]

% of adults delaying or not getting prescriptions

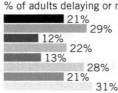

19%
30%
8%
9%
10%
23%
15%
21%

Health Disparity #4: LGB Latino adults are least likely to have a regular source for basic healthcare.[7]

% of adults not having regular health care source

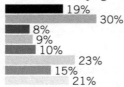

9%
12%
n/a[8]
14%
23%
26%
9%
12%

Health Disparities Among Transgender People of Color

While there is almost no data about the health disparities faced by transgender people of color, the combined impacts of racism and transphobia undoubtedly lead to worse health outcomes. The few statistics that do exist around the health disparities faced by transgender people focus almost exclusively on transgender women and incidence of HIV/AIDS.

These statistics show drastically high rates of HIV/AIDS among transgender women. In California, for example, publicly funded counseling and testing sites report that transgender women have higher rates of HIV diagnosis (6 percent) than all other risk categories, including men who have sex with men (4 percent) and partners of people living with HIV (5 percent). African-American transgender women have a substantially higher rate of HIV diagnosis (29 percent) than all other racial or ethnic groups.[15] In addition, according to a 2008 Minority Council report on AIDS, nearly 57 percent of all HIV-positive transgender women are African American.[16] For both transgender and LGB people of color, data collection is a matter of life and death: It is impossible to improve the health and well-being of LGBT people of color without the understanding and prioritization that comes with enhanced data collection

We Need More Comprehensive Data on LGBT Health Disparities

The CHIS statistics above are based on one of the few government public health surveys in the United States that regularly asks questions about sexual orientation. Much of the research to date on LGBT health issues has focused on sexually transmitted diseases—including HIV/AIDS—and has neglected to study other health concerns, such as the importance of mammograms for lesbians and bisexual women or how high rates of harassment affect the mental health of LGBT youth.

Health Disparity #5: LGB African-American women are the least likely to have had a mammogram in the past two years.[9]

% of women receiving a mammogram in past two years

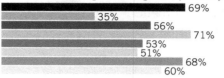

Health Disparity #6: LGB African-American adults are most likely to have diabetes.[10]

% of adults with diabetes

Health Disparity #7: LGB Asian or Pacific Islander adults are most likely to experience psychological distress.[11]

% of adults experiencing psychological distress in past year

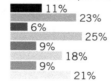

Health Disparity #8: LGB Latino adults are much more likely to abuse alcohol.[12]

% of adults reporting alcohol abuse

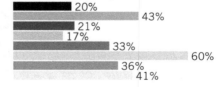

For example, a review of 3.8 million citations of articles in the National Library of Medicine published between 1980 and 1999 found that just 3,800 (0.1 percent) related to LGBT issues. Of these articles 2,300 (61 percent) were disease specific, with a focus on sexually transmitted diseases, mostly HIV/AIDS. Moreover, 85 percent of the articles failed to include any mention of the racial or ethnic background of the individuals studied.[17]

Recommendations

As proposed in the original "How to Close the LGBT Health Disparities Gap," the U.S. Department of Health and Human Services should establish an Office of LGBT Health. This office would take the lead in coordinating a consistent and scientifically driven response across HHS to LGBT health disparities and overall health care for people in these populations.

The office should first act to ensure that any federally funded health study that collects demographic information—on age, sex, race, ethnicity, primary language, or socioeconomic status—must also include questions about sexual orientation and gender identity.

THREADS OF COMMONALITY IN TRANSGENDER AND DISABILITY STUDIES

By Ashley Mog

The button pictured above says: "Crips & Trannies Need to Pee Too" (Koyama et al.). I originally learned about this button from a zine called *Restricted!! Voices on Disability and Sexuality*. Created in Bowling Green, Ohio in 2005, the zine contains twelve essays from people who are queer or transgender and have disabilities. This button is simultaneously catchy, funny, and thought-provoking by pointing to something quite everyday, using the bathroom, as a site where people whose bodies differ in some way from the norm are often excluded. Bathrooms are segregated by binary gender, and unless otherwise marked, are often inaccessible because of the gender designation or because the space is not large enough to accommodate different bodies. In addition to the physical barriers, limited bathroom options for people with disabilities and transgender people does discursive violence by not acknowledging the existence of disabled and transgender people. Public bathrooms are just one of the sites where transgender and disability meet, and activists communities are making connections already, such as the safe2pee website (*safe2pee*), which contains interactive maps of accessible bathrooms all over the United States, Mexico, and Canada.

This paper discusses some of the other important ways that transgender and disability issues overlap and intersect in academic and non-academic communities. I came to this topic because I have been heavily involved in transgender and disability activism and communities in my undergraduate career at the University of Washington. I identify as queer and I have a psychiatric disability, so these issues are personal and academic interests of mine. I have been involved in activism around trans-inclusive healthcare and gender neutral bathrooms. In the gender neutral bathroom activism I have participated in, we made connections between bathrooms that are physically accessible for people with disabilities and bathrooms that are accessible for people with a wide variety of gender identities. My own activism and connections to activists who are working on these issues helped inform how I wanted to approach the topic of intersectionality.

Scant published work specifically addresses the connections between transgender and disability studies. The limited scholarship on this connection concerns disability and sexual queerness, in a broad sense. Robert McRuer's book, *Crip Theory: Cultural Signs of Queerness and Disability*, begins to address the intersections between queer theory and disability studies, and he uses concepts such as Judith Butler's "performativity" and Adrienne Rich's "compulsory heterosexuality." Eli Clare's book, *Exile and Pride: Disability, Queerness, and Liberation*, also discusses intersections between queerness and disability. Clare writes about transgender people; however, the focus of this piece involves broader understandings of "queer" and intersectionality among a myriad of identities. My aim is to specifically address transgender and disability studies together in a way that has not been done before.

To explore the intersections between transgender studies and disability studies, I begin with a discussion of the terms I am going to use for my analysis, including how I will define "transgender" and "disability" and how I will use works that talk about queerness and disabilities. The next two sections are about medical and societal systems that strive to normalize people with disabilities and transgender people. I focus on medical systems, social institutions, and passing because these mechanisms are used to punish embodied difference in a broad sense. In the two sections that follow, I talk about community-level intersections between transgender and disability communities around hierarchies, labeling, communities, and coalitions. These connections are important to examine because of the potential for social change exemplified within building ties across communities. By understanding the ways transgender studies and disability studies intersect, we can have a deeper understanding of both fields and recognize the potential for changing inaccessible societal systems.

Thoughts on Terminology and Existing Fields

Terminology is a critical concern for both transgender and disability communities because naming indicates operations of power. Historically in the West, people with disabilities and transgender people have rarely been able to name themselves. I am using the word "transgender" as an umbrella term to talk about transsexuals, genderqueers, intersexuals, and other people who do not fit into a traditional gender binary. I define "disability" as an umbrella term to talk about people with mobility, psychiatric, learning, developmental, and sensory disabilities. These terms are both community/self-defined, as well as legally defined in some cases. I will go more into the meanings, histories, and ideas that shape use of terms later in this paper.

I am going to be using person-first language in order to avoid labeling a group of people solely based upon their disabilities. In *Claiming Disability*, Simi Linton discusses language which has been used to talk about people with disabilities and how it has been harmful and claimed as a site of resistance. The disability community has begun to take control of the words that have been used to describe disability and disabled people, both the words that name oppression and name groups. The words used to describe disability have been and are still used to mark a medicalized label, but they also name an identity and provide a rallying point for activism and a collective group. Linton calls for people to talk about their disabilities; to move beyond the shame and fear, to make the personal political.

While "queer" has functioned as an umbrella term, it is this precise function that can exclude people who are supposed to be "covered" under the umbrella for the sake of a singular unity. Judith Butler discusses this issue in *Bodies That Matter* when she states, "[A]s expansive as the term 'queer' is meant to be, it is used in ways that enforce a set of overlapping divisions" (228).

Butler points out that "queer" aims to cover many groups of diverse people and because of the massive tasks involved in doing that, there are always going to be problems. This is not to say that "queer" should be eliminated altogether; however, we have to recognize the limits of the term in its current usage.

Queer studies addresses the materiality and corporeality of sexuality; however, it does not do an adequate job of analyzing the ways in which this is informed by, and intersects with, gender's corporeality. Transgender studies emerged, in part, because "queer" and queer studies have been unable to fully address the issues involved in looking critically at transgender experiences. Susan Stryker refers to transgender studies as queer theory's "evil twin" to explain similarities and differences between the two. She states that "'transgender' increasingly functions as the site in which to contain all gender trouble, thereby helping secure homosexuality and heterosexuality as stable and normative categories of personhood" because they are still bound up in binary gender (214). She argues that queer theorists often use transgender identities to legitimize their own aims, either by claiming trans people as a part of a "cohesive" queer community or by using trans identities as the measure of abnormality. (For more on this, see Namaste; Jagose).

Transgender studies, much like disability studies, works with the lived bodily experiences of people who fit outside of hegemonic gender norms and the ways in which people negotiate corporeal experiences that run up against societal barriers that only privilege certain bodies. Transsexuality is often thought of as a primarily bodily experience because of its association with changing bodies, despite transsexuals' broader definitions (Bornstein 8). Specifically, because transsexuality is seen as pathological (e.g. "Gender Identity Disorder," as cited in the DSM IV), and other queer identities are most often not anymore, transsexuals' stories do not fit under dominant representations of "queer." Trans (short for transgender) identities are used to talk about the ways in which queer identities intersect with gender, while de-emphasizing the specifically physical aspects of talking about who are considered "men" and "women." Similar to the uses of disability, the word "transgender" is a result of claiming an identity and has been used to talk about a large group of people. The word "transgender" is a fairly new term "that emerged in its current usage as a collective category of personhood in the early 1990s," developing from activism in New York and San Francisco (Valentine 229-230). People with various trans identities can and do use the word and concept of "transgender" to bind together and have more political power.

I am not arguing that queer theory is not trying to be inclusive or is always delegitimizing transgender identities. But a more comprehensive understanding of gender identities must be taken up if the word "queer" is to fully represent trans identities. This issue is important to my work because a good deal of the scholarship I have referenced here that involves intersectionality uses the word "queer" in making connections to disability. However, a connection that is necessary to make between transgender studies and disability studies is the specific corporality and marked bodies of people in these categories, and how such bodies function in medical, societal, and community spheres.

The Medical Model and Institutionalization of Identity

People within disability and transgender communities share histories of medicalization and institutionalization, and the medical model of disability can serve as a jumping-off point for a discussion of medicalization. The medical model of disability states that disability is a purely medical affliction, and "this model defines disability as a personal problem, curable and/or treatable by the medical establishment" (Clare *Exile* 81). The "problem" of such bodily difference lies solely with the individual person, as though it is an intrinsic characteristic of the person. The medical model of disability asserts that a "cure" would make the person's body "normal." In *Exploring Disability*, Colin Barnes, Geof Mercer, and Tom Shakespeare suggest that the discourses behind the medical model of disability came out of nineteenth century's advancements in "the scientific medical profession" after large-scale industrialization (19). Lennard Davis further explains that because of the medical profession's ascendancy during this time, the goals of "curing" and determining how to make the human body function in an optimal way were privileged, hand in hand with the rise of the eugenics movement and efforts to do away with difference that was outside of the average (13). Such ideas have persisted into the twenty-first century.

Medical documentation is central to the medical model of disability. Dean Spade, who is a lawyer and activist, articulates the ways transsexual people navigate the law in order to receive medical treatment, and he points out that no matter the subject of a legal case, "medical evidence will be the cornerstone" of determining the rights of the trans person because of the ways trans bodies have been medicalized (18). There is significant overlap between trans and disability studies relating to documentation, investment in normality, and the ties between disability law and transsexuality. For instance, as Dean Spade points out, medical documentation is necessary in order to be recognized as a transsexual. To obtain this, one needs to have a "transsexual story," a need to change one's body, and what are called "real feelings" (Spade 19). Whether a person wants to change one's own body or not, a medical diagnosis is necessary to access the category of transsexual, thus making transsexuality something that is pathological—a personal difficulty of the individual and not something to be accounted for in society. This is also true for disabled students accessing services for academic accommodations in schools. In order to receive extra time for tests or note-takers, one must have a medical diagnosis (for which students must usually pay themselves) to register with the disability services office at their school. Disability is made into a medical diagnosis in this instance, much like transsexuality is pathologized in order for individuals to access services.

Images of people whose bodies fall outside of a constructed norm—whether that be social gender, medically-defined sex, and/or disability—are often employed in an effort to create a picture of what is and is not considered a medical condition. Visual representations of medicalized bodies in textbooks, both of disabled people and transgender people, help to create a specific paradigm within the medical field, "to locate the sight/site of deviance on the bodies of a wide array of social outcasts" (Singer 601). The obsession with locating and photographing what qualities the "social outcasts" embody and finding ways to eradicate or normalize these bodies has roots in eugenics. Images of "abnormal" bodies help uphold ideas of what "normal" bodies look like; they provide a point of comparison. Author Ben Singer analyzes older medical images of intersex and transgender people that represent the ways bodies have been pathologized and the ways in which different bodies have been represented as freakish or abnormal. These clinical photographs are taken in a way that showcases bodies and dehumanizes the actual people in them. For instance, many of the photos show people's bodies and a bar across their eyes, and the subsequent dehumanization of people creates a context where disrespect and discrimination are permissible. Singer juxtaposes medical photos with pictures taken by transgender and intersexual people as a reclamation of their bodies, including photographs of people with physical disabilities (Cameron). By taking their own pictures and displaying them in a different context, the trans, intersexual, and disabled people pictured reclaim their bodies from the medical context in which they have been historically placed and demonstrate that having a variation of bodies is not "wrong" or something to be "fixed."

The issue is not that intersexuals, people with disabilities, or trans people are not "natural"; the issue is that these people and their bodies are seen as threatening to dominant cultural ideals (Kessler 25). Medical systems focused on "fixing" what is "wrong" with non-normative bodies have existed for so long that binary assumptions take precedence over the realities of human variation. Because of bodily difference, these differences are seen as a medical condition that can be "fixed" or altered in order to normalize bodies. Despite this common assumption, those who are being medicalized find ways to exercise forms of resistance.

Societal Perceptions: Passing and "Compulsory Able-Bodiedness"

The social implications of disability and of being transgender result in innumerable social barriers. Disability has been historically seen as a deficit of the individual, as "there remains the persistent belief that the cause of social disadvantage is within individuals and that change is based on personal transformation" (Linton 143). Historically, this has also been the case for queer people, and as I will argue, for people who fall under the transgender umbrella. The dominant sentiment is that if you just try hard enough, you can overcome having a disability or you can be gender normative, with the assumption being that this is the "natural" and "right" way to be. In this section, I address passing and the concept of "compulsory able-bodiedness" because they provide excellent frameworks for thinking about the drive to subscribe to bodily norms. Indeed, passing is often the manifestation of the stronghold "compulsory able-bodiedness" has in the world.

Passing is encouraged when society does not easily accept difference, and it consists of being able to succeed in being perceived as part of the dominant group and therefore not noticed most of the time. For people with disabilities this typically consists of passing for non-disabled, and for trans people it means passing for normatively-gendered. Jamison Green talks about some  of the issues surrounding passing within female-to-male transsexual communities; he says in order to be considered a "successful" transsexual, you must appear to not be transsexual at all ("Look" 501). When he began to pass completely as a man, he would give lectures and people would marvel at how "normal" he is; however, on the other hand, the news media reporting on transsexuals would have less interest in him because he doesn't "look like a transsexual" ("Look" 502). As Green says:

> Denying our transsexual status is an acquiescence to the prevailing gender binary that will never let us fit in, and will never accept us as equal members of society. Our transsexual status will always be used to threaten and shame us. ("Look" 503)
>
> Green is reminding us that even when one can pass as something, there is always a risk that trans histories, which sometimes have nothing to do with self-identification, will be found out and the person will lose acceptance.

Simi Linton similarly talks about passing in regard to able-bodiedness and how children who use wheelchairs are often taken out of them for family photographs, while other children with invisible disabilities are told not to discuss them (20). She says that the message in this practice is that "you are like everyone else, but only as long as you hide your disability" (21).

Passing as non-disabled takes an emotional toll on the person passing, because it requires not talking about a critical part of themselves. This can be compared to the ways going stealth[1] as a transsexual means not talking about your past and transition. Also, it means that there is a piece of information that could possibly be used to shame an individual—being trans or being disabled. The shame, however, comes from the fact that disabled bodies and transgender bodies are devalued and are considered a deficit of the person. If the individual is the source of the difference that is regarded as undesirable, then passing as someone who does not have the difference is understood as the best way to deal with this situation. The existence of people with disabilities poses a threat to normative bodies because they are exposing the ways in which society produces social structures around one type of bodily ability while others are devalued.

Robert McRuer analyzes the intersections between disability and sexuality by posing a theory of "compulsory able-bodiedness" (8), building on Adrienne Rich's theory of "compulsory heterosexuality," and both relate to ideas about passing. "Compulsory heterosexuality" explores the sexuality of women and how society's expectations of heterosexuality serve to stigmatize and erase lesbian identity (Rich 229). McRuer explains "compulsory able-bodiedness" as the idea that the "natural" way for bodies to be is non-disabled and that one can "choose" this way of being. There is an implication that if you are disabled, you would rather not be disabled, and that "able-bodied identities, able-bodied perspectives are preferable and what we all, collectively, are aiming for" (9). In other words, you are always failing to be what you "should" be if you are a person with a disability. Both the concepts of "compulsory heterosexuality" and "compulsory able-bodiedness" speak to a culture that mourns the loss of the illusion of "natural," "normal" bodies. Difference in gender and ability are "natural" because so many people embody those differences; however, what is constructed as "natural" does not often match up with those differences. The idea behind Rich's and McRuer's use of "compulsory" is that ability, heterosexuality, and (in my analysis) gender roles, are obligatory, necessary, and carry punitive consequences if breached. Punishment in this sense means denied access to buildings, medical care, or full participation in society.

McRuer's critical and related concept of "ability trouble" (10) draws on Judith Butler's concept of "gender trouble." "Ability trouble" explores the ways in which disability challenges ideas about bodies and ability, much like the existence of drag and queerness poses a threat to gender normativity in Butler's work. Compulsory heterosexuality/compulsory able-bodiedness and gender/ability trouble can be extrapolated to think about trans identities as well. The loss of the idea that gender is a given natural is similar to the loss that being disabled invokes in a society that naturalizes able-bodiedness. When a person does not fulfill the expectations based on that person's assigned sex at birth, it is often considered a tragedy or a problem. Underlying this is the assumption that everyone "wants" to be normatively gendered, that this is the way to happily exist in the world.

Falling outside of societal norms of embodiment often results in an individualization of societal oppression: the individual is the source of the problem because of a personal deficiency and because they are not trying hard enough to eradicate the problem, which implies that society has nothing to do with oppression. Passing for a member of a dominant group in society is an example of this and leads to such questions as: Wouldn't you rather be normal? Being normal is the right way to be, wouldn't you choose it? These questions imply there is nothing positive or useful in falling outside of the norm; however, in reality, many people fall outside of the norm and find ways to reclaim and celebrate their positions in society.

Social Model, Hierarchy, and Social Change

The social model of disability explains that the societal barriers that people with disabilities face are not individual but are actually a result of artificial barriers that privilege certain bodies while failing to recognize others as legitimate. Eli Clare defines the social model of disability as "disability, not defined by our bodies, but rather by the material and social conditions of ableism" (*Exile* 60). Saying "artificial" here is not to say that these barriers are not real; it means that the barriers were socially constructed but have material effects. As in the case of societal ableism, barriers that trans people face, such as not having a safe bathroom to use, are not a result of the trans person being deficient in some way but are barriers created by society. The social model is a useful tool to analyze hierarchies within communities and the labels groups of people use for collective activity.

A way to define people is through individual and group identities in social contexts. Both "transgender" and "disabled" function as umbrella terms that are meant to encompass or cover many people with varying identities, but as a result, there are divisions within communities because it often proves difficult to serve the needs of everyone within a community with one term/concept. "Transgender" can mean transsexuals, gender queers, intersexuals, drag kings and queens, cross dressers, and many more (Green "Introduction" 3).[2] There are several similarities between people classified as "transgender," being groups that call into question the naturalization of binary gender and sex, and therefore, there are many connections to be made. That being said, the groups of people listed to be covered under the term "transgender" are quite diverse in experiences and therefore are not always united under a common goal. Divisions like this can make a cohesive community identity difficult to form.

Within trans and disability communities, there are also hierarchies of identifications. Kate Bornstein speaks of "an unspoken hierarchy" (67) that happens within groups of male-to-female transsexuals that creates situations where people feel like they are not "trans" enough because of lack of surgeries or hormones. This hierarchy reinforces other lines of oppression as well, such as race and class, with white transsexuals often at the top. Because of these hierarchies, collective organizing becomes a difficult task. Similar trends can be found among people with disabilities. While there is a specific legal code for how to define "disability" in terms of effect on one's life and impairment, disability also functions as an identity category and can encompass wheelchair users, people who are D/deaf,[3] people who are blind, people with autism, developmentally disabled people, and many more. Within the legal code, there are guidelines one must meet to be considered "disabled enough" to access services under the Americans with Disabilities Act. This legal definition of disability is used for purposes such as employment and academic accommodations in school, and it gives a way to talk about disability for purposes of legal and civil rights. There are limits to its efficacy, however, as it relies on medical documentation and the idea of disability as lack.

Within disability studies there are hierarchies as well—much of the scholarship in disability studies thus far has been produced by white males who have mobility impairments (e.g. Hockenberry). Also, some people within disability communities seek to legitimize their aims by stating the ways they are not like or are above other members of the disability community. For example, in the 2005 documentary *Murderball*, which follows a wheelchair rugby team going to the Paralympics, one of the members of the rugby team talks about how he wants wheelchair rugby to be considered and respected as a competitive sport. He says, "This is a real competition, it isn't the Special Olympics," thereby delegitimizing the Special Olympics.[4] Such divisions can make forming a cohesive community of people with disabilities difficult.

Social models of identity are not only about refuting medical perspectives, but are also about celebrating diversity and making social change, both of which require alliances. Political expediency, which involves leaving people out of a social movement with promises to fight for that group's rights later, often leaves disenfranchised groups to fight for their own rights. This exclusion has been an attribute of many social movements, such as second wave United States feminism, where white women excluded concerns about racism within the women's movement in order to facilitate a "unified" front of homogenized women, which alienated women of color from the movement (Hill Collins 14). The act of dividing up groups of women created a weaker movement, and "experience has shown that nothing is more destructive of efforts to win civil rights protections for our communities than internal conflicts and divisions" (Green 51). "Internal conflicts and divisions" are issues in transgender communities and disability communities as well. Examples of political expediency surrounding these issues can be seen in recent proposed legislation as well as in past civil rights movements.

Divisions in the face of political pressure are exemplified by the Employment Nondiscrimination Act (ENDA), where transgender people were excluded from the official bill presented to Congress. The "T" of GLBT was taken off of ENDA because it was thought to be too risky in getting the bill to pass. Congressman Barney Frank and the Human Rights Campaign (HRC) were big proponents of this exclusion as they saw this reframing as a way to make the bill more marketable. However, 350 national queer organizations opposed the exclusion of gender identity from the bill in an act of solidarity with trans communities (*National*). When looking at the legal rights already won for GLBT people in the United States, Jamison Green points out that there has been no evidence that excluding transgender people makes a bill proposal more easily passable; he states that "civil rights for trans people have been won in a broad range of local jurisdictions [...] particularly when GLBT advocates present a united front and work together to plan and implement a coordinated strategy" ("Introduction" 51).

Much like transgender people being pushed to the margins of social movements, people with disabilities have also been marginalized. Several social movements have gained their salience by claiming that they are not disabled. As historian Douglas Baynton argues, "[D]isability has been used as the defining tenet in denying people rights to citizenship and participation in society, disability has functioned for all such groups as a sign of and justification for inequality" (34). Baynton argues that African Americans were considered best suited for slavery because they did not have the capacity to be independent, and that "African Americans were often lumped with the 'defective,' 'delinquent,' and dependent classes" (41)—and all such features are linked to the assumed negative of disability. As Baynton notes, people within movements fighting for civil rights had to separate themselves from the image of being disabled, and this separation did not challenge the oppressive structures behind discrimination based upon disability but occurred because of the stigma attached to being classified as having a disability (51). Challenging hierarchies around privileged bodies, whether for disability or non-normative gender expression, is the way to making real change, instead of dividing communities for the sake of the rights of one group within the community.

While creating distance between groups for the sake of social change has been and still is a part of the way many movements work, there are always instances where successful coalitions are formed. In my experience of working in coalitions between groups of people, one of the biggest advantages is in strength in numbers. For example, during the University of Washington's annual Transgender Awareness Week over the last three years, we worked on making many of the events marketable to a diverse group of people. One way we did this was having sponsorship from the diversity commission for disabilities sponsor events. In the campaign for more gender neutral bathrooms, the uniting issue is access to a public bathroom. The details of access issues for people with disabilities and transgender people differ in some significant ways in terms of spatial room versus gendered markings. However, the issue of inaccessibility based on embodied difference is the important one that creates a point for uniting to change.

Conclusion

In doing any type of intersectional academic work, it is important to acknowledge that while connections can be drawn, some of the specific facets are not the same in the comparison of two subjects. As Eli Clare notes, "[S]ystems of oppression work through similar mechanisms, but the details differ" ("Gaping"). The interconnections I developed in this paper between transgender and disability are meant to be a way to think about coalition-building and framing similarities. I draw attention to and actually name what I would consider to be an organic relationship between two groups. While containing many different people, these groups can be thought of in similar ways because of similar threads of oppression.

Issues of embodied difference cut across many lines of identification and social classification and have implications for those bodies not privileged as "normal." These implications include lower employment rates, inaccessible social institutions and public spaces, civil rights, and social stigma, among many other things. None of these points are new. Many scholars and activists have argued about the importance of investigating these forms of discrimination; my contribution here is to begin to show how connections among these implications play out in transgender communities and in disability communities, although further analysis is necessary. Another example is the emerging transability movement, people who "want to become disabled" (http://www.transabled.org), which is a site where issues about changing bodies and societal norms from disability studies and transgender studies meet. Because of stigma around having a disability, being a transabled person is particularly contentious. This movement could certainly be used to demonstrate further connections between transgender and disability communities.

Both transgender studies and disability studies are becoming more widely studied within universities in the United States. As disability studies and transgender studies grow larger and find more space within academia, attention to the similarities among those and other movements for social change will help facilitate deeper analyses of the workings of oppression as well as means for achieving socio-political change. While in activist circles, coalitions between disability and transgender communities are facilitated all of the time (gender neutral bathroom activism being one of the examples), academia has yet to explore the potentially powerful change connections like this can make.

Works Cited

2009 World Games. "FAQs: How are the Special Olympics Different Than the Paralympics?" 7 June 2008 <http://www.2009worldgames.org/Mission/FAQs>.

Barnes, Colin, Geof Mercer, and Tom Shakespeare. *Exploring Disability: A Sociological Introduction*. Malden, Mass: Polity Press, 1999.

Baynton, Douglas. "Disability and the Justification of Inequality in American History." *The New Disability History: American Perspectives*. Eds. Paul K. Longmore and Lauri Umansky. New York: New York University Press, 2001. 33–53.

Bornstein, Kate. *Gender Outlaw: On Men, Women, and the Rest of Us*. New York: Vintage Books, 1995.

Brueggemann, Brenda Jo. *Lend Me Your Ear: Rhetorical Constructions of Deafness*. Washington D.C.: Gallaudet UP, 1999.

Butler, Judith. *Bodies that Matter*. New York and London: Routledge, 1993.

Cameron, Loren. *Body Alchemy: Transsexual Portraits*. Pittsburgh: Cleis Press, 1996.

Clare, Eli. *Exile and Pride: Disability, Queerness, and Liberation*. Cambridge: South End P, 1999.

—. "Gaping, Gawking, Staring: Living in Marked Bodies." DASA. Eli Clare Public Lecture. University of Washington, Seattle. 10 June 2008.

Davis, Lennard J. "Constructing Normalcy: The Bell Curve, the Novel, and the Invention of the Disabled Body in the Nineteenth Century." *The Disability Studies Reader*. Ed. Lennard Davis. New York: Routledge, 1997. 1–28.

Green, Jamison. "Introduction to Transgender Issues." *Transgender Equality: a Handbook for Activists and Policymakers*. Eds. Paisley Currah and Shannon Miller. New York and San Francisco: National Center for Lesbian Rights and the NGLTF Institute, 2000. 1–12.

—. "Look! No, Don't! The Visibility Dilemma for Transsexual Men." *The Transgender Studies Reader*. Eds. Susan Stryker and Stephen Whittle. New York: Routledge, 2006. 499–508.

Hill Collins, Patricia. *Black Feminist Thought: Knowledge, Consciousness, and the Politics of Empowerment*. 2nd ed. New York: Routledge, 2000.

Hockenberry, John. *Moving Violations: War Zones, Wheelchairs, and Declarations of Independence*. New York: Hyperion, 1995.

Jagose, Annamarie. "Queer Theory." *New Dictionary of the History of Ideas*. Ed. Maryanna Cline Horowitz. New York: Charles Scribner's Sons, 2005. 1980–85.

Kessler, Suzanne. "The Medical Construction of Gender: Case Management of Intersexed Infants." *Signs* 16.1 (1990): 3–26.

Koyama, Emi, Diana Courvant, Thea Hillman, Leslie Bull, Nomy Lamm, and Qwo-Li Driskill. "Trans/Genderqueer Buttons." *Confluere: A Network for Social Change*. 21 Apr. 2008 <http://www.confluere.com/store/button-trans.html>.

Linton, Simi. *Claiming Disability: Knowledge and Identity*. New York: New York University Press, 1998.

McRuer, Robert. *Crip Theory: Cultural Signs of Queerness and Disability*. New York: New York University Press, 2006.

Murderball. Dirs. Henry Alex Rubin and Dana Adam Shapiro. *Murderball*. ThinkFilm, 2005.

Namaste, Viviane K. *Invisible Lives: The Erasure of Transsexual and Transgendered People*. Chicago: University of Chicago Press, 2000.

National Gay and Lesbian Task Force. 28 April 2008. <http://www.thetaskforce.org>.

Restricted!! Voices on Disability and Sexuality. 29 June 2005. 28 April 2008. <http://restrictedzine.tripod.com/>.

Rich, Adrienne. "Compulsory Heterosexuality and Lesbian Existence." *The Lesbian/Gay Studies Reader*. Eds. Henry Abelove, Michele Aina Barala, and David M. Halperin. New York: Routledge, 1993. 227–254.

Safe2pee. Bathroom Liberation Front/Genderqueer Hackers Collective. 21 Apr. 2008 <http://www.safe2pee.org/beta/>.

Singer, T. Benjamin. "From the Medical Gaze to Sublime Mutations: the Ethics of (Re)Viewing Non-Normative Body Images." *The Transgender Studies Reader*. Eds. Susan Stryker and Stephen Whittle. New York: Routledge, 2006. 601–620.

Spade, Dean. "Resisting Medicine, Re/modeling Gender." *Berkeley Women's Law Journal* 18.15 (2003): 15–37.

Stryker, Susan. "Transgender Studies: Queer Theory's Evil Twin." *GLQ: a Journal of Lesbian and Gay Studies* 10.2 (2004): 212–215.

Transabled.org: Talking About Body Integrity Integrative Disorder—Just Another Disability. 19 Aug. 2008 <http://transabled.org/>.

Valentine, David. "We're 'Not About Gender': The Uses of 'Transgender.'" *Out in Theory: The Emergence of Lesbian and Gay Anthropology.* Ed. Ellen Lewin and William Leap. Urbana: University of Illinois P, 2002. 222–245.

Notes

1. Stealth is a word commonly used in transsexual communities and refers to passing as a gender without publicly (and sometimes privately) acknowledging having transitioned from one gender to another.

2. I am choosing to use intersex individuals in this definition of transgender because intersexuals have created alliances with other members of transgender communities, and intersexuality is often included when talking about who is "transgender."

3. "Deaf" with a capital "D" refers to someone who identifies with Deaf culture whereas a lowercase "d" refers to physical deafness (Brueggemann 6).

4. According to the official Special Olympics website, "Special Olympics and Paralympics are two separate organizations recognized by the International Olympic Committee. The principal differences between the two lie in the disability of participating athletes and levels of ability in sports participation" (2009 World Games).

POSITION STATEMENT ON TRANSGENDER/TRANSSEXUAL/ GENDER VARIANT HEALTH CARE

By American College of Nurse-Midwives

The American College of Nurse-Midwives (ACNM) supports efforts to provide transgender, transsexual, and gender variant individuals with access to safe, comprehensive, culturally competent health care and therefore endorses the 2011 World Professional Association for Transgender Health (WPATH) Standards of Care.

It is the position of ACNM that midwives

Exhibit respect for patients with nonconforming gender identities and do not pathologize differences in gender identity or expression;

Provide care in a manner that affirms patients' gender identities and reduces the distress of gender dysphoria or refer to knowledgeable colleagues;

Become knowledgeable about the health care needs of transsexual, transgender, and gender nonconforming people, including the benefits and risks of gender affirming treatment options;

Match treatment approaches to the specific needs of patients, particularly their goals for gender expression and need for relief from gender dysphoria;

Have resources available to support and advocate for patients within their families and communities (schools, workplaces, and other settings).

To facilitate these goals, ACNM is committed to

- Work toward the incorporation of information about gender identity, expression, and development in all midwifery educational programs;
- Make available educational materials that address the identities and health care needs of gender variant individuals in order to improve midwives' cultural competence in providing care to this population;
- Support legislation and policies that prohibit discrimination based on gender expression or identity;
- Support measures to ensure full, equal, and unrestricted access to health insurance coverage for all care needed by gender variant individuals.

Background

Gender variant people face multiple barriers to accessing health care and suffer disproportionate disparities in health outcomes. Gender variant individuals experience higher rates of discrimination in housing, education, and employment and lower rates of health insurance coverage than the general population.[1] As many as one-fourth of gender variant people avoid health care services due to concerns about discrimination and harassment.[2] HIV infection within the gender variant community is 4 times the rate of the general population; rates of drug, alcohol, and tobacco use, and depression and suicide attempts are also higher.[2,3] These outcomes disproportionately affect gender variant people of color.

When gender variant individuals are able to obtain health insurance, most find that their insurance providers specifically exclude gender affirming therapies (eg hormonal or surgical procedures), deny basic preventative care services on the basis of gender identity, and refuse to cover sex-specific services due to perceived gender incongruence (eg a man with a cervix may be refused coverage for a pap smear).[4-6] Few legal recourses exist because gender identity and expression are excluded from federal and most state non-discrimination protections.

In addition, the under-reported and under-researched reproductive health care needs of gender variant individuals are of particular interest to midwives. Qualitative studies and anecdotal evidence confirm that gender variant individuals desire parenting roles and can and do create biological families.[7]

Midwifery Practice and the Gender Variant Patient

As many as half of gender variant individuals report having to educate their health care providers about their health care needs, but gender variant people do not by default have unique or complicated health issues. Most members of this community require the same primary, mental, and sexual health care that all individuals need.[8] The most important thing all midwives can do to improve the health care outcomes of gender variant individuals is to use their skills to provide care that is welcoming and accessible.

Musculoskeletal, cardiovascular, breast, and pelvic care for individuals who have undergone hormonal and/or surgical therapy is typically straightforward but in some cases requires additional training. Similarly, administration of hormone therapy for gender affirmation is appropriate for primary care providers, including certified nurse-midwives/certified midwives (CNMs®/CMs®) who have undergone appropriate training. The World Professional Association for Transgender

Health (WPATH) "strongly encourages the increased training and involvement of primary care providers in the area of feminizing/masculinizing hormone therapy."[9] Seeking hormone therapy is the entryway to health care for many gender variant individuals. According to WPATH, "medical visits relating to hormone maintenance provide an opportunity to deliver broader care to a population that is often medically underserved."[9]

CNMs/CMs should seek to provide evidence-based, welcoming, and accessible care for gender variant individuals in accordance with ACNM Standard of Practice VIII[10] and their state regulatory bodies.

References

Grant JM, Mottet LA, Tanis J, Harrison J, Herman JL, Keisling, M. *Injustice at Every Turn: A Report of the National Transgender Discrimination Survey*. Washington, DC: National Center for Transgender Equality and National Gay and Lesbian Task Force; 2011.

Grant JM, Mottet LA, Tanis JT. (2010). National transgender discrimination survey report on health and health care. http://transequality.org/PDFs/NTDSReportonHealth_final.pdf. Published October 2010. Accessed November 13, 2012.

Dutton L, Koenig K, Fennie K. Gynecologic care of the female-to-male transgender man. *J Midwifery Womens Health*. 2008; 53:331–337.

Transgender Law Center. Recommendations for transgender health care. http://www.transgenderlaw.org/resources/tlchealth.htm. Accessed November 13, 2012.

Gehi PS, Arkles G. Unraveling injustice: race and class impact of Medicaid exclusions of transition-related health care for transgender people. *Sex Res Social Policy*. 2007; 4(4):7–35.

National Coalition for LGBT Health. An overview of U.S. trans health policies: a report by the Eliminating Disparities Working Group. http://transequality.org/PDFs/HealthPriorities.pdf. Published August 2004. Accessed November 13, 2012.

Wierckx K, Van Caenegem E, Pennings G, et al. Reproductive wish in transsexual men. *Hum Reprod*. 2012; 27(2):483–487.

Feldman JL, Goldberg J. Transgender primary medical care: Suggested guidelines for clinicians in British Columbia. http://transhealth.vch.ca/resources/library/tcpdocs/guidelines-primcare.pdf. Published January 2006. Accessed November 13, 2012.

World Professional Association for Transgender Health. Standards of care for the health of transsexual, transgender, and gender nonconforming people. http://www.wpath.org/documents/Standards%20of%20Care%20V7%20-%202011%20WPATH.pdf . Accessed November 13, 2012.

American College of Nurse Midwives. Standards for the practice of midwifery. Published December 4, 2009. Accessed November 13, 2012.

Resources

1. American Medical Association. (2008). Removing financial barriers to care for transgender patients. Resolution 122(A-08). http://www.gires.org.uk/assets/Medpro-Assets/AMA122.pdf. Accessed November 13, 2012.

2. Bernhard LA. (2011). Gynecologic health for sexual and gender minorities. In Schuiling KD, Likis FE, eds. *Women's Gynecologic Health*. 2nd ed. Burlington, MA: Jones & Bartlett Learning; 201: 185–208.

3. Brown Boi Project. *Freeing Ourselves: A Guide to Health and Self-Love for Brown Bois*. Oakland, CA: Brown Boi Project; 2011.

4. Fenway Institute. Understanding the T in LGBT: Caring for transgender patients. Fenway Guide to LGBT Health, Module 7 http://www.fenwayhealth.org/site/DocServer/Handout_7-A_Resources_final.pdf?docID=6221. Accessed November 13, 2012.

5. Gay & Lesbian Medical Association. Guidelines for care of lesbian, gay, bisexual, and transgender patients. http://www.glma.org/_data/n_0001/resources/live/GLMA%20guidelines%202006%20FI NAL.pdf. Accessed November 13, 2012.

6. Gorton RN, Buth J, Spade D. Medical therapy & health maintenance for transgender men: a guide for health care providers. http://www.nickgorton.org/Medical%20Therapy%20and%20HM%20for%20 Transgender%20Men_2005.pdf. Accessed November 13, 2012.

7. Institute of Medicine. The health of lesbian, gay bisexual and transgender people: Building a foundation for better understanding. http://www.iom.edu/Reports/2011/The-Health-of-Lesbian-Gay-Bisexual-and-Transgender-People.aspx. Published March 31, 2011. Accessed November 13, 2012.

8. Lambda Legal. When health care isn't caring: Lambda legal's survey on discrimination against LGBT people and people living with HIV. http://data.lambdalegal.org/publications/downloads/whcic-report_when-health-care-isnt-caring.pdf. Accessed November 13, 2012.

9. Steinle K. Hormonal management of the female-to-male transgender patient. *J Midwifery Womens Health*. 2011; 56:293–302.

10. Tom Waddell Health Center: Protocols for hormonal reassignment of gender. http://www.sfdph.org/dph/comupg/oservices/medSvs/hlthCtrs/TransGendprotocols122006.pdf. Revised December 12, 2006. Accessed November 13, 2012.

11. Center of Excellence in Transgender Health. Primary care protocol for transgender patient care. http://transhealth.ucsf.edu/trans?page=protocol-00-00. Published April 2011. Accessed November 13, 2012.

12. Vancouver Coastal Health. Transgender health program. http://transhealth.vch.ca/. Accessed November 13, 2012.

Note. The term "gender variant" is used throughout this document to reflect a broad range of gender non-conforming identities, expressions, and experiences. This term is used as an umbrella term for all individuals whose gender expression or identity differs from the sex assigned at birth.

Source: Task Force on Gender Bias; Clinical Standards and Documents Section DOSP

Developed: November 2012

Board of Directors Approved: December 2012

IT GETS BETTER, UNLESS YOU'RE FAT

By Louis Peitzman

I never had to come out as fat.

When you grow up overweight, everyone notices — not just your classmates, who are too young to have mastered the art of tact, but also friends' parents and teachers. I knew I was fat because people told me I was fat, either directly (a slap to the stomach and an unkind word) or in subtler ways (having a teacher rifle through my lunch box and comment on the contents). I felt shame over my size long before I had any concept of my sexuality, and years after coming out as gay, I still feel anxious identifying as fat.

As an openly gay writer, one of the questions I'm asked most often is, "Were you bullied growing up?" And the answer is yes, but it's never the answer they're looking for. In many ways I was lucky to have come of age in a liberal enclave where my sexuality was accepted if not embraced. Oh, sure, I've had the word "faggot" hurled at me — and the sad truth is, I'd be shocked if a gay man hadn't — but it was always secondary. The real source of my bullying was the extra weight I've carried since childhood. I can count on one hand the number of times I've been called a "faggot" to my face, but I couldn't tell you how often someone has made a dig about my weight.

Outside of anonymous internet comments, the gay slurs have stopped almost entirely. Remarks about my weight, however, are a depressing constant.

I share this not for sympathy but for context. It's an answer to the people who seem surprised when I explain that no, I was never really bullied for being gay, but instead got made fun of for being fat on a daily basis. They are open-minded progressives, and I appreciate their fixation on the way LGBT people are treated; obviously, I share their concern. But the treatment of overweight people is, for the most part, lost on them. And that's largely because so many of my allies and fellow gay men championing equality — compassionate, forward-thinking individuals — are the same people delicately suggesting I lose some weight.

What it comes down to is good intentions. Call someone a gay slur and you're homophobic. Use a racial slur and you're a racist. But when you wonder out loud why I can't just lose some weight, you're looking out for me. At least, that's the perception. The hurtful degradation becomes socially sanctioned, because being fat is considered to be innately wrong. The common understanding is that fatness is unhealthy and unnatural and always the fat person's fault, despite the fact that science does not agree with these assessments. And suddenly, otherwise good people — those who are proud to not have a bigoted bone in their bodies — feel no shame in condemning us fatties. It's not bigotry if we deserve it.

Being fat is never easy, but in the spirit of National Coming Out Week, I'm offering this potentially controversial perspective: As hard as it is to be gay, being fat and gay makes everything so much worse.

I was once told that coming out as a gay man was like being welcomed into the best club in the world. It was maybe an overstatement, but I understand the sentiment: When you first come out, you're automatically granted inclusion — if not by friends and family, then by the gay community as a whole. They get it. They get you. And they're eager to let you know that you're not alone, and that you have a seat at the table. Unless, of course, you're also fat, in which case, no, you can't sit with us.

Certainly this isn't true of all gay men: I'm speaking in generalities based on what I have experienced. There are, of course, gay men who don't obsess over their weight or the weight of potential sexual partners. There are also those for whom going to the gym is not an activity to build one's days around. But the stereotype of the gay obsession with body image and a six-pack is not unfounded. There is a widely held understanding that being gay means maintaining a certain standard of physical beauty, with very little room for deviation from the norm.

I can't speak for all gay men, but I can tell you what I have faced as an overweight gay man. I can tell you that when I lost 15 pounds due to depression, a well-meaning older gay man told me I had done the right thing, because my only other option would have been to gain weight and become a bear. I can tell you that one person I tried to date helpfully offered, "You could be really attractive if you lost some weight." And I can tell you that I deleted Grindr after one night when a stranger messaged me to let me know that if I shed a few pounds I "might actually be cute."

It would be comforting to dismiss these as isolated incidents, but based on conversations with other gay men like me, I don't think they're all that unusual. The truth is, the gay community isn't interested in embracing overweight people because we're a blemish on the image of perfection. And much in the same way progressives as a whole can get away with ignoring anti-fat bigotry, gay men never bother examining the way they treat their overweight brothers. Ignore us or relegate us to the butt of hackneyed jokes: We just don't matter. It doesn't get better for us.

From the beginning, the "It Gets Better" campaign has been fairly criticized for its limited scope: Yes, it does get better, provided you're an attractive, able-bodied white cisman. I want to be clear — it has gotten better for me since I came out. I don't for a minute regret being an openly gay man, and I consider my life now to be a drastic improvement over life in the closet. At the same time, I can't help but grimace at the "it gets better" trope for the way it glosses over so many problems within the gay community. Just because it gets marginally better doesn't mean it ever gets good enough.

The internalized shame I feel about my weight is largely a credit to society, where all fat people are treated like second-class citizens. But adulthood should be about repairing those wounds and learning to love myself as I am. Instead, I'm surrounded by people who, despite having faced the same oppression I have as gay men, largely refuse to embrace me at my current size. The end result is that I've been out for nearly a decade, and I still feel like an outcast within the gay community. I wish I had faith in that getting better any time soon.

A DOCTOR WALKS INTO A BAR: FINDING A NEW DOCTOR WHEN YOU DON'T LIKE THE DOCTOR IN THE FIRST PLACE

By Marianne Kirby

Alas, this is not a post about Doctor Who.

Going to the gynecologist. Ah, that imperative ritual of having a uterus.

It's just about that time of year for me again—but because my doctor moved out of state, I have to find a new person I can trust to examine my area, inside and out, for general healthfulness. Finding someone to poke at my parts in a medical sense is actually way more aggravating to me than the examine itself. So I have some techniques for making the whole process a lot less painful. Metaphorically. If there's physical pain, there's something else going on. I thought it would be a good idea to share these tactics—I know going to the doctor is almost always fraught. It can be even more so when you're going to wind up wide-legged on a table.

PREP WORK

Before I take my pants off with anyone, I need to know a little bit about them.

This counts for dates and it counts for doctors, too. In fact, it counts EXTRA for doctors—they're working for me and I'm paying them!

Before I go to any doctor, much less one who expects me to get naked on a table and submit to invasive exams, I call and do a quick phone interview. These are the questions I ask:

What is your office policy when it comes to the treatment of fat patients?

Is the practice familiar with and do you support Health At Every Size (HAES)?

What's the largest size gown you have readily available?

How likely are you to market weight loss surgery to me?

Do you have large-size blood pressure cuffs in your exam rooms?

How do you respond if patients refuse to be weighed? Do you allow people to be weighed standing backwards?

These are some pretty straightforward questions. Not knowing what HAES is doesn't have to be a dealbreaker—but the reaction of whoever is on the phone with me can be very revealing about the culture of that particular doctor's office.

Remember—if you have any other concerns, this phone screening is a good time to mention them. Are you a trans man? This is a vital chance to make sure no one is going to give you any grief. Are you disabled? This is a vital chance to make sure they'll accommodate you as needed without making you feel like shit. And so on.

Note that, at this point, you're probably talking to whoever is on the phone. That is totally cool. Nurses and nurse practitioners are a huge part of creating and maintaining the environment and atmosphere of a practice. Even if the doctor is friendly, if the nurses aren't, it might not be an office you want to visit.

Make sure to have a couple of offices you can call—don't put all your eggs in one, um, ovary. So to speak. It's also best to make these calls when you don't have a particularly urgent issue. Remember, this person is going to be working for you. You want to come at this from a place of comfort and power, not a place of fever and emergency.

Once I have my list, I'll go over my impressions. I don't have the fiscal luxury of making appointments with multiple doctors, but if I did, I would absolutely schedule consults with a couple of different people. Schedule a consultation—not an exam—if at all possible. That'll give you a chance to get to know this doctor in person, even if it's just for ten or fifteen minutes, when you aren't under the gun of illness. That's important.

SETTING UP THE FIRST VISIT

I like to schedule appointments in the morning. I don't really like going to an office after I've been running around all day—always makes me worry I'm sweaty and gross. Rather than worry, I schedule for my prefered time as often as possible.

Remember, you want to arrange this appointment in a way that minimizing your own anxiety. Doctor's are busy, absolutely. But you have to ask for what you need—if you need to arrange a time when you won't be waiting in the lounge out front for very long, tell the person scheduling the appointment that and explain it's due to anxiety. They'll often be very willing to work with you.

And if they aren't, it might be a good idea to move to the next doctor on your list.

THE FIRST VISIT ITSELF

Remember all that advice people give to teenagers about to take tests like the SAT and the ACT? That's pretty good advice for your first visit to a new doctor, too.

If you're able, get a good night's sleep beforehand. If you're able, eat something small and easy on the stomach to help settle you.

Have your important paperwork (insurance cards, any necessary medical documents, etc.) ready beforehand so you aren't scrambling to find it once you get to the office.

Remember, you can take a letter to be included in your file (I think I got this from Stef at cat-and-dragon). It can include your history with doctors, any discussion of your anxiety that you wish to share, your stance on weight loss, and the purpose of the your visit. It can include anything you want it to. And you can hand that to the doctor and expect them to read it. If you're comfortable having a conversation, go for it. But it's always good to have this stuff documented.

This first visit is a good time to let the nurse and/or doctor know if you prefer not to be weighed. If you are comfortable being weighed, or with being weighed backwards, that's a good conversation to have, too.

AFTER THE FIRST VISIT

Evaulate—how'd it go? Did the doctor treat you with respect? Did the doctor make eye contact? Would you feel comfortable going to this person with an actual medical issue? If yes, schedule an appointment for an exam! If no, if at all possible, repeat the process with a different doctor from your list.

This applies no matter what kind of doctor you're seeing. You are putting yourself in a vulnerable position when you go to the doctor, particularly the gynecologist. That means it needs to be someone you can at least trust not to abuse you.

An actual gynecological exam isn't running through a field with rainbows and kittens. But it also tends to be fairly quick, and most doctors seem to be at least cognizant that it isn't a happy fun position to be in. Doctors conduct exams differently, of course. But most will do the initial intake exam before you have to take off your clothes. A good doctor will talk to you and let you know what's going on throughout the exam—which, again, shouldn't take all that long once they get going. If you are ever uncomfortable or feeling panicky, tell the doctor to stop. Even when they're in the middle of an intrusive exam, they work for you.

CIVIL MARRIAGE V. CIVIL UNIONS: WHAT'S THE DIFFERENCE?

By Gay & Lesbian Advocates & Defenders (GLAD)

FRAMING THE CONVERSATION: WHAT'S REALLY AT STAKE?

First, let's be clear. This discussion is about substance—not symbols. The human stakes are enormous. This document explains why civil marriage, and not civil unions, is the only way to make sure gay and lesbian couples have all of the same legal protections as other married couples.

Second, the discussion is about ending governmental discrimination against gay and lesbian families with respect to civil marriage and its legal protections and responsibilities—not about any religious rite of marriage. Every faith is and will remain free to set its own rules about who can marry and on what terms.

Third, marriage is many things to many people. But it is also a legal institution in which governmental discrimination has no place.

Let's compare civil marriage as a legal institution to civil unions as a legal institution.

What is Marriage?

Marriage is a unique legal status conferred by and recognized by governments the world over. It brings with it a host of reciprocal obligations, rights, and protections. Yet it is more than the sum of its legal parts. It is also a cultural institution. The word itself is a fundamental protection, conveying clearly that you and your life partner love each other, are united and belong by each other's side. It represents the ultimate expression of love and commitment between two people and everyone understands that. No other word has that power, and no other word can provide that protection.

What is a Civil Union?

A civil union is a legal status created by the state of Vermont in 2000 and subsequently by the states of Connecticut, New Hampshire, New Jersey, Rhode Island, Illinois, Delaware and Hawaii. It provides legal protection to couples at the state law level, but omits federal protections as well as the dignity, clarity, security and power of the word "marriage."

What are Some of the Limitations of Civil Unions?

Civil unions are different from marriage, and that difference has wide-ranging implications that make the two institutions unequal. Here is a quick look at some of the most significant differences:

Portability

Marriages are respected state to state for all purposes, but questions remain about how civil unions will be treated in other states since very few states have civil unions.

Ending a Civil Union

If you are married, you can get divorced in any state in which you are a resident. But if states continue to disrespect civil unions, there is no way to end the relationship other than by establishing residency in a state that respects the civil union.

Federal Benefits

According to a 1997 GAO report, civil marriage brings with it at least 1,138 legal protections and responsibilities from the federal government, including the right to take leave from work to care for a family member, the right to sponsor a spouse for immigration purposes, and Social Security survivor benefits that can make a difference between old age in poverty and old age in security. Civil unions bring none of these critical legal protections.

Taxes & Public Benefits for the Family

Because the federal government does not respect civil unions, a couple with a civil union will be in a kind of limbo with regard to governmental functions performed by both state and federal governments, such as taxation, pension protections, provision of insurance for families, and means-tested programs like Medicaid. Even when states try to provide legal protections, they may be foreclosed from doing so in joint federal/state programs.

Filling Out Forms

Every day, we fill out forms that ask us whether we are married or single. People joined in a civil union don't fit into either category. People with civil unions should be able to identify themselves as a single family unit, but misrepresenting oneself on official documents can be considered fraud and carries potential serious criminal penalties.

Separate & Unequal—Second-Class Status

Even if there were no substantive differences in the way the law treated marriages and civil unions, the fact that a civil union remains a separate status just for gay people represents real and powerful inequality. We've been down this road before in this country and should not kid ourselves that a separate institution just for gay people is a just solution here either. Our constitution requires legal equality for all. Including gay and lesbian couples within existing marriage laws is the fairest and simplest thing to do.

How Real are these Differences between Marriage and Civil Unions, given that a Federal Law and some State Laws Discriminate against all Marriages of Same-Sex Couples?

Right now, a federal law, the Defense of Marriage Act (DOMA) denies recognition of same-sex unions conferred by any state for purposes of all federal programs and requirements. Only married same-sex couples have the right to challenge this discrimination, and, in fact, GLAD filed two federal lawsuits to do just that. For more information see www.glad.org/doma. It is anticipated that the United States Supreme Court will hear a DOMA case during it 2012–2013 session and issue a decision by July 2013. If the Supreme Court rules DOMA unconstitutional, or if Congress repeals DOMA, then married same sex-couples will have access to the 1138 laws that pertain to marriage, but civil union couples will still not have this access.

About 40 state laws have laws and/or constitutional amendments that prevent same-sex couples from marrying. Using the term "marriage" rather than "civil union" is an essential first step to opening the door and addressing whether continued governmental discrimination against civil marriages of gay and lesbian people makes sense.

Marriage and civil unions remain different, both in practice and in principle.

First, a few states have not taken a discriminatory position against civil marriages of gay and lesbian couples. In those states, civilly married gay and lesbian couples should be able to live and travel freely and without fear that their relationship will be disrespected.

Second, even as to those states with discriminatory laws and/or constitutional amendments, legally married gay and lesbian couples from those states may well face some discrimination in some quarters, but their marriages will also be treated with legal respect in other arenas. Marriages are far more likely to be respected by others than newly minted "civil unions."

Using the term marriage also prompts a discussion about fairness. Allowing same sex couples to marry (rather than enter a separate status) will allow gay and lesbian people to talk with their neighbors, their local elected officials, and the Congress about whether discrimination against their marriages is fair. Where gay and lesbian people and their children are part of the social fabric, is it right to continue discriminating against them in civil marriage? The federal government and states that have taken discriminatory positions against marriages of gay and lesbian couples could rethink those policies and go back to respecting state laws about marriage, as they have done for hundreds of years. In the end, we will not be able to have this discussion until gay and lesbian folks have what everyone else has: civil marriage.

QUEER AND DISORDERLY

By Gustavus Stadler

I n 1991, Eve Kosofsky Sedgwick published "How to Bring Your Kids Up Gay: The War on Effeminate Boys" in the "Fear of a Queer Planet" issue of *Social Text* (*ST* 29). The immediate prompt for Sedgwick's essay was the first Bush administration's repudiation of its own Department of Health and Human Services's 1989 report drawing attention to the exceptionally high rate of suicides among gay and lesbian youth. Interested in what a depressed queer teenager or child might encounter if seeking, or being forced to seek, help from psychological clinicians, Sedgwick discovered that while homosexuality had been withdrawn (with much self-congratulation) from the official catalog of pathologies, psychiatrists' approach to gender was now guided, at least officially, by something called Gender Identity Disorder (GID). "Help" was synonymous with steering kids toward acclimation to the supposed order of "traditional" gender roles. Sedgwick asked "how it happens that the depathologization of an atypical sexual object-choice can be yoked to the new pathologization of an atypical gender identification." In a series of bracing readings of major work in the field, some of which claimed to affirm "healthy" (read: normatively gendered) forms of homosexuality, she made clear the compatibility of this diagnosis with a broad structure of thinking and feeling designed to eliminate queerness in its initial stages, before it had a chance to live beyond early childhood. Her powerful polemic labeled this work "a train of squalid lies. The overarching lie is the lie that they are predicated on anything but the therapists' disavowed desire for a non-gay outcome."

Here and throughout the essay, Sedgwick's writing reflects the energy of a time in which the possibility of disappearance was very much the driving force of queer activism—a movement both ravaged and galvanized by the AIDS epidemic. Now it would seem that, at least according to a powerful sector of that activism's inheritors, gays and lesbians are beyond that, fighting what the *Advocate* called in the subheadline to its 16 December 2008 issue "The Last Great Civil Rights Battle," the struggle to legalize same-sex marriage. (The presumptive whiteness of that sector is made clear in the main headline's awesomely insidious, newsstand-friendly declaration that "Gay Is the New Black.") Yet the GID diagnosis remains on the books, one of the many sore

Gustavus Stadler, "Queer and Disorderly," *Social Text*, vol. 27, issue 100, pp. 210–213. Copyright © 2009 by Duke University Press. Reprinted with permission.

points that threaten the coherence of such one-more-river-to-cross rhetoric. Thus, in the current *Diagnostic and Statistical Manual of Mental Disorders* (DSM), psychiatrists are advised to watch children for certain patterns of behavior:

> They may have a preference for dressing in girls' or women's clothes or may improvise such items from available materials.... They particularly enjoy playing house, drawing pictures of beautiful girls and princesses, and watching television or videos of their favorite female characters. Stereotypical female-type dolls, such as Barbie, are often their favorite toys.... They avoid rough-and-tumble play and competitive sports and have little interest in cars and trucks.... They may insist on sitting to urinate and pretend not to have a penis by pushing it in between their legs.
>
> Their fantasy heroes are most often powerful male figures.... [They] prefer boys as playmates, with whom they share interests in contact sports, rough-and-tumble play, and traditional boyhood games. They show little interest in dolls or any form of feminine dress-up or role-play activity. A girl with this disorder may occasionally refuse to urinate in a sitting position.

Conjuring, in a quasi–cold-war tone, little spectral armies of Barbie-averse biological girls and princess-obsessed biological boys, these passages sound almost satirical, as though lifted from an episode of the television series *Mad Men*. But in their purported goal of rescuing children from the pain of growing up different, they reflect shockingly impoverished attitudes toward not only gender, but also play and fantasy, not to mention children and parents themselves. And, as of early 2009, they appear destined to remain the official word of the American Psychiatric Association (APA).

The DSM is revised every fifteen to twenty years; work has already begun on the fifth edition, slated for publication in 2012. In May 2008, the APA named Dr. Kenneth Zucker to head the DSM-V work group on gender and sexuality. Zucker and another member assigned to the group, Ray Blanchard, are among the most prominent of a number of vocal, well-published clinicians whose work arises from, and is dedicated to maintaining, the belief that the behaviors comprising GID are indeed pathological and ought to be submitted to corrective treatment. Zucker considers gender variance, or what he calls "gender dysphoria," a symptom of some root problem in a child's development—absent fathers and overbearing mothers heavily populate this diagnostic landscape. According to a November 2008 article in the *Atlantic*, his chosen modes of treatment have included advising a family to turn their household "into a 1950s kitchen sink drama, intended to inculcate respect for patriarchy, in the crudest and simplest terms." As one element of this cure he advised the parents to tell the GID-diagnosed child, "Daddy is smarter than Mommy." In another publication, Zucker approvingly quotes work describing a mother who "inadvertantly induced a gender identity disorder in her four-year-old son by allowing him to overhear her anti-male speeches to her feminist discussion group."

Is there really any connection between the current marriage-centric state of lesbian/gay/bisexual/transgender politics and the DSM issue? The latter is certainly a more oblique, less visible fight, played out not in the courts and electoral politics but in largely Internet-based awareness raising and appeals to the APA to open the details of its revision process to the public. Yet the high visibility of the marriage issue in the media, like the (to some) easy translation into a triumphalist narrative modeled on a superficial understanding of the black civil rights movement, threatens to obscure every aspect of queer politics that is messy, conflicted, or unsuited to the mainstream media's terms and representational strategies. More important, those working for marriage need to be careful to recognize their cause's susceptibility to a shorthand of family values rhetoric, however appealing it may seem to employ at certain junctures. Appeals to Adam and Steve's ability to raise a stable family just like Adam and Eve (oh, sorry, bad example) may hold a good deal of currency within the grand tradition of sentimentalism in the U.S. cultural-political sphere, but for a lot of straight people, "stable" means boys raised as boys and girls raised as girls. Sociologist Mary Bernstein, for instance, examining efforts by lesbian and gay couples to change family law, has described a tendency to "circumvent rather than embrace the challenge to heteronormativity, thus leaving dominant norms in tact."

My main question is this: just what will the marriage fight do to the struggle to develop and live what Judith Butler calls "a new legitimating lexicon for the gender complexity we have always been living"? The answer may not be clear yet, but the contemporaneousness of the same-sex marriage issue and the DSM issue illustrates a developing shift, if not fracture, in the relationship of transgender people to gay and lesbian politics as articulated by the *Advocate* or a group like the Human Rights Campaign. Many trans activists feel the focus on marriage both discourages challenges to gender normativity and pulls energy away from their major concerns: violence (and inclusion in hate-crimes legislation), employment discrimination (the status of transgender people's inclusion in the Employment Non-Discrimination Act currently under debate in Congress is, as I write, uncertain), and fair and decent treatment by the medical institution: doctors, psychiatrists, and health insurance companies. The climactic, end-of-days rhetoric of the "Last Civil Rights Battle" is particularly alienating as trans people continue to be consigned, in many quarters of society, to nonexistence.

POLYAMOROUS FAMILIES, SAME-SEX MARRIAGE, AND THE SLIPPERY SLOPE

By Elisabeth Sheff

ABSTRACT

Opponents of same-sex marriage identify multiple-partner families as the pivotal step that, were same-sex marriage legalized, would propel society down a "slippery slope" to relational chaos. Like the families of same-sex partners, polyamorous families—or those with adults in openly conducted multiple-partner relationships—demonstrate alternate forms of kinship not necessarily dependent on conventional biolegal kin, sexual connections, or even chosen kin ties as previously understood. This article extends sociological knowledge by detailing characteristics of relatively unknown family form; comparing original data on polyamorous families with published research on same-sex families instead of heterosexual families, a contrast that decenters heterosexual families as the sole measure of legitimacy while simultaneously expanding knowledge about same-sex families and explaining how polyamorous families' differences have implications for the same-sex marriage debate and how these shifting social norms implicate changes for the field of family studies and larger society

KEYWORDS

polyamory, same-sex, gay, marriage, divorce

Elisabeth Sheff, Excerpts from: "Polyamorous Families, Same-Sex Marriage, and the Slippery Slope," *Journal of Contemporary Ethnography*, vol. 40, no. 5, pp. 487–489, 501–503, 507–508. Copyright © 2011 by SAGE Publications. Reprinted with permission.

Recent events such as the ongoing dispute over same-sex marriage, the legal prosecution of Latter Day Saints (Mormons) in polygynous relationships, and media attention (such as the television series Big Love about a husband with three wives) have propelled multiple-partner relationships into public attention. In the United States, the conflict over same-sex marriage is the latest installment of an ongoing debate over the meanings, configurations, and social implications of family forms. This discussion has grown increasingly shrill as the confluence of major social shifts in gender norms, sexuality, and the economy culminate (for the moment, at least) at the question of whether people of the same sex should be allowed to legally marry. At stake in this debate are what defines a family as legitimate, and who gets to decide. The social and political implications of these changes have significant consequences, for families and other institutions as well.

A growing body of scholarship on varieties of families addresses these dramatic shifts. Most germane to this discussion, research on families of sexual minorities, primarily those of lesbians, bisexuals, and gays (henceforward *lesbigays*,[1] Carrington 1999), indicates the importance of what Stacey (2003, 145) describes as "a historically unprecedented variety of family life." Lesbians, gay men, and bisexuals differ not only in gender and desire, but vary tremendously in a number of other ways including by race (Anzaldua 1987; Hemphill 2007), social class (Gamson 1999), and geographic locale (Oswald and Culton 2003).

Polyamory is a form of relationship in which people openly court multiple romantic, sexual, and/or affective partners. With an emphasis on long-term, emotionally intimate relationships, practitioners see polyamory as different from swinging—and from adultery—with the poly focus on honesty and (ideally) full disclosure of the network of relationships to all who participate in or are affected by them. Both men and women have access to multiple partners in polyamorous relationships, distinguishing them from polygynous ones in which only men are allowed multiple (female) partners.

The emergence of self-consciously polyamorous families follows the rise in lesbigay families, though to date academic examination of polyamorous families has been minimal. Polyamorous communities are smaller, less organized, and appear to be far more homogeneous than the larger and more diverse lesbigay communities, with the majority of (identified) polys being white, middle- or upper-middle class, well-educated people with relatively high socioeconomic status (Sheff and Hammers 2011). Most of the women in my sample of mainstream polyamorous community members are bisexual, and the majority of the men are heterosexual (Sheff 2005a, 2005b, 2006). In

this article, I compare polyamorous families to those of lesbigays for four reasons: (1) poly families follow directly in the social wake of the lesbigay challenge to heterocentric family forms; (2) as stigmatized sexual minorities, lesbigay and poly people face similar challenges and use many of the same strategies to navigate family life; (3) conservative politicians and journalists frame arguments against same-sex marriage as leading to a "slippery slope" that inevitably sanctions multiple-partner marriage, bestiality, and incest; and (4) this comparison decenters heterosexual families as the sole comparison point while simultaneously expanding knowledge about lesbigay families.

Polyamorists and lesbigays face many similar challenges—disclosure, stigma, custodial issues, and relationships with families of origin—and use comparable strategies to navigate them. One major difference between lesbigays and polyamorists is that the mainstream public is relatively oblivious to polyamory, with poly people remaining virtually invisible to society at large. Whether they embrace, despise, or are indifferent to lesbigays, almost everyone in the United

States today is aware of the existence of lesbians, gay men, and (to a lesser extent) bisexuals. The same cannot be said of polyamorists, and this affords them a measure of protection from social stigma that is not as readily available to the more easily recognized lesbigay people in same-sex relationships.

I argue that the many similarities between polyamorous and lesbigay families are indicative of adaptive strategies that have evolved in response to the same social circumstances, and that such flexible approaches to family life can provide positive role models for other groups in society and thus merit legal recognition as legitimate families. I begin with a review of relevant family and kinship literature and then detail my research methods. Next I describe the characteristics of poly families and discuss the manners in which polyamorists organize their relationships with biolegal (consanguine and/or legal; Carrington 1999) families, marriage, commitment, and divorce. Using my original data on polyamorous families, I draw comparisons between my sample and those in others' published studies of lesbigay families. Finally, I conclude with an analysis of the impact of polyamory on the same-sex marriage debate and the implications of the increasing public awareness for polyamorists and society at large. This article extends sociological knowledge by (1) detailing some characteristics of a relatively unknown family form; (2) comparing same-sex families to poly families rather than heterosexual families; (3) contributing an alternative to the debate on same-sex marriage; and (4) exploring some of the implications these families hold for sociological theory and society.

[...]

Commitment and Marriage

While marriage and commitment used to be combined as a single process, social changes have separated them into distinct life events. Now it is common for people to cohabit in committed relationships without being married, and many others no longer see marriage as the lifelong commitment it once was when life spans were shorter and women's choices more constrained.

In contrast to the clear dedication to marriage equality displayed by some same-sex marriage advocates, polyamorists appear to be far less personally or politically devoted to plural marriage than lesbigays are to same-sex marriage. In the only study of polyamory and attitudes toward plural marriage of which I am aware, Aviram (2007) finds that most of the 35 polyamorous activist interviewees did not see plural marriage as a desirable or attainable goal. Aviram (2007, 282) asserts that this indifference to marriage stems in part from the cultural background of poly communities that emphasizes free-form, fluid, almost Utopian relationships among individuals who are suspicious of institutions, disdain mainstream homogeneity, and "equate the public official aspects of marriage with legal rights" that regulate and limit relationships, leading ultimately to "submission to an archaic, rigid, undesirable social order." Although Aviram did not address the relevance of class, race, or socioeconomic status, elsewhere I argue that race and class privileges provide polyamorists some buffer against discrimination (Sheff and Hammers 2011), making the rights associated with legal marriage less important for polys than they would be to others with fewer social privileges. Polys' desire for plural marriage might also be diluted or negated by their access to ostensibly heterosexual, dyadic marriages. Such access grants polys greater social maneuverability than those in recognizably same-sex relationships, a latitude that is reflected in polys' views of marriage. Some reject marriage as inherently flawed; others are married but accord it little import; and still others view marriage as profoundly important in shaping their relationship structures and interactions.

Commitment ceremonies. My respondents report a variety of views pertaining to marriage and commitment ceremonies. Like some lesbigay couples, polyamorists occasionally formalize their commitments with public ceremonies that acknowledge the group as a family unit. For some, ceremonially announcing that they are "fluid-bonded" (a negotiated safer-sex agreement that allows people to share bodily fluids with specific lovers) signals their lasting pledge to their partners and communities at large. One trio of two women and a man who had dated for several years gleefully informed the attendees at their ceremony/party that marked their fluid-bonding that "We are a family now!" Other polys choose alternative forms of union such as handfasting, a pagan ritual in which people are ceremonially bound wrist to wrist with soft cord for three days and thereafter considered to be married.

Occasionally large and stable families like the Wyss quad deal with the lack of official recognition by creating corporations or trusts to manage taxes, child custody, medical power of attorney, inheritance, and joint property ownership. As scholars documenting lesbigays' attempts to secure similar legal rights find (Dalton 2001; Hequembourg 2007; Wright 1998), such arrangements require extensive legal documentation in an attempt to address every foreseeable contingency, from the division of property in case of "divorce," to the assurance of continued custody of children should the biological parents die. The high cost of this legal documentation makes this route prohibitive for those without the financial resources for such extensive legal preparation.

Marriage. Because many in polyamorous relationships can legally marry in ostensibly monogamous, heterosexual dyads, they have different relationships with marriage than do most lesbigays. While lesbigays may also elect to marry someone of another sex in a similarly ostensibly monogamous and heterosexual dyad, it requires a far greater effort to maintain a closeted gay life than it would for polys with other-sex partners—a configuration that makes them socially intelligible as heterosexual couples with "close friends." This ability to remain closeted almost effortlessly is a resource to which many people in same-sex relationships do not have access, and thus functions

as a form of (often misattributed) heterosexual privilege that provides a buffer against effects of stigma against sexual nonconformists.

Few of my respondents mention legal plural marriage at all, and none identify it as an important goal. Some respondents eschew and occasionally ridicule monogamous marriage as an ill-conceived experiment. Dylan, a 40-year-old white costume designer and mother of one, opines: "I think [marriage] is an institution, and that's fine if you want to be institutionalized." Others deride people in monogamous marriages as "coasting" or "on automatic pilot." Thaddeus, a 41-year-old white musician, casts marriage as detrimental to the health of relationships: "The thing that ruins their marriage was a piece of paper saying that they were married. . . . There wasn't communication, that these were things that they certainly couldn't talk about because they felt stuck." Polyamory provides Dylan and Thaddeus a vantage point from which to critique monogamous families and relationships, much like those who oppose same-sex marriage because they contest all marriage or advocate decoupling social benefits from relationship status (Card 2007; Emens 2004; Polikoff 1993).

Like the majority of polyamorists who have participated in research (Sheff and Hammers 2011), Dylan and Thaddeus are both white, well educated, and middle class—enjoying the privileges that allow them to focus on rebellion against the patriarchal norms of conventional families. Their socioeconomic status and cultural cache provide the kind of security that is scarce for lesbigay and/or working-class people. The larger and more diverse lesbigay community has a broader range of people, and the social privileges that attend legal marriage can be far more important to those who have few other privileges. The more scarce the privileges, the more precious each becomes. Mainstream polyamorists' myriad privileges allow them to downplay or eschew marriage in favor of rebellion precisely because they are so well endowed in other areas.

In some cases, legally married polys downplay their marriages. Phoenix and Zach, a white couple in their early sixties, date their relationship from its inception over thirty years ago, rather than the date of their actual legal marriage, which Phoenix sees as "pretty much just a piece of paper. We did it so he could get health insurance—at the courthouse." Many legally married polys mention it only in passing and do not identify it as important in their interviews, but are still able to avail themselves of its advantages and secure benefits that remain unavailable to their counterparts in same-sex relationships. This near-universal poly disinterest in legalizing multiple-partner marriage, or even investing heavily in conventional marriage, stands in sharp contrast to the significance many lesbigays accord same-sex marriage.

[...]

Lack of access to legal divorce. While divorce and its polyamorous proxy of separation exert a mixed impact on polyamorous people and their children, the lack of access to official divorce can sometimes be as difficult as a divorce itself. The Mayfield quad, composed of Alicia, Ben, Monique, and Edward, all white and in their late thirties or early forties, was together for 11 years before breaking up. Ben, Monique, and Edward had all been employed during their term in the quad, but Alicia's back injury prevented her from performing paid labor. Instead, she cared for their home and Monique and Edward's biological children who were five and seven years old when the quad coalesced as a family. When the quad disbanded, Alicia had no access to the usual recourses available to women whose monogamous legal marriages end. Without legally recognized relationships to any other quad members except her soon-to-be ex-husband, formalized access to the children she had cared for during the last 11 years, or recourse to seek the alimony traditionally awarded to homemakers who divorce a wage earner, Alicia was in a difficult position indeed. While legal protections would not have shielded

Alicia from the emotional impact of the family's dissolution, they would at least have allowed her visitation of the children she reared, and financial compensation for the years she spent raising them and maintaining the household to facilitate the waged work of her spice. Lack of official recognition of her polyamorous family contributed to Alicia's personal and financial devastation.

No marriage means no divorce, and in many cases, no mediated negotiation of custody and property issues. Legal divorce is clearly far from perfect, but it does provide some protections for nonbiological parents and homemak- ers that are unavailable to people in relationships denied official sanction. For both polyamorists and lesbigays who wish to marry or divorce, institutional recognition remains a double-edged sword: it constrains the forms families are able to take, but the lack of those institutional protections can be costly for those who fall outside its purview. In this case, the inflexibility of external society inhibits adaptability and hinders families' abilities to retain kinship ties in the face of crises like divorce.

[...]

'OUTRAGE' DRAGS POLITICS' CONSERVATIVE WINGTIPS OUT OF THE CLOSET

By Dan Zak

The maybe-not-so-new news: Congress is peppered with toe-tapping closet cases who have sex with men but champion anti-gay legislation in the light of day. Our source goes by the name of "Outrage," a crisp, efficient, sometimes petty but often damning documentary about allegedly gay politicians who actively campaign and vote against gay rights.

Depending on your sensibilities, the film is either a rallying cry for truth or a pitiable bit of muckraking. Or both. Yes, much of its artillery is rumor and innuendo that have circulated for years inside the Beltway, but the mission is respectable. "Outrage" tries to expose harmful hypocrisy in American government by laying all the evidence on the table. During the film's brisk 86 minutes—as it connects the dots of deceit to indict a whole generation of white, middle-aged Republican males in power—a levelheaded, fair-minded viewer will respond with contempt, skepticism, empathy and uncertainty. But never boredom.

"Outrage" caters to our desire to see powerful people stripped of their righteousness. Despite the explosive subject matter, it's a very classical documentary. Talking heads are mixed with news footage, buttressed with some basic reporting and assembled to address one politician at a time. Through a series of corroborated anecdotes, the film proves, at least to itself, that a certain politician is gay, and then follows each outing (or re-outing) with an itemization of the politician's "no" votes on gay rights. It is a methodical public shaming.

Do these men deserve their privacy? No, the film says. They "have a right to privacy but not a right to hypocrisy," as openly gay Rep. Barney Frank (D-Mass.) puts it on camera. Other interviewees include former New Jersey governor Jim McGreevey, Rep. Tammy Baldwin (D-Wis.), D.C. Council member David Catania and a host of other media figures, activists and current and former politicians from both sides of the aisle.

The film's targets are recognizable, high-profile politicians at the city, state and federal levels. The long, sordid saga of former Idaho senator Larry Craig is the axis on which the movie spins, but "Outrage" comes down hardest on another prominent politician whose name we won't print here. Why? He has denied repeatedly that he is gay, and there has been no substantiated reports in mainstream media about any homosexual relationships or transgressions. (Director Kirby Dick would hate this last sentence, since his movie also targets the media for their laziness and bias.) Dick has structured "Outrage" around this particular politician, gathering compelling evidence and interviews to support his case and suggesting that this man's hypocrisy is all the more dangerous because he may be bound for a 2012 presidential run.

But in the absence of an admission, or irrefutable evidence, "Outrage" does not arrive at many truths. It is, rather, a desperate plea *for* truth.

Dick has zeroed in on abuses of power in previous documentaries like "Twist of Faith," in which he went after the Catholic Church, and "This Film Is Not Yet Rated," in which his target was the Motion Picture Association of America. With "Outrage," he outs Capitol Hill as one giant glass closet that has perpetuated discrimination for too long. While he convincingly indicts some of his targets, others do not receive a thoughtful, thorough treatment, and are therefore as good as slandered. At one point in the film, the blogger Michael Rogers, who's made a career of outing closeted politicians, calls them "horrible traitors," and walks the hallways of a House office building, pointing to nameplates of congressmen he says are closeted gays. It's a teensy bit Michael Moore-ish.

The film, however, is mostly without venom. It's sad and serious. It synthesizes and sources decades of supposition. It bemoans missed opportunities wrought by deceptive politics. It laments the violence faced by gay teens because an older, more powerful generation refuses to relinquish righteousness for rightness. And it has a dreadful logic to it: If our leaders aren't true to themselves, how can they possibly be true to us?

Outrage (86 minutes, at Landmark's E Street Cinema) is not rated. Contains sexual themes.

DON'T ASK, DON'T TELL, AND DON'T BE TRANS

By JAC

History is being made today for the lesbian, gay, bi, and respective non-heterosexual communities the US Military policy Don't Ask, Don't Tell (DADT) officially is repealed. Everyone is celebrating, and I'm celebrating too, but I have to admit I'm more jaded than joyful. Today as the LGB military is coming out, trans* military is being left out.

As an activist rooted in the anti-war/anti-military movement, even I recognize the significance of the USA's largest employer (the federal government) removing a grossly discriminatory policy that *theoretically* places sexually queer people on equal footing with non-queer people. That's a big deal. And I think it is an even bigger deal that this momentously important event for the "LGBT" community completely leaves off the T. One would like to believe that if high schools can create gender identity and expression inclusive policies then congress can too, but apparently not. An early Department of Defense report on DADT, referenced by several blogs and articles, stated: *"Transgender and transsexual individuals are not permitted to join the Military Services. The repeal of Don't Ask, Don't Tell has no effect on these policies."* After media attention the report was removed from the government's website. According to the US Military, trans* people are "unfit to serve" primarily (categorically) because of our good friend, Gender Identity Disorder. As mentally ill people, trans* communities are not medically fit to serve.

A common thought about DADT, or now in this case with trans* people in the military, is that the "military problem" isn't really a problem because it is better if our people don't join up—it's better to protect our precious queers. I can't help but think this sometimes ... or most of the time ... but I force myself to remember that there are people out there who actually like the military—(like a pre-teen Midwest GenderQueer who associated fighter pilots with a desirable yet (continually) unobtainable masculinity—thank you Top Gun). My freshman year of college I met a guy who was determined to have a military career; he said it was his calling. He was also gay. This was years before I came out but even a "straight girl" could see how problematic the situation was. I remember asking him why he wanted a job where he would have to hide who he

was his entire life. He looked very sad, yet very determined and said "It's not ideal, but I can do it." Now he doesn't have to, but no such luck if it were me.

Revisiting the "military problem," in my experience people think that it is easy to fix: If you don't like the military, then don't join. This is the number one pillar upholding the classist, global mirage that choosing to join the military is always a choice. Speaking strictly for America, our economic system promotes dependency and servitude towards positions in power. We tell our people to succeed, but don't enable them to do it. With jobs disappearing and public funds being non-existent, we're left with a mass population of the under-educated, unsupported, and unemployed. Our trans* community is especially vulnerable because, like other oppressed groups, we are more likely to be poor, unemployed/underemployed, and more likely to lack personal and/or societal support and resources. In other words, we are a population in need and in comes the secure, sturdy military to solve all our problems. I have personally known several young trans* folks who can't pay for groceries let alone for college; who may struggle to get a job because they are gender non-conforming; sometimes they are trying to escape an unaccepting home; maybe they are desperate to get money to transition; they are people willing to give up everything to get a better life, and that's exactly what they do by joining up. It was not a choice for them. They felt they had no other options, and perhaps they didn't. Being trans* in the military has it's own unique issues that no one talks about. A fascinating 2008 study by Transgender American Veterans Association (TAVA) showed that all military branches have trans* people, the Army being highest at 38%. If you're trans* in the military you live in fear of being outed (resulting in losing your job, your home, and/or friends and chosen family). You can't transition in any form, medical or otherwise, and rigidly sexist uniform codes forbid expressing your actual gender (you can even be court-martialed for "cross-dressing"). If you've taken hormones or had surgery before enlisting but don't report it (which you wouldn't because it would keep you from being admitted) you will be discharged when it was inevitably found out in your records. The military has no protections against harassment over gender expression or perceived gender and if you went to complain to a higher up (that is, if it wasn't the higher up who was harassing you) their solution is to tell you that "if you aren't trans, you have nothing to worry about." You also can not confide in religious or medical personnel because, as military employees, they are not required to practice confidentiality on the subject. Quiet the opposite. In the TAVA survey, 40% of the trans*military personnel stated they were unhappy with their lives.

I also believe that repealing DADT won't change much for your average LGB (or perceived to be LGB) trans* military employee. It's against military law to harass, beat, and rape people, but it still happens; and like everywhere in society it is extremely under-reported and often left without any reprisal. Rules changing doesn't mean that people change, and people are who you see every day. Just like any place of business (and it is a business) without an aggressive campaign of combined education and no-tolerance policies the military will never be a safe place for anyone, "gay" or not. We must continue to address the military industrial complex for what it is, as an institutional system of oppression that preys upon our poor, our young, our disenfranchised, and our communities of color. It is a presence that manipulates the global society in order to serve a small percentage, and that is the top 1% of the US elite.

What bothers me more than the issues within the military is the greater "LGB" community's reaction, or lack their of, to the exclusion of trans* communities. I'm so glad today is here so I won't be invited to another "Yay DADT! All Our Problems are Over!" facebook event; after months of it I'm fed up. Yes, we should be celebrating, but its downright lousy to rub it in trans people's faces saying "we don't have to worry anymore" and "problem solved." If you're going to go that far you might as well just call today what it is, yet another "We Forgot You, Again" day, or "We Matter More" day. And yes, I do have to remind people that our problems are not over. I'm not a downer, I'm an activist. I'm not bitter, I'm fucking furious. The LGB community knows what it's like to be ignored, passed over, discriminated against, but that doesn't mean they aren't capable of taking their rights and privileges for granted. The LGB community makes strides with the help of the trans* community, the trans* community is booted out, and what should be our joy becomes a part of our pain. But in of every disappointment there is room for action. It holds me together when people do speak out and recognize that we are not done yet. We must continue to work, continue to fight, and never be satisfied until we all are equal.

I've heard today described as "the light at the end of the tunnel." If this is your truth, I celebrate joyously for you. And as you reach that light at the end of the tunnel, I hope you remember that some of us have been left behind and we are still working in the dark.

DAN SAVAGE UN-WELCOMING PARTY! PAMPHLET

By The Homomilitia

A word of advice: your words and be-haviours, ranging from dismissive to downright hateful, have no place in any movement claiming to counter homophobia and sex-negativity. As a matter of fact, they have no place anywhere. Here are a few ways you can start to hold yourself accountable:

Acknowledge the impact of your words and actions.

Listen and learn from the people who have taken the time and energy to call you out and challenge you to change your behavior.

Apologize, publicly and sincerely.

Take action to MAKE things better! Actively fight for an end to all forms of oppression in our communities and in the world.

We are queers and allies coming together to form an un-welcoming party for Dan Savage, noted for his ableism, ageism, classism, misogyny, racism, rape-apologism, serophobia, sizism, trans-phobia and, oh yeah, that column.

We express solidarity with glitter bombers in Eugene, Oregon and Irvine, California and seek to join our voices with all those calling out Dan Savage, his apologists, and a broader culture of oppression that legitimizes his words and actions. We will not band together behind a man or a movement that refuses to acknowledge the realities of poverty, racism, colonization, ableism, criminalization, transphobia, and other forms of violence experienced by queer communities.

We're joining together to tell Mr. Savage that he's not welcome in our city, in our hearts, or in our bedrooms. We're fed up with him being held up as a spokesperson for sex-postive, GLBTQ politics and we want to make it clear—to him and to everyone else who will listen—that

*I'm probably the world's preeminent advice columnist, but right now I need some advice myself. You see, I've been accused of **ableism, ageism, classism, misogyny, racism, rape-apologism, serophobia, sizism, transphobia,** and almost every other "-ism" there is, I've already dismissed these claims as ridiculous, but now it's getting extreme. There's a whole website devoted to showcasing my oppressive behaviour (http://fucknodansavage.tumblr.com/) and I've been glitter-bombed twice by social justice activists! (Yes, that means they threw glitter at me … trust me, it's even messier than it sounds.)*

Why is this happening to me? And how can I stop it?!

Defending Against Nags

Ableism

When a reader asked Dan to stop using the word "retarded" as an insult, Dan decided to use a substitution for the word, replacing this derogatory term with "leotarded." Rather than take this as an opportunity to reflect on the power of language, acknowledge the impact of his words, apologize, and stop using the term, Dan decided to make light of the issue with a mocking response.

Rape-Apologism

In his column, Dan responded to a reader asking for advice on supporting a woman in an abusive marriage. Dan counseled the reader to interrogate her "story." Part of rape culture is the tendency for people to disbelieve and question sexual assault and abuse survivors, even though it is a known fact that sexual assault and abuse are vastly underreported and coming out as a survivor can be an incredibly painful and difficult process. Dan's advice frequently reinforces an attitude of sexual entitlement. While instructing his readers to "GGG" (good, giving, and game), Dan fails to consider how power dynamics shape intimate relationships.

Racism

Dan has repeatedly placed blame on Black and Latino communities for the success of homophobic legislation in the USA. During the Prop 8 debate in California, Dan said "I'm done pretending that the handful of racist gay white men out there–and they're out there, and I think they're scum—are a bigger problem for African Americans, gay and straight, than the huge numbers of homophobic African Americans are for gay Americans, whatever their color."

This statement clearly plays on racist stereotypes that portray people of colour as intolerant, sexually conservative, and backwards. Despite being called out by queer people of colour for the racism underlying these claims (as well as statistical data disproving his claims), Dan refuses to apologize.

Fat-Phobia

Dan has repeatedly made derogatory and pathologizing comments about fat people and has gone as far as implying that weight gain is a legitimate reason for divorce/separation. Dan has defended his fat-hating prejudice, despite being called out for body-policing and despite significant research calling into question dominant understandings of the relationship between fat and health.

Serophobia

(Discrimination against HIV+ people) Dan has described HIV positive people who have unprotected sex with HIV negative people as "deadbeat infectors," advocating for mandatory drug-support payments from people who transmit the virus. By arguing for policy that targets individuals and criminalizes HIV positive people, Dan contributes to discrimination, stigmatization, policing, and marginalization already experienced by HIV positive people on a daily basis.

Transphobia

Whether he's throwing around words like "shemale," "bad/selfish/stupid tranny," and "freak," advocating that trans people postpone transition to make things easier for their kids, or insulting trans folks for insisting that people use their preferred pronouns, Dan Savage is no friend to trans communities and their allies. No, he is part of a broader trend of privileged cis-gendered gays who routinely ignore trans issues and transphobia in "GLBTQ" and sex-postive organizing.

SYLVIA RIVERA'S TALK AT LGMNY, JUNE 2001 LESBIAN AND GAY COMMUNITY SERVICES CENTER, NEW YORK CITY

By Sylvia Rivera

Latino Gay Men of New York (LGMNY), a social group established in 1991, invited the Bronx-born, Venezuelan/Puerto Rican Stonewall veteran, transgender activist, and Young Lords member Sylvia Rivera (1951–2002) to be a guest speaker at its monthly "First Friday of the Month" meeting in June 2001. This meeting was organized as a celebration of LGBT Pride month, in commemoration of the Stonewall riots of 1969, a landmark event in the history of gay liberation. The meeting was held at the temporary building that the Lesbian and Gay Community Center was occupying near Gansevoort Street while its main building on 13th Street was being renovated. Since Sylvia was banned from entering the Center (see transcription), we had to secure a special permit in order for her to gain admittance. She came with her life partner Julia Murray. The meeting began with small group discussions of the legacy of Stonewall, followed by Sylvia's talk. The gathering concluded with a surprise rendition of "Happy Birthday" and the eating of cake and strawberries, an advance celebration of Sylvia's 50th birthday, which was to occur in July. Sylvia passed away from liver cancer several months later, in February 2002. The recording of Sylvia's talk unfortunately does not include the very beginning of her presentation. Particularly interesting, in addition to Rivera's recollection of the Stonewall riots, of early 1970s activism, and of the 1973 schism regarding the inclusion of drag queens in the broader movement, is her discussion of current trans politics in New York and of her participation in World Pride (Italy, 2000), her critique of gay normalization and gay marriage, and her comments on the activism generated by the murders of Matthew Shepard (1976–1998) and Amanda Milan (1975?–2000).

Sylvia Rivera, "Sylvia Rivera's Talk at LGMNY, June 2001 (Lesbian and Gay Community Services Center, New York City)," *CENTRO Journal*, vol. XIX, no. 1, introduced by Lawrence La Fountain-Stokes, transcribed by Lauren Galarza and Lawrence La Fountain-Stokes, pp. 117-123. Copyright © 2007 by Centro de Estudios Puertorriqueños, Hunter College, CUNY. Reprinted with permission.

Note on the editing: We have attempted to limit editing solely to clarify meaning and eliminate redundancy. Some (minimal) rearrangement of phrases in sentences has been done, to simplify syntax. Otherwise, we have respected the talk as it was presented. We have also attempted to maintain Rivera's distinctive grammatical usage, such as the plural of you (yous) and her occasional use of double negatives. Also please note that the Lesbian and Gay Community Services Center was renamed in July 2001 and is now known as the Lesbian, Gay, Bisexual and Transgender Community Center.

We did have connections with the Mafia. You must remember, everyone was doing drugs back then. Everybody was selling drugs, and everybody was buying drugs to take to other bars, like myself. I was no angel. I would pick up my drugs at the Stonewall [Inn] and take them to the Washington Square Bar on 3rd Street and Broadway, which was the drag queen third world bar. Even back then we had our racist little clubs. There were the white gay bars and then there were the very few third world bars and drag queen bars.

The night of the Stonewall [riots], it happened to be the week that Judy Garland had committed suicide. Some people say that the riots started because of Judy Garland's death. That's a myth. We were all involved in different struggles, including myself and many other transgender people. But in these struggles, in the Civil Rights movement, in the war movement, in the women's movement, we were still outcasts. The only reason they tolerated the transgender community in some of these movements was because we were gung-ho, we were front liners. We didn't take no shit from nobody. We had nothing to lose. *You* all had rights. We had nothing to lose. I'll be the first one to step on any organization, any politician's toes if I have to, to get the rights for my community.

Back to the story: we were all in the bar, having a good time. Lights flashed on, we knew what was coming; it's a raid. This is the second time in one week that the bar was raided. Common practice says the police from the 6th Precinct would come in to each gay bar and collect their payoff. Routine was, "Faggots over here, dykes over here, and freaks over there," referring to my side of the community. If you did not have three pieces of male attire on you, you were going to jail. Just like a butch dyke would have to have three pieces of female clothing, or *he* was going to jail. The night goes on, you know, they proof you for ID, you know, back then you could get away with anything. Fake IDs were great back then (*audience laughter*), because I wasn't even 18 yet; I was gonna turn 18. We are led out of the bar. The routine was that the cops get their payoff, they confiscate the liquor, if you were a bartender you would snatch the money as soon as the lights went on because you would never see that money again. A padlock would go on the door. What we did, back then, was disappear to a coffee shop or any place in the neighborhood for fifteen minutes. You come back, the Mafia was there cutting the padlock off, bringing in more liquor, and back to business as usual.

Well, it just so happened that that night it was muggy; everybody was being, I guess, cranky; a lot of us were involved in different struggles; and instead of dispersing, we went across the street. Part of history forgets, that as the cops are inside the bar, the confrontation started outside by throwing change at the police. We started with the pennies, the nickels, the quarters, and the dimes. "Here's your payoff, you pigs! You fucking pigs! Get out of our faces." This was started by the street queens of that era, which I was part of, Marsha P. Johnson, and many others that are not here. I'm lucky to be 50 in July, but I'm still here and I'll be damned if I won't see 100 (*laughter*).

One thing led to another. The confrontation got so hot, that Inspector [Seymour] Pine, who headed this raid, him and his men had to barricade themselves in our bar, because they could not get out. The people that they had arrested, they had to take into the bar with them, because there was no police backup for them. But seriously, as history tells it, to this day, we don't know who cut the phone lines! So they could not get the call to the 6th precinct. Number one, Inspector Pine was not welcome in the 6th precinct because he had just been appointed to stop the corruption and, you know, what they called back then, we were a bunch of deviants, perverts. So he was there for that purpose, so who knows if one of his own men didn't do it, that was, you know, taking a payoff himself.

The police and the people that were arrested were barricaded inside this bar, with a *Village Voice* reporter, who proceeded to tell his story, in the paper, that he was handed a gun. The cops were actually so afraid of us that night that if we had busted through that bar's door, they were gonna shoot. They were ordered to shoot if that door busted open. Someone yanked a parking meter out the floor, which was loose, because it's very hard to get a parking meter out of the ground (*laughter*). It was loose, you know, I don't know how it got loose. But that was being rammed into the door.

People have also asked me, "Was it a pre-planned riot?," because out of nowhere, Molotov cocktails showed up. I have been given the credit for throwing the first Molotov cocktail by many historians but I always like to correct it; I threw the second one, I did not throw the first one! (*laughter*) And I didn't even know what a Molotov cocktail was; I'm holding this thing that's lit and I'm like "What the hell am I supposed to do with this?" "Throw it before it blows!" "OK!" (*laughter*)

The riot did get out of hand, because there was Cookie's down the street, there was The Haven, there was the Christopher's End. Once word of mouth got around that the Stonewall had gotten raided, and that there's a confrontation going on, people came from the clubs. But we also have to remember one thing: that it was not just the gay community *and* the street queens that really escalated this riot; it was also the help of the many radical straight men and women that lived in the Village at that time, that knew the struggle of the gay community and the trans community.

So the crowds did swell. You know, it was a long night of riots. It was actually very exciting cuz I remember howling all through the streets, "The revolution is here!" (*laughter*), you know? Cars are being turned over, windows are being broken, fires are being set all over the place. Blood was shed. When the cops did finally get there, the reinforcements, forty five minutes later, you had the chorus line of street queens kicking up their heels, singing their famous little anthem that up to today still lives on, "We are the Stonewall girls/we wear our hair in curls/we wear our dungarees/above our nelly knees/we show our pubic hairs," and so on and so forth.

At that time, there were many demonstrations. They were fierce demonstrations back then. I don't know how many people remember those times, or how many people read of the struggle in this whole country, what was going on. So then the tactical police force came and heads were being bashed left and right. But what I found very impressive that evening, was that the more that they beat us, the more we went back for. We were determined that evening that we were going to be a liberated, free community, which we did acquire that. Actually, I'll change the 'we': *You* have acquired your liberation, your freedom, from that night. Myself, I've got shit, just like I had back then. But I still struggle, I still continue the struggle. I will struggle til the day I die and my main struggle right now is that my community will seek the rights that are justly ours.

I am tired of seeing my children—I call everybody including yous in this room, you are all my children—I am tired of seeing homeless transgender children; young, gay, youth children. I am tired of seeing the lack of interest that this rich community has. This is a very affluent community. When we can afford to rerenovate a building for millions and millions of dollars and buy another building across the street and still not worry about your homeless children from your community, and I know this for a fact, because the reason that I have to get clearance every time to come into this building is because I saw many of the kids before the building was being renovated up the street, many of the children are sleeping on the steps of that church. I went in there with an attitude. I raised hell. Yes, maybe I did try to destroy the front desk, but I did not attack anybody. But what did this community center do to me? My thanks for everything I have done for this freakin' community? Had me arrested and put in Bellevue! So I'm supposed to kiss their asses? No, I don't kiss nobody's ass cuz I haven't lived this long, because I don't kiss nobody's ass.

That night, I remember singing "We Shall Overcome," many a times, on different demonstrations, on the steps of Albany, when we had our first march, where I spoke to the crowds in Albany. I remember singing but I haven't over-come a damn thing. I'm not even in the back of the bus. My community is being pulled by a rope around our neck by the bumper of the damn bus that stays in the front. Gay liberation but transgender nothing! Yes, I hold a lot of anger. But I have that right. I have that right to have that anger. I have fought too damn and too hard for this community to put up with the disrespect that I have received and my community has received for the last thirty-two years.

And a point of history, you know that it took the Gay Rights Bill here in New York seventeen years to pass. [It was approved in 1986.] But I'll go through the beginning. When we were petitioning for the Gay Rights Bill, there was only one person that was arrested. That was me. Because I had the guts to go into the Times Square area on 42nd Street and petition the people to sign that petition. And the only reason I did it was because that bill did include the transgender community. Two or three years into the movement and the bill is being presented and we're going back and forth to City Hall. They have a little backroom deal without inviting Miss Sylvia and some of the other trans activists to this backroom deal with these politicians. The deal was, "You take them out, we'll pass the bill." So, what did nice conservative gay white men do? They sell a community that liberated them down the river, and it still took them seventeen years to get the damn bill passed! And I hate to say it, but I was very happy. Every time that that bill came up for a vote, I said, "I hope it doesn't pass," because of what they did to me. As badly as I knew this community needed that bill, I didn't feel it was justified for them to have it on my sweat and tears, or from my back.

So Stonewall is a great, great foundation. It began the modern day liberation movement, like we spoke before about the Daughters of Bilitis and the Mattachine Society. Yes, there were lots of other little groups but you had to be what they called themselves the "*normal* homosexuals." They wore suits and ties. One of the first demonstrations that they had, lesbians who'd never even worn dresses were wearing dresses and high heels to show the world that they were normal. Normal? Fine.

One of my best friends now, who has employed me for the last seven years before I changed jobs, is Randy Wicker. Randy Wicker was a very well-known gay male activist in 1963. He was the first gay male—before any real movement was there—to get on a talk show and state to the world that he was a *normal* homosexual. I give him credit for that. He has done a lot of different things, but he also in 1969 and for many years trashed the transgender community. It took him a lot of years to wake up and realize that we are no different than anybody else; that we bleed, that we cry, and that we suffer.

But this has been going on for the longest time. I mean, before gay liberation, it was the same thing: "drag queens over there, we're over here." The world came tumbling down in 1969 and on the fourth anniversary of the Stonewall movement, of the Stonewall riot, the transgender community was silenced because of a radical lesbian named Jean O'Leary, who felt that the transgender community was offensive to women because we liked to wear makeup and we liked to wear miniskirts. Excuse me! It goes with the business that we're in at that time! Because people fail to realize that—not trying to get off the story—everybody thinks that we want to be out on them street corners. No we do not. We don't want to be out there sucking dick and getting fucked up the ass. But that's the only alternative that we have to survive because the laws do not give us the right to go and get a job the way we feel comfortable. I do not want to go to work looking like a man when I know I am not a man. I have been this way since before I left home and I have been on my own since the age of ten.

Anyway, Jean O'Leary started the big commotion at this rally [Christopher Street Liberation Day, 1973]. It was the year that Bette Midler performed for us. I was supposed to be a featured speaker that day. But being that the women felt that we were offensive, the drag queens Tiffany and Billy were not allowed to perform. I had to fight my way up on that stage and literally, people that I called my comrades in the movement, literally beat the shit out of me. That's where it all began, to really silence us. They beat me, I kicked their asses. I did get to speak. I got my points across.

There was another speaker that day, Lee Brewster (she passed a year ago), very well known to the trans community and to the cross dressing community. She got up on stage, threw her tiara to the crowd and said, "Fuck gay liberation." But what people fail to realize was that Lee Brewster put up the majority of the money for the Gay Pride March of 1970, which was our first one. And it was once again, out of maybe two or three hundred of us that started from the Village, up 6th Avenue, up two little lanes of traffic, that we were the visible ones. We were the visible ones, the trans community. And still and yet, if you notice where they keep pushing us every year, we're further and further towards the back. I have yet to have the pleasure to march with my community, for the simple fact that I belong to the Stonewall Live Veterans group, I march in the front.

But until my community is allowed the respect to march in the front, I will go march with my community because that's where I'm needed and that's where I belong. And yes, I'll wear my big sash that says "Stonewall." And people are gonna ask. And I'm gonna tell why; because this is where the Heritage of Pride [the group that organizes the march] wants to keep us. You see, I don't pull no punches, I'm not afraid to call out no names. You screw with the transgender community and the organization Street Transgender Action Revolutionaries [STAR] will be on your doorstep. Just like we trashed the HRC [Human Rights Campaign] for not endorsing the Amanda Milan actions, and then when they threw us a piece of trash, we refused to accept it. How dare you question the validity of a transgender group asking for your support, when this transgender woman was murdered? No. The trans community has allowed, we have allowed the gay and lesbian community to speak for us. Times are changing. Our armies are rising and we are getting stronger. And when we come a knocking (that includes from here to Albany to Washington) they're going to know that you don't fuck with the transgender community.

Mainstreaming, normality, being normal. I understand how much everybody likes to fit into that mainstream gay and lesbian community. You know, it used to be a wonderful thing to be avant-garde, to be different from the world. I see us reverting into a so-called liberated closet because we, not we, *yous* of this mainstream community, wish to be married, wish for this status. That's all fine. But you are forgetting your grass roots, you are forgetting your own individual identity. I mean, you can never be *like them*. Yes we can adopt children, all well and good, that's fine. I would love to have children. I would love to marry my lover over there [Julia Murray], but for political reasons, I will not do it because I don't feel that I have to fit in that closet of normal, straight society which the gay mainstream is going towards.

This is why they don't want the transgender people to have rights. This is why they always tell us, "Oh let us get ours, and then we'll help you get yours." If I hear that one more time, I think I'll jump off the Empire State building. (*laughter*) But I'm sure a lot of people would like that, especially the old-timers, because I have actually mellowed down through the years. I used to be a bitch on wheels. (*laughter and applause*)

But these are days that we have to reflect on. This is a month that's very important. I may have a lot of anger but it means a lot to me because after being at World Pride last year in Italy, to see 500,000 beautiful, liberated gay men, women, and trans people and being called the mother of the world's transgender movement and the gay liberation movement, it gives me great pride to see my children celebrating. But I just hope that—and I've heard a lot of positive things in this room tonight, as far as people realizing that the trans community was your benefactor and that people are opening up their eyes. But you got to remember, don't just say that because we're here; show your support when we send out a call for action to support our actions, the things that we plan to do.

I mean, it was a hurting feeling that on May 4th [2001] we had history-breaking civil rights in for city council. Our bill was finally introduced. Wow! We waited this long! But where were my sisters and brothers? Where were my children that I liberated? Very few allies showed up. But what made me proud was that the trans community showed up in numbers, and the girls that work these corners even got the nerve enough to come into public and go onto something that they would never consider doing, which was to walk on City Hall because they are all afraid of the police, but they were there. So, that goes to show the rest of the community, that technically when we ask for your support, we want your support. But in the long run, if it's not there, we will acquire what we need.

But, we must remember: Amanda Milan's actions are coming up. I hope to see a lot of you there. But remember one thing, when you all fell out en masse, including myself, for Matthew Shepard, and many of us went to jail, I only got to see maybe five minutes of the whole thing because being the person who I am, a front liner, as soon as I sat down in the street, one of the white shirts that has known me for years, the person he says, "When the order goes down, get that bitch right there, get her off the street and into the paddy wagon." So that's the way that went.

But it seemed like everybody and their mother came out for Matthew Shepard. A white, middle class gay boy that was effeminate! Amanda Milan got killed last year, five days before Gay Pride. We waited a month to have a vigil for her. Three hundred people showed up. What kind of a—doesn't the community have feelings? We are part of the gay and lesbian community! That really hurt me, to see that only three hundred people showed up. And it's not like it was gonna be a long vigil, I mean we went from 36th Street to 42nd Street. So, when we call people, not only to sponsor our actions, we expect to see bodies there. I mean, but like I said, we're capable of doing it on our own because that's what we're learning now, after thirty-two years, that we cannot depend on nobody, except our own trans community, to keep pushing forward.

But remember that as you celebrate this whole month, of how you are liberated. And I feel so sorry for those that are not able to read the history of the Stonewall around the world. And we have to blame once again all the publishers and whatnot. I tried to push Martin Duberman's publishers [Plume/Penguin] to have the Stonewall book translated into Spanish [*Stonewall* (New York: Plume, 1994)]. But they felt that the book would not sell in Third World countries, in Latin countries. Which is a lot of crap! Because the only way that you're going to learn the history, especially if you're far away and just coming out, is to be able to pick up a book and read about the history of the Stonewall and how you were liberated. I know many of our countries are not as liberated as the United States, as far as the gays are concerned, especially Latin American countries, because once again you got to remember that we have to play that big macho role, you know, men, we have to make lots of babies! But it's a shame that it has taken thirty two years for people to finally realize how much we have given to you, to realize the history of the trans involvement in this move-ment. And in that note, I hope to see yous when I send out the e-mails to you, and I hope you pass that on. That I hope to see a lot of yous there for the Amanda Milan actions and I once again wish yous all a very happy gay pride day but also think about us (*the audience claps*).

CPSIA information can be obtained
at www.ICGtesting.com
Printed in the USA
LVHW05s1914030918
589034LV00017B/225/P